Inferno in the French Quarter

On Gay Pride Day in 1973, an arsonist set the entrance to a French Quarter gay bar on fire. In the terrible inferno that followed, thirty-two people lost their lives, including a third of the local congregation of the Metropolitan Community Church, their pastor burning to death halfway out a second-story window as he tried to claw his way to freedom.

A mother who'd gone to the bar with her two gay sons died alongside them. A man who'd helped his friend escape first was found dead near the fire escape. Two children waited outside a movie theater across town for a father and "uncle" who would never pick them up.

During this era of rampant homophobia, several families refused to claim the bodies, while many churches refused to bury the dead. Author Johnny Townsend pored through old records and tracked down survivors of the fire as well as friends and relatives of those killed to compile the first full account of a forgotten moment in gay history.

This second edition on the 50th anniversary of the fire includes additional research and information not available previously.

Praise for Johnny Townsend

"In [*Inferno in the French Quarter*] author Johnny Townsend restores this tragic event [the UpStairs Lounge fire] to its proper place in LGBT history and reminds us that the victims of the blaze were not just 'statistics,' but real people with real lives, families, and friends."

Jesse Monteagudo, *The Bilerico Project*

In *Inferno in the French Quarter*, "Townsend's heart-rending descriptions of the victims...seem to [make them] come alive once more."

Kit Van Cleave, *OutSmart Magazine*

Inferno in the French Quarter: The UpStairs Lounge Fire is "a gripping account of all the horrors that transpired that night, as well as a respectful remembrance of the victims."

Terry Firma, Patheos

"[*Inferno in the French Quarter*] is a one-of-a-kind piece of history. Without Townsend's diligence and devotion, many details would've been lost forever. With his tremendous foresight and tenacious research, Townsend put a face on this tragedy at a time when few people would talk about it....Through Townsend's vivid writing, you will sense what it must've been like in those final moments as the fire ripped through the UpStairs Lounge. [*Inferno in the French Quarter*] is a chilling and insightful glimpse into a largely forgotten and ignored chapter of LGBT history."

Robert L. Camina, writer and producer of the documentary *Upstairs Inferno*

Johnny Townsend

Inferno in the French Quarter:

The UpStairs Lounge Fire

Johnny Townsend

Print ISBN: 979-8-9880847-2-3
Ebook ISBN: 979-8-9880847-3-0

Printed on acid-free paper.

2023

Second Edition

Cover design by Isabel Beeson Design

Contents

June 24, 1973

It would've been better for Luther Boggs if he hadn't gone to the beer bust that afternoon at the UpStairs Lounge. Or perhaps if he'd gone only to the beer bust and then headed home immediately afterwards. After all, *Mannix* was on TV that night back in June of 1973. He could have watched *MASH*. Or perhaps *Gunsmoke*. If he left now, he could be home in time to watch *Here's Lucy*. But her special guest that week was fifteen-year-old Donny Osmond. Luther might have been gay, but he was certainly no pedophile, despite what mainstream society believed about "degenerates."

Luther Thomas Boggs was born on March 1, 1926, to Allen and Agnes Blanchard Boggs, his mother still living in Sulphur, Louisiana. His ex-wife and sixteen-year-old son had moved to Denver, where the woman continually spoke poorly of Luther, creating in the boy just the opposite effect she desired, making him instead think Luther must have been a good man to leave her fifteen years earlier.

In 1973, Luther was forty-seven years old, a computer programmer who'd recently left Pan American Life Insurance Company, whose pastime was tending his garden. 5'8" and weighing 125 pounds, Luther belonged to the Patio Planters, a group which conducted walking tours through the French Quarter in the Spring, showing off many of the beautiful private patio gardens. Luther had lived on Madison, one street below Jackson Square, so his building was directly behind the famous Pontalba apartments. He did move around a bit, though. In 1967, he lived at 638 Royal St., apartment 205, and in 1973, he finally bought a house and lived at 6424 ½ Louisville St.

He enjoyed seeing other patios in the Quarter and liked the idea of letting people see his patio as well. Just walking down French Quarter streets and seeing the front of the buildings was quite enchanting, but Luther knew that no one could gain a full appreciation for the Vieux Carre' without seeing the inside, too.

The late June evening was hot, as summer nights always were in New Orleans, and the sky clear. Along the Mississippi River or beside Lake Ponchartrain, there might be a slight breeze, but on Iberville, just off Canal Street, there were too many buildings for much of a breeze to get through. It was just hot.

At least the UpStairs had air conditioning. That meant they had to keep the windows closed, of course, but that was just as well. Because the windows went all the way down to the floor, and there was no balcony, the bar's previous owners had needed to install bars across the windows. They couldn't let someone get drunk and just fall out onto the street, could they? There wasn't much danger of that now, with half the windows covered with plywood, bars, or air conditioners.

The UpStairs had a decidedly friendly atmosphere, with bartender Buddy Rasmussen never hesitating to ask Luther or any of his other customers to do a little something for him. Luther went to the UpStairs almost every day after work, so he was enough of a fixture that Buddy felt free to be casual. "Could you go tell that cab driver downstairs no one sent for him?"

"Could you please tell that guy to stop standing in the doorway and letting all the cold air out?"

"Could you help me wash these glasses while I fill the pitchers with beer?"

Whatever. And Luther and the other customers felt just as much at ease at Buddy did. "Hey, Buddy, can I put my record of 'Crocodile Rock' in your jukebox?"

"My kid's selling Girl Scout cookies. Would you like some?"

This evening, Luther was sitting at the end of the bar near the jukebox, which was next to the door. He and Buddy and a few of the other customers were chatting. The beer bust had been over for a while now, and Buddy could relax a bit. There were often a hundred or more people at the UpStairs every Sunday afternoon, but now the crowd had started to thin out. There were probably only sixty-five people still in the bar. Enough to keep Buddy occupied, but sixty-five was a number he could handle.

It's hard to say what Luther, Buddy, and the others were talking about. America had declared a cease fire in Viet Nam earlier that year, and some of the POWs had returned home. The Supreme Court made its landmark ruling in January on the Roe v. Wade case, legalizing abortion. In the Spring, there was major flooding along the Mississippi River, endangering New Orleans. Skylab was currently circling the Earth. Billie Jean King was scoring points in tennis, Stephen

Sondheim recently made the cover of *Newsweek,* and Tatum O'Neal just found fame in *Paper Moon.* The book *Sybil* had just been published. Meat prices were soaring. Loretta Lynn, Carly Simon, and Roberta Flack were popular artists of the day. And Secretariat recently won both the Kentucky Derby and the Preakness.

But the real news, of course, was Watergate, as it had been the day before, and the day before that, and every day, week after week, for several months. Most likely, after having a few drinks, Watergate was not exactly the topic Luther wanted to discuss. He probably wasn't talking about his ex-wife, either. Everyone was most likely just gossiping, chatting about what they'd done that day, trying to enjoy the last of their weekend before Monday morning came all too soon.

Gay Liberation hadn't reached New Orleans yet, so probably few people even noticed that this was Gay Pride Day. In New York, people were celebrating the anniversary of the Stonewall riots, which had taken place four years earlier. Instead, for most of the crowd at the UpStairs, this Sunday was much like the previous ones, with friends greeting friends and everyone trying to calculate just how much they could drink and still be able to function the next morning at work.

The bar was noisy that evening, what with Dave and Bud both banging away at the piano at the other end of the room, and the jukebox blaring away near the entrance. The sound of sixty voices mingled together in the smoke-filled air, but soon there was another noise which began to intrude. Phil Esteve, the bar's owner, had installed a buzzer outside. The bar was on the second floor, with a stairway leading up from the street entrance down on the first floor. When the bar was closed, Phil locked the gate, and anyone making deliveries would have to press the buzzer, which rang upstairs in the bar. Closing the gate kept out transients in this not too respectable part of the Quarter. It also kept out anyone who might try to burglarize the place. There was always money in the cigarette machine and the jukebox, and the alcohol itself, of course, was worth a small fortune.

In addition to alerting anyone inside of deliveries, though, the buzzer could also be used by cab drivers who'd been called to pick someone up. And naturally, the buzzer was also used at times by pranksters, by jerks just trying to be irritating. It was ringing now. Not in repeated bursts, but in a long, continuous, aggravating ring. No one had called for a cab, and there were certainly no deliveries coming on a Sunday. If it was a customer, all he'd have to do was walk up the stairs and open the door. No need to be such a pest by leaning on that buzzer.

Buddy figured he knew who it was. Almost surely that asshole he'd thrown out of the bar earlier that evening for fighting. The guy was weird, always trying to cause trouble. And Buddy would have none of it here at the UpStairs. Now the pest was back, ringing and ringing and ringing.

"Luther," Buddy said wearily, "would you go see who in the hell is ringing that buzzer?"

Luther nodded his agreement. It would be the second to last favor he would ever do. Within moments, twenty-nine people would be suffocated or burned to death, with three more patrons dying painfully over the following two weeks.

Another fifteen people at the UpStairs would suffer terrible burns or other injuries. And a close-knit community would be shaken to its core.

This is the story of those impacted most by the tragedy. It's also the story of the bar itself, which held a unique place in LGBTQ French Quarter culture.

While the arson took place during Gay Pride weekend, the attack wasn't a hate crime as we usually understand it, perpetrated instead by a disgruntled patron. But the tragedy became a hate crime nevertheless as a result of the city's response.

At Buddy's request, Luther stood and walked the few remaining feet over to the entrance, preparing to call out to whoever was at the bottom of the stairs. He put his hand on the doorknob of the fire door at the top of the stairwell, unaware of the 700-degree inferno boiling upwards on the other side. As he pushed open the door, flames shot instantly through the opening. Luther stumbled backwards into the room, but the door remained open, closing slowly on its automatic hinge before jamming, with the flames rushing in after him, shooting furiously into the bar.

Jim Hambrick

James Walls Hambrick never knew his paternal grandmother, as she died shortly before he was born in Lexington, Kentucky, on September 13, 1927. He did get to know his grandfather and many of his father's nine brothers and sisters, however. He also was able to visit his maternal grandparents often in Mt. Washington, Ohio, near Cincinnati, as he grew up. Grandfather James L. Walls was an insurance broker, sold real estate, and owned a wharf along the Ohio River in Cincinnati.

But what Jim remembered most as a child was the farm in Mt. Washington, the big red barn behind the house, and his grandfather raising crops and fantail pigeons. Jim's two oldest siblings, sisters Agnes and Bennie, were born there in Mt. Washington.

Bennie was perhaps a strange name for a girl, but when Jim's mother, Alma, was pregnant with her second child, her husband, Benjamin H. Hambrick, was set on having a son. After all, he already had one daughter. Fair was fair. But the baby was a girl. Set on having that boy, though, Benjamin insisted on naming the infant Bennie. He did relent a little, however, in allowing her middle name to be Helen.

Benjamin, Jr. came next, in 1926, followed by James, and then by John, Raymond, and Joseph Henry. With seven kids in the house, Jim had ample opportunity to learn how to get along with others, and this was something he picked up at an early age. There was the added incentive of avoiding their father's strap to keep Jim and his siblings playing agreeably with one another.

Jim's father owned two grocery stores in the 1920's and '30's. None of the children ever worked there, but they were aware that times were hard. No one had any money. A twenty-five-pound bag of flour sold for twenty-five cents during the Depression, pork chops were five cents a pound, and a live chicken cost only twenty cents. Still, many people couldn't pay and would charge their groceries, asking for thirty-day credit, since many employers, including the railroad and the racetrack, only paid their employees every thirty days. But even after their next paycheck, many customers didn't pay their bills, or paid only a portion.

Things began looking bleaker and bleaker. Then one of the two grocery stores burned down. Jim's father had let the insurance lapse because he could no longer afford it. Now with the added financial strain of losing this store, he lost the second one, too. Jim's father went to work as a meat cutter in someone else's grocery store.

By 1940, things were finally looking up a bit, but then Jim's parents divorced. Alma took the two youngest boys back to Cincinnati, but the five oldest children stayed with their father on Limestone in Lexington, though Agnes soon married a career Army man and moved out. Bennie followed her example later by marrying a major.

As a teenager, Jim decorated walls at Purcell's, a department store in town. He also decorated windows at Tots-n-Teens, a clothing store, and at Kresge, a dime store.

He learned interior decorating, becoming rather good at that as well. He lived for a while with two schoolteachers, paying his way in part by getting up early every morning in the winter to light the furnace for the others.

After two years of high school, Jim joined the Navy in Louisville on July 3, 1945, and was first stationed at the USN Training Center in Sampson, New York. Afterward, he was stationed at Patuxent River in Maryland, his rank SN V6. The war ended shortly after he joined, so his enlistment would not last as long as he expected. He wasn't able to complete even that shorter commitment, though, because he developed rheumatic fever and was discharged with a hole in his heart. He recovered enough, however, to join the Naval Reserve, so he remained part of the military, just not on active duty.

Jim returned to Lexington but didn't move back with his father. He lived instead with a friend, Dr. Johnston, and his wife. After recuperating a bit more, Jim traveled with some of his family to visit Bennie up in Milwaukee, but he suffered a relapse and Benjamin had to carry him off the train when they returned to Lexington.

By 1948, Jim's doctor advised him to move south, suggesting that a warmer climate might help him avoid further relapses. Jim didn't want to go just anywhere further south, however. By this time, he realized he was gay and knew that being gay would be easier in a larger city. And he also wanted to be far enough away from his family that his homosexuality would cause them as little trouble as possible.

Jim moved to New Orleans in 1948, reporting to the Headquarters of the Eighth Naval District, since he would remain in the Reserves until August 6, 1954. Jim hoped that

New Orleans would be more accepting of "decadence." He didn't come alone, however. He'd made some friends in Lexington, and they all decided to make the move together. That way they could combine adventure with a little bit of safety, too.

Fun for gay men in the 1950's always felt risky. Not dangerous in the sense of being caught in a raid—Jim never did know anyone personally who was arrested in a raid—but dangerous in the sense that homosexuality was completely unacceptable to society, and going to a gay bar was a rebellious and bold thing to do, since the risk of trouble was always there.

At the same time, New Orleans had to be one of the most tolerant cities in the nation during the '50's and '60's, though perhaps this wasn't saying much. When gay men were dancing in New Orleans, they still couldn't touch in San Francisco, as far as Jim could tell. When a friend of his returned from Los Angeles, the friend told Jim of a visit he made to a gay bar there. The friend had met someone and shaken his hand. The bartender had jumped in quickly, saying, "Hey, now, cut that out. No touching in here."

Yes, overall, things were okay in New Orleans. Of course, it helped that Jim was far from the stereotypical gay male. He had no affectations or effeminate mannerisms. He was instead tall, 6'2", strong, and quite "masculine." He wasn't the most handsome man in the world with his hairline receding, and with his waistline also growing as his love for New Orleans food grew. But without being prissy, he did keep his appearance neat and clean, so he was able to carry his 215 pounds reasonably well. His dark brown hair was always neatly combed, and he almost always wore a clean, pressed suit, even when he went out to the bars.

Of course, wearing a suit to the bars was commonplace in New Orleans until the mid-1960's. Jim was slow to give up a habit of years but did manage to adapt and flow with the times.

In the mid-1950's, there were eight gay bars within a two-block area of the Quarter. There was the Rendezvous, a bit rough, and Dixie's Bar of Music, diagonally across from the Rendezvous on the corner of St. Peter and Bourbon. Dixie's, run by Yvonne Fasnacht, was the most famous gay bar in New Orleans and one of the most famous in the country at the time. One didn't go into Dixie's unless one didn't mind entering an establishment that many of the tourists passing by knew was a gay bar.

Just down the block was Pat O'Brien's, famous then as now for its Hurricanes. What many people didn't realize is that for years the main bar in Pat O'Brien's was mostly gay. Again, people didn't go there unless they didn't mind becoming a gay tourist attraction. This was one of the oddities about New Orleans gay life.

Many cities with gay bars had them in sleazy areas to attract as little attention as possible. But for New Orleans gays, being inconspicuous was more difficult, as the "sleaze" of the Quarter was itself one of the main tourist attractions. So despite a more oppressive atmosphere in some respects, in other ways New Orleans was quite open to gay subculture.

Jim liked Pat O'Brien's and often went for social drinking, beer and scotch his favorite drinks. Then there were the other bars in the area, Papa Joe's, Tony Bicino's, Candy Lee, Pete's, Galley House, and Lafitte's, which was literally a bar inside of Jean Lafitte's old blacksmith shop on St. Philip and Bourbon, or at least the building where many people believed he'd had the shop he used as a front during his pirating days. When the lease ran out for the bar in the early '50's, Lafitte's opened up in 1953 one block further toward Canal, calling itself now Cafe Lafitte in Exile since it could no longer meet in the blacksmith shop.

As far as sex, certainly it was easily available throughout the '50's and '60's. There were no "back rooms" in the bars then, so sex didn't take place inside except on special occasions such as Mardi Gras or New Year's Eve, Mardi Gras a time of sexual abandon throughout the Quarter for both heterosexuals and homosexuals. While Jim was no exhibitionist, he did enjoy having a good time. He enjoyed sex and would go home with someone or take someone home with him if there was a mutual attraction and interest.

And there was something about a fireman. Sometimes alone, sometimes with his friend, John, Jim would go to various fire stations and chat with some of the men or cruise them until he got a favorable response. "Ooh, look at that one," Jim would tell John. "He can slide down my pole any time." Some of the firemen were too macho to admit being gay, but they'd let Jim do oral sex to them, and that was fine with Jim, too. "After all, they're serving the community, aren't they?" Jim reflected. "Doesn't that give me an obligation to serve them in return?" And he'd smile.

Jim never did have a lover during those years, and he didn't particularly want one. He had a few boyfriends, some one-night stands, and a few regular sex partners who weren't romantic interests. He also had a good circle of friends who provided companionship. And the bars were always there for socializing, so Jim went out often to see friends and acquaintances. Because of his casual, down-to-earth, outgoing manner, he had no trouble striking up conversations with anyone new he wanted to meet. He wasn't lonely.

Back in 1956, a friend introduced Jim to Richard Davis, from Hammond, Louisiana. Dick had just finished college and wanted to live in a larger city than his hometown. Jim liked Dick, partly because he was also masculine or "straight appearing," partly because he was a "go-getter" like himself, and because their personalities just seemed to complement each other.

After some discussion, Jim decided to ask Dick to move in. Together, they paid the $80 a month rent on their St. Charles apartment, a large house with two baths and seven rooms. They were never lovers, but they did become increasingly better friends. Certainly, they argued over the normal roommate topics such as how to squeeze the toothpaste tube or how to properly hang the toilet paper, but overall there were few arguments.

For years, every morning at breakfast, Jim and Dick talked about their problems with work or friends or how they'd dealt with realizing they were gay, or whatever else they felt like discussing in depth. Jim became a kind of mentor to Dick, and when Dick came to cry on Jim's shoulders one evening over a man who didn't return Dick's interest, Jim tried not to sound too condescending as he said,

"Richard, let me tell you from experience, three years from now, you won't even remember his name."

After a few years, Jim decided to buy a house at 5005 Coliseum Street in a pleasant Uptown neighborhood. Dick wasn't in a position financially to help buy it but agreed to continue paying rent. Jim, though, was already a successful salesman, having started at J.D. LeBlanc and now selling office furniture with Hanson Flotte, just down the block from Dameron Pierson on Camp Street.

Jim enjoyed his work and was good enough to avoid being hassled by his boss. He was well liked by his coworkers, as least some of whom knew he was gay, and he made friends with some of the people working at Dameron Pierson, too. Jim was an outside salesman. He attracted his own customers, set his own hours and appointments, and courted his customers, enjoying every minute of it.

After Jim bought the house on Coliseum, he began renovating. The place was in pretty good shape, but several years later, he bought another house, on Robert Street, which needed more substantial work. Over the next year, working on weekends and sometimes in the evening, Jim did major renovations on the second house and then began renting it out. He had further opportunity to use his carpentry skills when Hurricane Betsy blew the roof off their house in 1965.

For Christmas, he was as likely to get an electric saw or a sander as a shirt or sweater from Dick or his other friends.

Jim and Dick continued as roommates throughout the end of the '50's and through the 1960's. Twice, Dick went off to the army, where he worked with artillery, but even during those periods, Jim was glad Dick still considered the house in New Orleans his permanent address, and Dick always seemed glad to get back home.

Jim and Dick had other roommates at the house for various periods, including Jim's brother, John, who lived with them a couple of years before moving to Dallas, but the other residents were always temporary. Jim did acquire one other permanent roommate in 1962, when he took in a puppy, a brown dachshund he named Rocky, whom he adored and who adored him right back. Jim and Dick made up the real household, despite the occasional roommates, and some people assumed they were lovers rather than just good friends.

Neither Jim's family nor Dick's ever implied that, however. Neither man ever brought up the subject of homosexuality with family. If the family figured it out, that was great. If they didn't, that was fine, too. Who he slept with was hardly a subject Jim felt he needed to bring up at dinner during a holiday visit.

By the early '70's, some of the bars had changed. There were still Pete's Place, at 800 Bourbon, the Galley House Bar, at 542 Chartres, perhaps the oldest gay bar in the city, Cafe Lafitte in Exile, at 901 Bourbon, into which an irate customer drove a pickup through the wall in 1971, and the Golden Lantern at 1239 Royal.

Some of the other gay bars and meeting places included Kitty's Grog at 718 N. Rampart, which in 1972 still had customers coming in wearing a coat and tie, the Caverns at 801 Bourbon on the corner of St. Ann, Diogenes at 940 Conti Street, Milord at 740 Burgundy, Rod's at 625 St. Philip, the

Safari Lounge at 706 Iberville, Wanda's at 704 Iberville, Wanda Stumpf's Lounge at 820 N. Rampart, Cruise on Dauphine near Orleans, Club Unique at 700 N. Rampart, Club New Orleans Baths at 515 Toulouse, Canal Baths at 512 Gravier Street, and Mom's Society Page at 819 St. Louis.

Some of the others, including lesbian bars, were Alice's Bar at 515 Ursulines, Ann's Bar Club at 507 St. Louis, the Burgundy House Bar and Restaurant at 600 Burgundy, Charlie's Corner, which was a black bar outside the Quarter, Storieville on Bourbon near St. Ann, Streetcar Bar and Restaurant at 901 Bourbon, and Vickie's Lounge on Toulouse and Decatur.

Certainly, Jim didn't go to all these places, but he enjoyed living in a city where so many gay establishments could exist. There were problems, of course. Just in January of 1971 alone, there were thirteen arrests and four beatings of gay men by police at Cabrini Playground, a cruisy area in the Quarter on Burgundy at Barracks, as well as other parts of the Quarter. Despite that, with so many places to go, this still had to be one of the better cities to live in, as far as Jim was concerned.

As Jim began to be more successful in his business, he traveled to New York regularly to see Broadway shows and to California to visit friends. He also traveled often to Houston, or to Pensacola to enjoy the beach, or back to Kentucky to visit his family and his friends, the Rogers and the Johnstons. He also returned in 1959 for his father's funeral, and to Cincinnati in 1964 for his mother's funeral.

Most of his trips were more pleasant, however. He flew to Mexico and Central America on a couple of trips, and he even made it to Europe once. In New Orleans, he became good friends with Dr. Jackson Beebe, and Jim often attended formal dinner parties with Beebe and other friends.

Jim, though raised Protestant, converted to Catholicism in the early 1950's but then rarely went to church. He had strong political opinions, yet while these were generally Republican, he voted for Kennedy. Despite his two serious crises with rheumatic fever in the mid-1940's, Jim was almost always in good health in New Orleans, except for the usual cold a couple of times a year and an occasional bout with the flu. And though Jim was easy going, he was no pushover. When a mugger attacked him once, Jim beat the man up and walked away.

Jim had his circle of friends, Dick had his own, and together they had yet another circle of friends. More often than not, when they went out, they went separately, frequently going to different bars. Jim wasn't a regular at the UpStairs but did go occasionally to the beer bust with friends. He knew Phil Esteve, the bar's owner, who'd lived for a while in the same neighborhood as Jim and Dick. On June 24th, Jim made no special plans to visit the UpStairs, but when a friend of his suggested it, he went along without protesting. It was a fun enough place, and that was what Sunday evenings in the Quarter were for. So around 7:50, only a few minutes before the fire began, Jim, laughing and telling jokes as always, climbed up the steps to the UpStairs Lounge.

Skip Getchell

Horace W. Getchell, a native of Maine, was born on October 6, 1937, to Horace Sr. and Thelma Coon Getchell. His grandmother raised him there in the northeast, and he remained close to her even after he moved to New Orleans. He also stayed close to his father and brother, who had moved to Olympia, Washington. Horace, nicknamed Skip, loved his brother's daughter and encouraged her with her education. He put her down as his beneficiary on his insurance, hoping to still be able to help her even if he were no longer around.

In the meantime, though, he sent cards and letters. He called his family in Washington and his grandmother in Maine. And every year, Skip drove up to visit his grandmother, getting to see the rest of the family as well if they all timed their visits correctly.

Skip worked in the International Trade Mart Building at the foot of Canal Street in New Orleans as a dispatcher for Gilscot Forwarding. The company specialized in moving freight across the country, so Skip was always working with train schedules and ship schedules. He asked his boss several times for a raise, but she would only tell him, "The business is in trouble right now, so we can't afford a raise for a while." Skip knew enough about the company to know it was doing well, and he grumbled regularly to his friends about the lack of recognition he received for his work.

He did do reasonably well, however, even without the raise. He and his lover of ten years, Bill Farrell, lived in a house at 1529 Crete Street. They owned a huge, top of the line, white Chrysler, and their house was filled with furniture. Bill, who worked for the school board, was also a piano player, and he often performed at the Galley House while owner Alice Brady sang. He earned enough to fill the house with bric-a-brac, mostly Mardi Gras related. Shelves were lined with glasses from different courts, and there were displays of numerous doubloons, not the cheap aluminum throws but the silver and bronze doubloons, expensive coins from a variety of the krewes. Stylish crystal vases and silver plates lined some of their other shelves.

Skip and Bill were both committeemen for several of the "straight" Mardi Gras balls. Skip loved to wear a tuxedo with tails, receiving frequent compliments on his appearance. At 6' 1", he cut a more dashing figure than his older, shorter, balding lover, but they both enjoyed dressing up.

Skip was one of the founding charter members of the Apollo krewe in New Orleans, an early gay krewe, but Bill did not join this one, preferring the straight balls. It was more common for the gay krewes to be satirical and campy with the balls, whereas most of the straight krewes took things seriously. Skip liked the idea of a kind of "crossover" krewe, a serious gay krewe that would perform the ball as pompously as the straight krewes did, hoping, as did Roland Dobson, another charter member, to get the straight community to accept gays.

But there were problems, so Skip only remained with Apollo a couple of years. One of the problems developed when Roland Dobson, again trying to gain respect for the krewe, had a television station photograph the ball. It was a nice gesture toward legitimizing the krewe, but one of the members lost a job when his employer learned he was gay.

Another problem was a difference of opinion with Dobson. Roland, a father, a former Church of God minister from Bogalusa, and a Burt Bacharach lookalike, was gay according to friends but had married the wealthy Mrs. Mayer. They maintained separate households, however, Roland keeping a place in the Quarter. Despite having money, Roland wasn't going to support the Apollo krewe singlehandedly, yet the bills kept piling up.

Skip complained, insisting they shouldn't spend money they didn't have, but Roland wanted to be extravagant. His captain's costume was covered with so many rhinestones that it seemed the world lit up wherever he walked. But it wasn't just the costume; Roland wanted every aspect of the ball to be extravagant. Skip was afraid that as a charter member he could legally be held responsible for the huge bills, so when Dobson, Glyce DiMiceli, and another member said they'd go ahead with the big plans, Skip and another charter member resigned.

Though Skip may have been disillusioned with Apollo, he still loved the other balls, and he and Bill continued attending regularly. But attending balls wasn't their only means of celebrating carnival. They also held an annual Mardi Gras party themselves, inviting dozens of people, until their home was packed with guests, some even from out of state. They had as many female friends as male, and as many straight as gay. The party would be held on the Sunday prior to Mardi Gras, there'd be food everywhere, and two bars for the guests.

Their cat was about the only one who stayed away during the parties. When just a few people were over, however, and anyone tried to go upstairs, their huge cat would swat at them through the railing, hissing and threatening. When Skip and Bill went out of town, they asked their friend, photographer Peggy Stewart, to take care of the cat, but she tried to give it as wide a berth as possible. Their cat was not the reason she liked Skip and Bill.

Tom Solieri's reason for liking Skip was not the cat, either. It had more to do with Skip's sparkling eyes and his great smile. Skip was at the Amon Ra Mardi Gras ball with Bill and some friends when he first ran into Tom. Skip liked him and so invited him to join his group when they all went out to eat breakfast after the ball was over. During the next few months, Skip continued to run into Tom at parties, usually Sunday get-togethers at the homes of various friends. Then one day, Skip asked Tom to go home with him.

As there were two bedrooms in the house, Tom was not immediately aware that Skip and Bill were lovers. He knew they were good friends, but they also separated sometimes at parties and talked to different people, so they could have just been housemates. They weren't, though. They were lovers. They simply had an "understanding" about other men, which was basically, "Play around if you want, but remember who your lover is."

Skip remembered, and he and Tom only had sex three times. Still, Skip did like him and so kept up a friendship. They all went to Lafitte's on Sunday afternoons together, and then afterward they'd walk over to the bar where Bill played on Sunday evenings. Once, Skip took him to the UpStairs, but as Tom didn't particularly like it, they usually just followed Bill to hear him play and sing, and maybe to sing along with him.

But they didn't just become bar friends. Skip knew Tom didn't have a car, and that he had to walk seven blocks to do his laundry, so Skip often insisted on driving Tom to the laundromat, sitting and talking with him as the clothes washed and dried, and then driving him back to his apartment.

He helped other friends with errands, too, and regularly called most of them, even if he'd seen them only a few days before. If he called Tom, "just to say hi," but could sense that Tom was sitting home alone feeling depressed, he'd stay on the line longer than he'd intended, telling jokes or telling him stupid things that had happened at work, trying to cheer him up, not only talking about himself but asking about Tom, too.

Tom, for his part, seemed amazed that Skip never appeared either angry or sad. "Is it an act?" Tom asked him once. "I put on an act for my other friends," Tom said. "I'm always a clown with them. But with you, I feel I can open up and tell you anything. But then you always seem so happy. Are you able to open up to me?"

Skip paused for a moment. "I guess no one's happy all the time. But I am most of the time. I decide to be happy. I think Auntie Mame has it right. 'Life is a banquet and most poor suckers are starving. Live! Live!'" It wasn't just a pep talk to cheer up a depressed friend. It seemed the only natural way to go through life.

Skip knew that one of the reasons for Tom's depression was that he'd been approaching thirty and still had no lover. When Peggy Stewart offered as a birthday present to take some photos of Tom for him to send to his family, Skip showed up at the studio during the shoot. "Just thought I'd pass by on my way home and say hi," he told them.

"But you live and work on the other side of town," Tom pointed out, laughing. Still, it never occurred to him that Skip might have popped in just to make sure Tom was feeling okay about his birthday. Or that Peggy had offered to shoot the photos for the same reason, making sure Tom looked both young and handsome in the final prints.

What helped Tom cheer up was finding a college he could attend for free, to finally get the education he wanted. The college was in Missouri, however, and most of Tom's friends discouraged the move, suggesting how much harder it would be to live gay in a small town. Skip knew that college was what Tom wanted, though, and probably what he needed as well. So he congratulated Tom on his acceptance to school. "Besides," added Skip, "it's probably good for you to get out of New Orleans. It's too easy to get jaded down here." So he left Tom looking at the bright side, and after Tom moved in January of 1973, Skip wrote to him regularly in Missouri, with Bill always adding a P.S. to the letters.

But Skip's remarks about getting jaded turned out to be a little prophetic. Though Skip laughed a lot, and he and Bill seemed to get along fine, a few months into 1973, problems began surfacing. It seemed that Bill was being romanced by another guy, and whether or not Bill was encouraging it, Skip felt he was and was furious. Bill had had sex with other guys, and it had never been a problem before. Sex was no threat to Skip. But a romance was.

Bill was the kind of guy who, if a friend asked for some help, he'd do whatever it took to find the information necessary. He was more than just an acquaintance to many people, he was a real friend to those he liked, much as Skip was. Perhaps his friendliness was being misinterpreted by an interested admirer, or perhaps he was truly involved in an affair. Skip tried not to jump to conclusions, but he didn't like what seemed to be happening.

Jimmy Willemet was one of their friends who could see the trouble brewing. He lived on Esplanade near Broad, just around the corner from Bill and Skip, and he spent most Saturday mornings at their place drinking coffee and chatting. He felt that Bill tolerated Skip's "friends," but that in return Skip became jealous awfully quickly of Bill.

But Skip could forget about it at least temporarily, especially while out barhopping. He and Jimmy often went out together, and once Skip coaxed Jimmy into going to the UpStairs, but Jimmy didn't like it and refused to return. "How did you ever start going there anyway?" he asked Skip.

Skip explained that he often had his hair cut at Murphy's, just down the block from the bar. "That's all there was to it. It was there." Then Skip patted his hair to make sure it was all in place, as he was always very proud of it, needing his hair always to be "just so."

For Jimmy, one of the problems connected with barhopping was that in 1973 Skip began drinking more heavily, and when he was drunk, the otherwise sweet Skip could be a bitch. Jimmy's grandmother professed psychic abilities, and Jimmy himself had had a couple of instances of deep intuition, but it didn't take any special talents to see that addiction problems were in the future for Skip if something didn't shake him up soon. Other friends noticed the drinking, too, and Skip had confided to one that he'd gone to a couple of different doctors to get prescriptions for Valium, so it looked like Valium was starting to become a problem, too.

In late Spring, Jimmy went to a function for the gay krewe Armeinius and became instantly enamored with the idea of joining. Friends told him to throw a big party and get to know more members, since he'd need to be elected into membership. Knowing Skip and Bill loved anything Mardi Gras related, he wanted to invite them both, but Jimmy knew they wouldn't get along at the party, and he was afraid Skip might get drunk and make a scene. Bill, on the other hand, often volunteered to play the piano for little or no money for Amon Ra's Miss America contest and other functions, so Bill seemed to deserve some recompense. But then, Jimmy was closer to Skip and generally preferred his company. And yet...

After debating with himself a while longer, Jimmy finally invited Bill to the party on Friday, June 22, and crossed his fingers.

The next morning, he knew he should go over for coffee as he usually did and try to explain his reasons to Skip, but instead he spent the day cleaning up after the party. Late Sunday morning, though, he did finally go over.

"He knows," said Bill as he opened the door.

Jimmy sighed. "I guess I'd better try to apologize."

"He won't speak to you."

But he did. Jimmy explained the reasons, adding that Skip would be invited to his next party without Bill, and Skip then seemed okay. For the most part.

So they went to Lafitte's to start the afternoon off with a couple of drinks. After a while, Skip suggested they head over to the UpStairs, but Jimmy declined, saying two Bloody Marys was his limit, and explaining that he had to get ready for his first krewe meeting. Skip shrugged but asked Jimmy to drop him off at the bar.

Jimmy did so, and as Skip stepped out of the car, Jimmy experienced another of the few psychic events of his life, as he saw a black, cloud-like aura over Skip's head. Maybe Skip was in for a really drunk, bitchy evening this time. Or maybe he was still mad about that party. Jimmy blinked, and the cloud was gone, probably just something in his eye and not a sign of anything. Skip waved good-bye and turned toward the dark entrance leading to the UpStairs Lounge.

Perry Waters

A native of Florida, Perry Lane Waters, Jr., was born on May 1, 1932, to Perry Sr. and Gertrude Wadcock Waters, and his mother still lived in Pensacola. Perry had spent some time in the Air Force, and then he'd attended Loyola Dental School (later LSU Dental School) in New Orleans. His senior picture is in the 1960 annual, though the Louisiana Dental Association has 1961 as his graduation date.

Perry was a member of the Dental Association in Florida while he lived in Pensacola after graduating, but he transferred back to New Orleans in 1965. Perry never married, and at forty-one he was living at 189 Hibiscus Place in Harahan, a suburb of New Orleans.

Dr. Waters had several patients he met in the gay community. He enjoyed having his social and professional lives overlap, but this also made him a soft touch at times. He charged less if he knew his patients didn't have much money, and at times he might even do some work for free.

Perry received 3rd and 4th degree burns over 75% of his body. The skin over his abdomen was intact, but almost all other skin and fat on his body was gone, except for a few pieces of skin attached to a couple of his fingers. His secretary, Jacqueline Best, identified him by a ring and a watch found on his body.

Bill Richardson and the Memorial Service

"They're fruits. Bury them in fruit jars."

Gays reeling from the loss of their friends soon faced another problem—no one wanted to bury those friends. Ministers and priests from several churches refused to give "Christian burials" to these men who'd been committing mortal sins and who'd died as a "direct result of their sinful nature." Those few religious leaders who did want to acknowledge the dead were afraid of repercussions from both their congregations of morally upright citizens and from their religious superiors. But one man in New Orleans did take a stand.

Father William P. Richardson, Jr., was the rector officiating at St. George's Episcopal Church in Uptown New Orleans. Born in 1909 to a forty-year-old mother and fifty-eight-year-old father, the first-born in the newlywed couple's marriage, Bill was a sickly child for years. This led him early to a life of contemplation rather than youthful activity, and he decided to enter the seminary and lead a life of service. He had one brother, who became a concert pianist.

Like his parents, Bill married late in life, in his mid-thirties, and while he knew something was different about him sexually, he didn't know what it was. He did love his wife, and they had two children, a son and a daughter. Bill and his wife were happily married for almost twenty years, until 1963, when his wife developed a blood clot, which lodged in her heart and killed her instantly.

Over the following years, Bill became involved in more activities, such as taking high school students on tours through Europe. Then he began taking Hindu and Muslim college students from India into his home. He liked helping young people, and he also liked the way these experiences helped broaden his mind.

In the early 1970's, Bill was presented with another experience, one which changed his life. His seminary in New York offered a summer course on homosexuality, women's liberation, and communal living. "Well, I don't know about any of that," Bill thought, "so I'd better go." He did gain some insight into the ideals behind communal living and a greater sensitivity for women's rights, but though he was years away from accepting his own bisexuality, he was greatly struck by what he learned about gays and of the oppression they faced.

He observed a gay marriage at Holy Apostles on 9th Avenue, with twenty to thirty clergymen witnessing the union of two men wearing white suits, who walked up the aisle and were blessed in a largely Episcopal ceremony. Bill was a bit taken aback when the two men kissed, but he returned to New Orleans with a strong feeling he needed to teach tolerance and help oppressed gays in his congregation and city.

Bill hired a down-and-out handyman to help with chores, and one day the man assaulted him. It was the first time Bill experienced penetration, and though the rape was a horrific experience, he did not report the incident or even fire the man. There was no further violence, and the experience left Bill with much to consider.

While Father Richardson was on one of his trips to Europe with high school students, he left his assistant, Stewart Wood, in charge of St. George's. When he returned, Bill learned that a man named Bill Larson had come to the church bookstore while Bill was gone and asked Wood to come to a gay bar, the UpStairs Lounge, one Sunday and preach to a small congregation that met there. It seemed a rather odd request, but Bill gave his permission, so Wood went to preach, making sure to bring his wife along with him.

When Larson learned of Bill's understanding attitude, he approached Bill with some of his concerns. "A bar isn't really a good place for a church meeting," Larson said. "Some of my members won't come. We need another meeting place. Could you help us?"

Bill had been the rector at St. George's for twenty-three years and felt he had a right to use some of his power. There was a chapel with a separate entrance at St. George's, and since the elected representatives in the vestry did not officially have a say in who met there, Bill authorized the use of the chapel for meetings of the Metropolitan Community Church. There was some commotion in Bill's Episcopal congregation, with one woman refusing to return until the chapel had been exorcised, but the grumblings didn't get loud and didn't last long because Larson soon bought a double shotgun, a typically narrow, New Orleans style house, at 1363 Magazine and moved the meetings there.

This didn't end the relationship between the two Bills. Larson still met with Father Richardson regularly for dinner and to discuss liturgy. William Ros Larson, who was born on January 5, 1926, to Anna Howell and Isadore Larson in Hamilton, Ohio, and had two sisters and a brother, had served in the Army for a time. He had originally been Methodist, and he'd been married and had one child.

When he felt a call to the ministry and became a Methodist lay minister, his wife left because she didn't want to be a minister's wife. Larson had wandered a bit after that, becoming an Episcopalian while learning to deal with his homosexuality. He moved to New Orleans in 1969. Bill eventually heard about MCC and joined that group, being ordained on April 24, 1972. Still, because of his limited background and the diverse needs of his congregation, Larson wanted to hear as many ideas as he could and enjoyed long discussions with the rector of St. George's.

At about 1:00 a.m. in the early morning of June 25, 1973, Father Bill Richardson received a telephone call. "Bill Larson's dead," the caller said. "He burned to death at the UpStairs."

Still groggy, Bill misunderstood and thought that Larson had died upstairs at his Magazine Street home. It wasn't until the next morning, after a sleepless night, that he realized the enormity of the tragedy. As he read the headlines announcing the deaths of twenty-nine people and looked at the gruesome photographs, the phone rang again. The friend who'd called the night before was asking now for Bill to hold a memorial service that evening.

"Yes, I can do that," Bill responded. "But let's keep this low key. Don't tell the media about it."

Bill knew his superiors wouldn't like the idea of doing anything that might sound to the public as if they were condoning homosexuality, but Bill also knew he needed to provide a religious setting where the mourners could grieve. Since grief was a personal, private issue, Bill didn't want the service to become a media event.

The Reverend Troy Perry, founder of MCC, flew in from California to attend the memorial service. Because there was so little time to advertise the meeting, though, only about eighty to ninety people (fifty, according to the newspaper, and two hundred according to Troy Perry) showed up at St. George's that evening. In addition to the mourners, however, Bill learned ten minutes before the service began that the media had arrived. Bill told them that this was not a publicity stunt, that no pictures were to be taken, and he begged the reporters not to write a sensational account of the service.

Morris Kight of the Gay Liberation Movement participated in the service, but it was Troy Perry many wanted to hear. "Someone said it was just a bunch of faggots," Perry said. "But we knew them as people, and as brothers and sisters, and will never forget them. This isn't the end," he went on. "My brothers and sisters who were destroyed in that fire, they're in peace now. The individuals who did this act, we have to pray for them, because they have to live with this. This will be on their consciences for the rest of their lives."

The following morning, Bill received a call from Iverson B. Noland, the Episcopal bishop of Louisiana. Noland, who strongly disliked sexually inappropriate people, not only gays but even anyone who'd been divorced, rustled his newspaper against the receiver.

"Is this true?" he shouted into the phone. "Is it true that you held a memorial service at St. George's?"

"Yes," Bill replied. "It's true."

Noland moaned. "What am I going to say when people call?"

"'Do you think Jesus would keep these people out?'" Bill suggested.

Noland was not appeased. He wanted to know why the service couldn't have been held at the MCC meeting place. It wasn't large enough, Bill explained. Noland still wasn't satisfied. He called again to let Bill know he'd received over a hundred calls from irate church members. Bill himself received a few hate calls and hate letters. His congregation was upset, and ministers of several fundamentalist churches called to tell him they were outraged at his improper actions. Only one member out of twelve in the vestry at St. George's supported Bill's decision to hold a memorial service.

Bill had expected to receive little support, but he wasn't prepared for all the antagonism. He wrote a letter to the vestry and the congregation saying he was upset at the anti-Christian attitude they displayed, that if he couldn't be Christian and a rector at the same time, he was going to hand in his resignation.

Bill's secretary telephoned Al Selph, the senior warden, the most important lay person, who convinced Bill not to send the letter, persuading him that his congregation loved him. Bill was still upset, but he had planned a month-long trip to India with two of his Indian students and decided to wait until he returned to see how things worked out. If his congregation continued to feel the same way, then he'd go ahead and resign after all.

Bill went out to take a walk and reflect on his choices. As he was walking, someone stopped him. "Thank you," said the woman and then walked on without further explanation.

Another woman stopped him further on. "I'm from Trinity Episcopal," she said, "and I think it was wonderful you did this."

Bill smiled wryly. "Could you call Bishop Noland and tell *him* that?"

She did. She also called her rector at Trinity and told him he should have held the memorial service there.

At the end of the week, Bill was approached to hold a second memorial service for all those who hadn't been able to attend the first. He told them he was sorry, but he was leaving the country and they'd have to find another place. The human relations committee for the Roman Catholic Church, even with proof that at least one of the dead was Catholic, wouldn't even issue a statement of regret about the fire, so they certainly weren't going to offer to host a service. Evelyn Barrett from the Unitarian Church Uptown offered her church's building, but the memorial service organizers decided it was too far from the Quarter and the service would therefore receive too small an attendance.

Finally, Reverend Kennedy, a black minister leading a white congregation at St. Mark's Methodist church on N.

Rampart on the fringe of the Quarter, offered to hold the memorial in his building. Three thousand leaflets were printed and distributed to reach as many of those who missed the first service as possible.

Not everyone who wanted to attend the memorial service showed up that night, however. Richard West had become physically ill when he saw the images of the dead on television. He really only knew one of those killed, Skip Getchell, having formerly been roommates with Skip's lover, Bill, along with their friends Lou Bernard and Nick. Richard didn't hear about the first memorial and so hoped to attend the second one. He wanted to publicly affirm his loss and share in the grief that so many others were feeling.

However, though Richard was a calm person by nature, he found himself feeling outraged and militant for the first time in his life the week after the fire, not so much over the fire itself, but over what he felt was Troy Perry's manipulation of the tragedy to boost his own image. Despite his love for Skip, Richard refused to attend the memorial service because of Troy Perry, and he attests that many others did likewise, sickened that someone could use so much pain and suffering to put himself in the spotlight.

One of those who did attend the memorial service that evening was the Reverend Finis Crutchfield, the fifty-six-year-old Methodist bishop of the Conference of Louisiana, responsible for all the Methodist congregations in the state. He claimed to have had several friends among those who died, and he wanted to show people by his presence at the service that Reverend Kennedy was not acting as a renegade without permission. Crutchfield had been married for thirty-two years and had a family, but he too was either gay or bisexual. He later moved with his family to Houston in 1976 to preside over the Texas Conference, and he died of complications resulting from AIDS in May of 1987. Kennedy and Crutchfield were the only two representatives of other denominations besides MCC present at the memorial, but during the service, a telegram of sympathy was read which had been received from the American Baptist Convention, less conservative than Southern Baptists.

Troy Perry spoke again at this second memorial service. John Gill of Atlanta, Georgia, Paul Breton of Washington, D.C., and Lucian Baril of New Orleans were other ministers who participated in the meeting, along with Morty Manford, a member of the Gay Activist Alliance in New York. Perry, addressing the mourners, said that "as long as one brother or sister in this country is oppressed, it's our problem."

Manford said that the victims "knew what it was like to live in a condemning society where churches call us sinners, psychologists call us sick, legislators call us criminals, where capitalists denounce us as subversive and communists denounce us as decadent." But, he added, "we know we are living, feeling, productive humans."

Near the end of the service, Breton said, "We need a time, a time to be quiet and think and to say to God what is deepest in our hearts, and for God to say to us what we need so much to hear."

What they heard from God came in a "still, small voice," but what they heard from other people came in loud and clear. Gays who heard comments on the street or at work like, "I hope they burned their dresses off" and "It was only faggots—why worry?" had to pretend not to take offense.

Many did argue or fight, but many more were afraid to lose their jobs if their sexuality became suspect over criticizing those who made light of the fire. So they'd hear jokes like, "What tragedy happened in New Orleans on June 24th? That only thirty faggots died and not more!" or jokes that began, "Did you hear the one about the flaming queens?" and try desperately to keep their rage inside.

Having a public place to vent their feelings and share their grief with others offered a way to do more than allow hatred and anger and fear build up inside. There was no way for a great deal of anger not to remain, but the two evenings of memorial services helped at least to keep the anger at a level the mourners could deal with and let them deal more fully with the grief itself that they also so desperately needed to face.

As the service came to a close, it was announced that the media was out front and that if they chose, the mourners could leave by a side exit. One woman stood up defiantly and insisted that she came in through the front and would leave through the front. Paul Killgore was there with his lover of three years, Frank Scorsone. They turned to each other and discussed what they should do.

They noticed the others around them debating as well. There was no sense among the group that it would be a failure to leave out the side entrance, only that they should decide what was best. Paul and Frank decided to leave through the front doors, and as it turned out, many others did, too. It may not have been a defining moment in gay New Orleans history, but it was a memorable moment at the very least. Thirty people had died, but now after two memorial services granting an opportunity for community grief, their friends and lovers could start to go on.

The UpStairs Lounge

Phil Esteve was at the Beverly Dinner Playhouse with his lover, Durel, and another couple, Hollis Wallace and his lover, on the evening of June 24th. *Damn Yankees* was about to begin. The foursome were eating and laughing, enjoying their night out, when a waiter came to their table.

"Mr. Esteve?"

"Yes?"

"Phone call for you, sir. You can follow me."

As the waiter led Phil to a phone, Phil wondered what the call could be about. Why would anyone bother to call him here? Who could it be, anyway? Buddy knew how to handle the bar. That's why Phil had made him manager. Many of Phil's friends should be at the bar right now, too. What could they need to call him for?

Phil hoped he wouldn't miss the beginning of the performance. Whoever was calling better damn well have a good reason.

"Hello?"

"Phil!"

"Yeah?"

"Phil, there's been a fire."

***

Phil's mother died in May of 1970. Phil was thirty-nine and began reflecting about life in general and about his in particular. Here he was almost forty and not getting anywhere. Now he'd inherited $15,000 from his mother. Maybe he should go into business for himself. It wasn't too late for him to make something of his life if he really tried.

But what should he do? Maybe some kind of shop. Perhaps a novelty shop on Royal Street. Perhaps a bar. Phil knew Alice Brady, who owned the Galley House on the corner of Chartres and Toulouse. One evening as he was still contemplating what he should do with his money, Phil stopped by to talk with Alice.

"What kind of shop do you think I should get?" he asked after presenting his options.

"Well," she replied, "if someone has a dollar, they'll buy a drink before they buy a gift."

So Phil began looking in the ads. He found a bar on the second floor of a building at 604 Iberville. There was a flop house on the third floor with a couple of rooms for rent. The bar was owned by Wanda Long and had been a gay bar before and at another time had been a merchant seaman bar. Nicky Gristina, a bartender who worked at Wanda's when the place was pretty much a hustler bar, said that Wanda was into witchcraft and would sometimes wipe a special ointment onto the bar to get customers.

Wanda had a reputation as a "big crook." She was always nice to Phil, though she did have a "vulgar mouth." She asked $15,000 for the bar, but Phil didn't want to spend his entire inheritance. He offered $7,500 and Wanda accepted, probably because she had lung cancer and wanted to start taking care of her affairs.

The UpStairs had been closed for a year when Phil took over. Of course, he knew nothing about running a bar, so he went to several bars to observe how things were done. He felt confident, though. You sold liquor and people drank it. It couldn't be *that* hard.

One night, Phil stopped at the Caverns and ordered a Manhattan. "I'm going to be opening a gay bar soon," Phil announced, a bit proudly.

"You better find a bartender you can trust," replied the bartender on duty, Buddy Rasmussen. They began talking. The UpStairs was well away from most of the other gay bars in the Quarter. No one was going to casually stop by. The UpStairs would need to be their destination. Well, perhaps anyone who took the Canal Street bus to get to the Quarter might walk by, or people coming from Uptown.

"If everyone from Canal Street to Carrollton stops by for just one drink on their way to Lafitte's," Buddy told him, "you'll be successful."

That was a pretty big if, though. The neighborhood was fairly sleazy, with a hustler bar in the next block. Since Phil had no intention of owning a sleazy bar, he'd have to work hard to create a different atmosphere at the UpStairs.

"Ugh." Buddy groaned as he took his first look at the four-foot-wide stairwell leading to the bar. Ugly plumbing jutted out everywhere, creating anything but a good first impression. Something had to be done about that. No one wanted to go someplace ugly. They went to bars to escape. "I know," he said. "I'll cover the plumbing with fabric. I'll drape it over the pipes all the way down along the ceiling and walls."

It might look a little strange, but better to create an odd first impression than an ugly one. Fortunately, there was a window at the top of the stairwell. They could leave that open to let the air flow, so it wouldn't get stuffy in the stairwell.

Upstairs in the bar, they looked about. The restroom, just to the left of the entrance, needed little more than cleaning. It was 5'4" wide and 6'11" long, big enough. From the restroom to the edge of the bar was about 8'7", with an eight-foot-high window in between, plenty of room to move about without feeling crowded. The bar, 28'4" long and 2'2" wide, jutted 6'4" out from the Iberville wall and ran parallel to it. And there were twenty-two chrome stools with padded red seats.

There were seven windows in that first room, all from the floor almost to the ceiling, and three similar windows in the second room. The three in the second room were covered with plywood, but what about these in the first room? My God, thought Phil, what if someone fell out the windows? Think of the lawsuits. But on closer inspection, he saw that the windows all had bars covering the lower portion. They weren't burglar bars, spaced too far apart for that, but they would alert people there was a window and that they'd better not walk out into empty air. Then he noticed the windows wouldn't stay open, anyway. The ropes connecting them to the counterweights had rotted, so the windows simply slid shut when opened unless propped open with a stick.

As hot as it got here in New Orleans, though, Phil didn't want to rely on windows for cooling the place down. They'd put in lots of air conditioning so the bar would be pleasant. One of these days he'd get around to repairing the ropes, but for now, a stick would do to hold the windows open on the few pleasantly cool days they might experience in New Orleans. Something more important was installing an automatic door closer for the fire door which led into the bar, so that no one would come in, leave the door open, and let all the AC rush out down the stairs.

An archway, 15'7" across, connected the first room to the second. This room was 21'6" across and 37' from the Iberville wall to the wall of the storage room and stairway to the third floor. A customer would still have easy access from the second room to the bar, but there was space here to maybe put a dance floor at the Chartres end of the room. They decided to elevate the dance floor by building a platform two feet high and six feet deep, spanning the width of the room.

They hoped that by raising the platform it would absorb the pounding of the feet on top of it. There was a bar below, and Phil didn't want to disturb the people beneath them. They bolted boards on the wall, laid rafters across, and nailed plywood down on top of the beams. There was still room for six tables with four chairs each in the second room as well as a cigarette machine against the wall to the third room.

As they looked at their completed platform, they decided to make a smaller, similar platform back in the first room for a piano to rest on, in the corner against the wall connecting the first two rooms, at the Chartres end of the bar, so the two platforms were next to each other, divided by a wall that came out to just past where the platforms ended. They purchased a white baby grand piano for the room and put it on the platform, with stairs leading up to it, and placed two columns with large candles on top of the stairs. The piano's platform blocked the bottom two feet of the window on the far right facing Chartres, but there was still plenty of light from the remaining window space reaching almost to the top of the twelve-foot ceilings. Maybe even too much light. Bars were supposed to be a little dim, weren't they?

There was more than enough room for the air conditioners they wanted, one in the top of the middle Chartres window, which was supported by plywood and beams that might block off a little more of the light from outside. The Iberville window in the corner seemed a good place for an icemaking machine, giving the bartenders easy access and blocking off yet more of that bright Southern sunlight. They also decided to cover the Chartres-side wall with the three plywood-covered windows with paneling to make that room hopefully a bit cozier. Now you couldn't even tell there *were* windows in the second room. Much nicer than plywood.

With a little more work, the bar was looking good. They'd fortunately been able to buy some things cheap, items from a flop house bar that burned down a couple of months before the UpStairs opened. They bought some oriental-looking hurricane lamps to place here and there. They put indoor-outdoor carpeting on the floors and along the stairs, which they'd keep clean by using muriatic acid. Buddy crawled through the bars on the windows in the front room, hooked his belt to one, and leaned out so he could clean the windows. Not too difficult, but Buddy hoped he didn't have to clean them often.

The bar counter was covered with a pink-orange formica, and Phil and Buddy put up red, flocked wallpaper along the walls. They set up a new wall against the Iberville side of the room behind the bar, covering two more of the windows, leaving four windows out of ten in the two rooms unobstructed. This new wall was brick and had a waterfall in the center. A bit gaudy, perhaps, but still rather nice, especially for this neighborhood. Some plastic lace tablecloths with some plastic roses in vases had been left on the tables by Wanda, but they looked so awful Phil and Buddy threw them out, putting instead big, teardrop-shaped candles on each table. At least there were no longer phones on the tables. Back when the earlier bar was in business, every table had phones. Someone would see someone else he liked and phone over to his table to introduce himself. Phil didn't want this to be a cheap pick-up bar.

The first two rooms were well set for now, but there was a third room to the bar. The only access to it was through a fire door in the second room. The three windows along the Chartres wall in this room were unblocked but painted, so there was no need to get any more plywood. The only problem was that the way the bar was set up made the first two rooms seem like one unit and the third room another. This room just didn't fit in with the rest of the bar. It might be hard to integrate it with the first two. No matter. They'd figure out something.

The UpStairs Lounge opened on Halloween of 1970.

At first, there weren't many customers. Sometimes, hustlers would bring their tricks from Wanda's (not the same Wanda who had previously owned the UpStairs) and have their johns buy them drinks. But no one was allowed to go about asking people to buy them drinks. If either Phil or Buddy saw any of that, they threw the guy out of the place.

Phil worked the day shift and Buddy worked at night. The bar wasn't open twenty-four hours a day like some Quarter bars, so when Buddy closed up around 4:00 a.m., he made sure the iron gate at the bottom of the stairwell was locked.

With only a handful of customers each night for the first few weeks after opening, Buddy had plenty of time between serving drinks to massage customers' shoulders or dance with them a few minutes. Phil had bought a jukebox and some records, charging ten cents a song, but when a customer asked if he could bring a favorite record, Phil and Buddy decided to have customers bring more of their favorites. They'd check on the back of the jukebox to see which songs were being played, and when they found one no one was playing anymore, they'd replace it with one a customer brought. They mostly brought in new songs, but there were a few oldies and even some opera. Even if a customer brought his own record, however, he still had to pay the ten cents to hear it play.

"We have to do something more," Phil said. "We still need more customers."

"We had a beer bust when I was in Houston," Buddy told him.

"A beer bust?"

They could put a pitcher of beer on each table, Buddy explained, and charge everyone a dollar to get in the bar. They could do it every Sunday afternoon, say from 5:00 to 7:00, refilling each pitcher until the beer bust was over. People would hear about it and soon they'd get a crowd coming every Sunday. Once the customers felt comfortable with the bar and came to know other folks there, they'd start coming on other days. The bar would lose money at first, but they'd make it up once they had those customers coming regularly.

There were no other beer busts in New Orleans at that time, so Phil was a bit dubious, but he decided to give it a try. They thought they'd use that third room for the beer bust, so Phil needed some more tables and chairs. He had a friend who worked with cables, so he was able to get fifteen of the huge wooden spools that cables were wrapped around, and Phil used the spools as tables. Because the floor area in the room was 26'9" by 54'8", the tables fit easily, and with four wooden chairs for each table, they could seat sixty people now if they needed. They started the beer bust, trying to be patient with its low attendance, but after a year, Buddy had to admit the idea just wasn't working well in this city.

Rather than give up the idea, however, they decided to try moving the beer bust from the third room to the second room. Suddenly, the beer bust flourished. Apparently, everyone had been feeling isolated back in the third room. Attendance swelled from a dozen or so to a hundred, and then at times to a hundred and twenty.

Phil hired Wayne to help during beer busts. Wayne was jovial and spirited and good for business. Wayne's lover, Lonnie, did outlandish drag for Mardi Gras, the only time Phil would allow drag in the bar. Lonnie once came in on Mardi Gras wearing a ten-foot-wide hoop skirt made of Saran Wrap. Together, Wayne and Lonnie befriended many of the customers, helping more people feel comfortable in coming.

After a while, though, Wayne moved to Alaska, and Phil hired Napoleon to help during beer busts. His lover was Stanley. Napoleon had worked for Clifford Construction previously. He also used to hustle before tending bar at the UpStairs but apparently never did any hustling once he started bartending. Certainly, Phil was never aware of it, and Phil made a point of checking up on things he suspected. He'd pop into the bathroom occasionally to make sure nothing was going on that shouldn't. A couple of times, Phil did find two guys getting a little too intimate. He kicked them out of the bar.

As attendance at the beer bust continued to grow, more of the customers became regulars. There was Adlai S. "Tad" Turner, who often came with his good friend, Luther Boggs. Tad was in his late forties and stopped in the bar every day after work. He'd stay for two to three hours, drinking gin and tonic every day, talking when he wasn't drinking. His friend Luther usually drank beer and rarely became drunk.

Tad liked routine. It was fun to have a regular bar to go to. It was comfortable to have a regular drink. He also had a favorite Mardi Gras costume he wore every year. Four heads on a kind of yoke he put over his head so it looked like a man with five heads was walking down the street.

Tad would drink from six to ten gin and tonics every day, and at one point he ran up a $200 bar tab. When Phil cut off his tab, Tad continued coming every day, only now coming with some money.

Then there was Uncle Al, a retired radioman who had worked at sea for years. Born in 1905, Albert Harold Monroe was in his upper sixties and only had two teeth in front. He'd buy a beer and nurse it for hours. A regular at every beer bust, Uncle Al loved to tell stories. He'd saved his money from his days as a radioman and bought land in the Rigolets. He had a farm there plus a house in the city, at 2265 N. Villere St., where his sister lived with him. Uncle Al grew extra vegetables on the farm so he could bring green onions and okra to his pals at the UpStairs.

And there was Gene, a silver-haired man in his fifties who always wore black, sometimes with a black cloak and carrying a cane. Single and living with his mother, Gene tried several time to pick Buddy up, but Buddy never went home with him, as getting picked up was not his goal.

Nila Latrell, who worked for South Central Bell telephone company, came to the bar regularly, and a Sophia Loren lookalike named Diane came occasionally with her friend Frank Dufrene, though women were certainly in the minority as customers. Max Barnett, who often worked for charities, came regularly, too, as did a male gossip columnist from the *Times-Picayune,* coming because he was a friend of Phil's.

Another regular was Bob McAnear, a narcotics agent with Customs who Buddy knew from his time working at the Holiday Inn. Bob wasn't gay, not even bisexual, but he and his wife Bettye liked Buddy. When Buddy invited them to the UpStairs, they went in a show of support.

Bettye Jo Bartlett McAnear was born in 1932 and was exuberant from the beginning. She was head of the cheerleading squad in high school and had her own radio show shortly thereafter. Even marriage and three kids couldn't keep her away from the stage. She sang in the church choir. She performed in local theater. She joined the New Orleans opera chorus.

When she and Bob saw the third room at the UpStairs, with a stage already built, Bettye couldn't stop herself from suggesting the bar put on plays.

"But no women come here," Buddy said. "We'd only have men in the cast."

"So what?" Bettye returned. "You guys are in drag half the time. You sew your own dresses for Mardi Gras. What's the problem?"

That third room in the bar had remained a problem for Phil. He'd let the Metropolitan Community Church meet there for a few months. That had ended up working out okay since now many MCC members were regulars at the bar. Probably half the members of the local congregation came to the beer bust every Sunday.

But after the MCC was no longer in the third room, Phil and Buddy wanted to do something else with it. Bettye soon added Director of Upstairs Melodramas to her resumé.

The stage in the third room was 18' by 26'9" and the patrons began performing their "nelly dramas" sometime in 1971.

Bettye wrote and directed the first of these plays. She worked at the Little Theatre and was happy to bring drama to the bar, even if it was just for fun. The "actors" used the storage room and stairwell to the third floor as the dressing room. There were no real drag shows yet at the bar, though the men would dress as women in the plays if portraying a woman. Many of the shows were literally melodramas, with exaggerated acting.

At other times, the group did slapstick comedy, but the melodramas were more common. Buddy put popcorn in bowls on the tables in the audience, and whenever the spectators saw a villain in the performance, rather than boo or hiss, they'd throw popcorn at the bad guy. "Egad, What a Cad," with an all-male cast, was quite a hit, as was "He Done Everybody Wrong, or The Deviate's Comeuppance," with characters such as Harry Deviate, Nellie Heaven, Miss Queenie, and the Infamous Memphis Queen.

In all, Bettye wrote and directed three melodramas for the Upstairs gang. She had a difficult time limiting their ad libs, which she felt weren't quite as good as the actual lines, but there was no real conflict. They were all just having a good time.

She tried to interest the local theater community to join in, but they weren't impressed with the idea of performing in a gay bar. After the plays became a success, though, more joined in and took over. Bettye was busy with work and her kids as well as her other music and theater projects, so she stepped back. She still felt her own plays were better, but the guys were enjoying themselves, and that was what really mattered.

Even without Bettye, Bob stopped by the bar two or three times a week in the afternoon for a drink. Sometimes at Customs, he'd hear about drug problems in the Quarter, and while chatting with other patrons at the bar, he'd get relevant information to pass on to the task force. Back in those days, documenting sources was a little looser. Once the rules changed and Bob was required to list his informants, he simply stopped asking questions. He wasn't going to put anyone in danger.

Bettye and Bob remained good friends with both Buddy and Phil. When Bob was out of town on an investigation, Buddy often helped babysit their kids. There was a special bond among many of the folks at the UpStairs, and one didn't need to be gay to fit in.

Besides the nelly dramas and church meetings and beer busts, there was also a tiny bit of activism. The Gay Liberation Front Theatre Workshop, with members Philip Schmidt and Charles Selber, from Shreveport, wanted to put on a play, but police gave the UpStairs trouble because the play was too political, so that particular play was never performed.

All in all, things were looking up. Phil hired David Gary to play ragtime on the piano. Customers would often gather around the piano to sing or dance. When the jukebox was playing, customers would dance to that music instead. The UpStairs was the first gay bar in New Orleans to obtain a dancing license, and people enjoyed the feeling of freedom they could experience by dancing in a public place.

But beer busts and plays and singing and dancing weren't quite enough. Buddy suggested a tricycle race. He'd seen one on the show *Laugh-In* and wanted to give it a try. He found a sturdy tricycle capable of supporting adults. Then he marked off a path on the floor with tape, winding the route among the tables, making sharp turns and going off in unexpected directions.

Buddy brought a stopwatch the day of the race, and one at a time, the contestants climbed aboard the tricycle. The only way they could reach the pedals was to drape their legs across the handlebars. Most fell over just trying to sit down. They had to keep the rear wheels astraddle the tape the entire distance, disqualified if they veered too far from the marked path. And Buddy timed each participant so he could declare the winner.

At other times, they'd hang a net from the ceiling, filling it with balloons. At a certain point during the evening, Buddy would release the balloons, and customers would pop them to see which ones had the half price or free drink coupons inside.

Week by week, the bar developed into an island of relative decency in a sordid neighborhood, into an oasis of friendship in a gay bar scene filled with superficiality.

Because the atmosphere at the UpStairs was so informal, many of the customers weren't just bar buddies. When Phil had Christmas dinner at his house, for instance, almost every guest was a customer from the bar. Phil Esteve went into the bar business to make money. But he made more than that. He made friends, and he and Buddy helped create an atmosphere where others could make friends as well.

In May of 1973, Phil and Durel went to Europe for a three-week vacation. Planning for it had kept Phil in a good mood. Things that usually bothered him didn't anymore. So what if that guy was being a little obnoxious? Phil was going to Europe. There was one incident, however, he couldn't overlook.

Phil had hired Donald E. "Mike" Wolf as a bartender not long before to replace Napoleon, who'd moved out of state. Mike was a good bartender, but he had a short temper. When he began an argument with Buddy and then struck Buddy, he still had to be restrained by customers to keep him from continuing to attack. Buddy fired him on the spot, and Phil stood behind Buddy's decision.

When things cooled off, though, Phil told Mike that if he apologized to Buddy, and Buddy accepted, that Mike could come return. Mike apologized, Buddy accepted, and things were okay for a few days. Then Mike started arguing with a customer and went outside to fight with him. This time, Phil refused to take him back. He fired him on May 17 and then left for three weeks to forget about everything except enjoying Europe.

When Phil returned, there was a new problem. The bartender hired to replace Mike, Joseph Dufrees, simply didn't show up for work one day. Joseph had decided to leave town and did so without giving any notice.

Phil put an ad in the paper but was not terribly impressed with the applicants. After two bad tries in a row, he wanted a bartender he could trust. A few days after the ad came out, on Saturday, June 9, a man named Hugh came in and asked Phil if there were any jobs around. As they talked, Phil became impressed by the man's personality.

Thirty-two-year-old Hubert Dean Cooley had been born on July 9, 1940, to Lawrence and Ruth Loveland Cooley, who lived in Hastings, Michigan by 1957 and still did in 1973. Hugh dropped out of school after the ninth grade and joined the Navy in Kalamazoo on July 25, 1957, as soon as he turned seventeen. He was given the rank of AR E-1 and was stationed at the U.S. Naval Training Center at Great Lakes, Illinois, leaving the service almost immediately afterward on November 4, 1957.

Hugh now lived at 1435 Polymnia Street, Apartment 3, just a few doors down from Mitch and Horace, regulars at the bar. Of medium build, perhaps a little on the thin side, Hugh had tried a heterosexual marriage but was now divorced.

"Stick around," said Phil. "Maybe I can use you."

Hugh's eyes lit up. He really needed a job, and knowing Buddy and several of the regulars made this job better than it might otherwise have been. Maybe his luck was changing.

Phil tried him out on an hourly basis for one week, to see if he would fit in, and then, finding that he did, Phil hired him full-time, to take the 8:00 p.m. to 4:00 a.m. shift.

Phil hired Bob Jordan at the same time he hired Hugh, also on a trial basis, but after five days, Jordan came to work drunk and fell behind the bar. Phil was willing to give him another chance, but when he came to work the next day even more drunk and fell again, Phil fired him.

"Give me the keys to the bar," Phil told him.

"No," said Jordan. "You pay me first."

They argued over the keys a few minutes, and finally Phil physically forced the keys from Jordan. Phil shook his head as he watched Jordan leave. At least Hugh was working out. That gave him two good bartenders, anyway. Buddy had sure been right that first time they spoke.

Friday, June 15, saw the start of a new play in the third room theatre, "High Spirits," which was a takeoff on a Noel Coward play. It seemed to generate a good response, appropriate laughs and a large crowd that seemed adequately thirsty. The play would probably run a few more months before they'd need to do another one. Someone from the Salt and Pepper Lounge, a straight bar, saw the play and liked it. He asked the UpStairs performers to use it one time at the UpStairs, on June 30, as a fundraiser for the Crippled Children's Hospital. The actors agreed.

Meanwhile, with Buddy and Hugh both scheduled to work on June 24, Phil knew he didn't need to be at the bar to check up on anything. They could both handle whatever came up. Phil and Durel got together with some friends and decided to have a nice, relaxing evening out at the Beverly Dinner Playhouse.

Tom and Paul

What could bring a man raised in Biloxi, Mississippi and a man raised in Milwaukee, Wisconsin together? Communication. Or rather, a Communications class.

Tom Struve, born April 17, 1950, could not stay in Biloxi like the rest of his family. He wanted a little something more out of life. He left for New Orleans and began attending Loyola University. There he met a pretty pre-med student and, after dating a while, became engaged because "it was the thing to do." He eventually realized, however, that a heterosexual marriage was not for him, and he called it off.

It was just as Tom was finally accepting his homosexuality that he signed up for a Communications course. He'd been a math major but realized that wasn't for him, either. He liked radio, however, and started to work at the student radio station. There, he was encouraged to change his major to Communications and did so. That led to his meeting with Paul.

Paul Doll, born August 17, 1945, had received his Master of Fine Arts in children's television in 1967 in Wisconsin and then moved to New Orleans for an associate professorship at Loyola. Paul grew up with a childhood friend, and as they matured, they realized they wanted to be more than best friends. They became lovers. When Paul moved to New Orleans, his lover moved with him. Nothing was going to separate them.

When Paul's blond, Jewish lover toured briefly as an accompanist for an opera singer, Paul thought of asking if they could arrange any future touring during summer or semester breaks if possible, so they could be together more. He didn't want to stand in the way of his lover's career, though, and if that meant being separated occasionally, he'd live with that. He knew that nothing was ever going to *really* separate them, at least not for long, after all their years as best friends.

Nothing, except maybe cancer.

Paul was still dealing with his lover's death when he noticed a cute young man in one of his classes. After they were both able to "communicate" the news they were gay, Paul invited Tom to go out with him some night to the bars. Tom accepted.

They became good friends, and in his senior year, Tom moved from his Uptown apartment to Paul's French Quarter place. He graduated from Loyola in 1970. Tom and Paul spent their "honeymoon" in Memphis, staying in the original Holiday Inn, and cuddling to keep warm against the snow outside, or well, cuddling just because they wanted to cuddle.

Paul left Loyola to become department chair at the University of New Orleans shortly before Tom graduated, and when Tom did get his degree, Paul hired him to work in ITV, or instructional television, while Tom worked part-time on his graduate degree. During the two years Tom worked with television, he and Paul taught several people who later moved on to local New Orleans fame, including Tom Fitzmorris, Fred Palmisano, Becky Allen, and Ricky Graham.

Soon, however, a new opportunity arose. Paul worked hard to ensure that UNO would operate a classical radio station, and in 1972, WWNO signed on, with Paul acting as general manager and Tom working as program director.

They needed some help finding people to host various musical programs, so they turned to one of their friends, Bill Farrell, who knew many of the musicians in town, as well as others who were simply knowledgeable and appreciative of music, being a pianist himself.

Tom and Paul often went with Bill and his lover, Skip Getchell, to the opera and theatre, visiting together afterwards at each other's homes. They also enjoyed sharing Mardi Gras balls together. Though Skip was in Apollo and Tom and Paul were in Amon Ra, they each supported the other's krewe by attending three or four major fundraisers for the other each year. If Tom participated in a drag show, he used the name Veronica, because his mother's cousin was the actress Veronica Lake. Other functions might include a prom night, or perhaps a casino night, with roulette and blackjack.

Tom and Paul didn't frequent the UpStairs Lounge as much as some of the other regulars, but they did make a point of going on Sundays for the beer bust, mostly because they enjoyed the singalongs around the piano so much. They knew Phil Esteve and liked to go to the bar to support him, and they also liked running into Skip and Bill or the numerous others with whom they liked to chat and gossip. It seemed as if everyone knew everyone, and that was an atmosphere they appreciated. Tom especially enjoyed singing "United We Stand" at the end of every beer bust. It seemed to mean something more than a slowly emerging gay pride. It was also a way of telling his friends there how he felt about them.

On June 24, as on almost every previous Sunday for the past year, Tom and Paul prepared for another evening of singing around the piano with their friends. They were already humming when they walked out the door.

Marti Bates

Marti Bates didn't want to go to the new bar on Iberville. Why Phil ever chose that sleazy neighborhood he'd never understand. But Marti had become friends with Buddy back at the Caverns, so he decided to go on over to the UpStairs to give it a try.

Why, it was a nice place, Marti realized after his first visit. He began telling his friends at Lafitte's about it, and little by little, with other customers also praising the bar, the numbers began to grow at the UpStairs.

One of the men who overheard Marti talking about the UpStairs at Lafitte's was Wayne Cottingham. He didn't particularly want to go to Iberville, either, but that guy Marti had sounded pretty convinced, so he thought he'd check it out. Besides, Marti was kind of cute, and maybe he'd run into him there.

They did meet at the UpStairs, and they both fell in love almost immediately. Soon they were living together in an apartment on Burgundy and St. Louis in the Quarter, and both became regulars at the bar, Marti going there almost every day.

For a while, especially in the early months of their relationship, Marti would stop by the UpStairs for a Bloody Mary on his lunch break. Then he'd go to his apartment, where he and Wayne would have energetic, heart-stopping sex, after which Marti would pass by the UpStairs yet again for another drink on his way back to work.

Before long, Marti knew most of the regulars, and as time went on, a few more joined the group, and those already in the group continually grew closer and closer. It almost felt like family, like being home when he was in the bar. He grew to love these people, feeling a special bond he never expected to feel with people he met in a bar.

Certainly, the melodramas helped. Everyone was able to cut up and have fun and interact in a way that would be impossible if everyone was just sitting on stools along the bar. It helped, too, when someone performed particularly well and Marti was able to recognize that his friends had talents he hadn't expected. Like the time Tad Turner played an old woman in one of the skits. He managed to be totally convincing even with that thick, walrus moustache.

When the bar put on a drag show, it was always campy, just for fun. Marcy Marcell did a pretty good Liza Minnelli, but Marti's Jeanette McDonald was pure camp. Of course, he was so nervous about performing that he drank a bit too much beforehand, so much that he wouldn't have been able to walk in loafers much less the spiked heels he was wearing. After he tripped, he jumped up to pretend it was all a part of his act, but everyone could tell he was just drunk.

Not that anyone cared. Sunday nights especially, after Buddy started the beer bust, people often got drunk. Marti and some of his friends would order a pitcher of beer each and chug-a-lug the whole pitcher at one time.

But of course they weren't always drunk. Marti's friend, Rusty Quinton, in particular liked to keep sharp enough to make puns and quip. Rusty, who'd previously run a bar over on North Rampart with his lover, Shelby Babin, always seemed to keep the group laughing. It wasn't even necessarily what he said as the way he said it. "Hi, Master Bates," Rusty might say when greeting Marti.

"That's Mister to you," Marti would reply.

"But Master Bates is the only thing I can think of when I see your cute face."

And there were the others Marti talked to at the bar. Diabetic Mitch and his lover Horace. David Solomon, the MCC guy who helped get the theater room at the bar for the church meetings. Jason Guidry, the bar dingbat. Bartender Napoleon and his lover Stanley, and bartender Wayne and his lover Lonnie. And there was that pleasant Philip Byrd, in his forties, plus the nice, dark-haired, rather effeminate Ferris LeBlanc, and lots of others.

Marti and several of the other regulars not only met continually at the bar but started meeting outside the bar as well. A group of them went to Pass Christian, Mississippi, one evening, had a little party and then slept on the beach. Another time, a group of them went on a steamboat cruise together.

More often, though, they'd get together for dinner. Adam, Buddy's lover, could be rather distant at times, but during dinner, he often loosened up and talked with everyone. And there was the Christmas when Marti and Wayne, Buddy and Adam, Wayne and Lonnie, and three other couples got together. Most of them were food and beverage people. Bartender Wayne was a chef, and both Marti and his Wayne were waiters. They borrowed some tables from Commander's Palace, decorated them with poinsettias, and each couple was tasked with cooking a meal and presenting entrees to the others.

Sometimes, it almost seemed as if Marti's whole life revolved around the UpStairs. He arranged his work schedule so he could be off every Sunday evening, because he wanted to be at that beer bust with his friends. Marcy was always there, and Rusty, and all the others, often gathering at the end of the bar nearest the door, which seemed to be the spot for his little group of friends. Marti might miss another day of the week, but he couldn't miss Sunday.

Wayne, though, grew a little tired of it at times. Their only days off from work were Sunday and Monday, and sometimes, Wayne wanted to go see a movie rather than just go to the bar like always, but Marti enjoyed the bar. If Wayne woke up after Marti and found that Marti wasn't in the house, he knew he could go on over to the UpStairs and find him.

Once, when Marti was at the bar, someone made a delivery. Marti looked down the stairs and saw two big boxes. Up came Wayne, saying, "Well, I know it's a little early, but Happy Birthday!"

In fact, it was four months early, but they dragged the boxes up the stairs and spent the next few hours putting together their identical bicycles as they sat on the bar floor, talking to friends and drinking a little while they worked. Marti looked around once during a break, wondering how it was possible for a bar to feel so much like his living room.

It had to be partly not just the other customers but also because he felt so close to both Buddy and Phil. They weren't just owner and customer. When Phil was short-staffed once, he felt comfortable asking Wayne to fill in for the day as bartender. Wayne accidentally knocked a bottle off the shelf, and when it crashed to the floor, a large splinter of glass cut through his pants and into his leg. Easily agitated Phil wasn't concerned about the alcohol but his friend and brought him immediately to the hospital.

Another time, Marti's appendix burst while he was working at Arnaud's. After a day or so in the hospital, he wanted very much to get out, demanding an early release. As he came out of his room in his wheelchair, he saw Phil Esteve, who'd come to pick him up. "My baby sister is in here," Phil was telling a nurse. "She just had a hysterectomy." Then Phil saw Marti approaching. "Oh, there she is!"

Phil offered to let Marti stay at his place for a few days rather than return to his own second floor apartment, but he left it up to Marti. "Want to go to my place then?" he asked.

"No," said Marti. "I want to go to the UpStairs."

Phil and Buddy let Marti run up a tab for the next few days until he could get back to work, and then once Marti was back waiting tables, they tore up the tab anyway.

On their second anniversary, Marti and Wayne ate dinner at Brennan's. They stayed three hours, finishing their meal and a bottle of champagne. Wayne wanted a little more, though, so after they left the restaurant, they headed over to the UpStairs. Perhaps it wasn't as elegant as Brennan's, but an anniversary would hardly be complete without visiting the place they'd first met. So they sat at the bar and enjoyed a second bottle of champagne. Two bottles for two years. Hmm, things might get tricky by their tenth anniversary.

Marti wondered sometimes if they drank too much. Helping 6'4" Wayne stagger home was not something he had to do often, thank goodness, but they sure did kick back and have fun at those beer busts they attended every Sunday as 1973 wore on, every week, throughout March, April, May, and on into June. Life wasn't perfect, but as long as they could keep sharing all those good times with friends, somehow everything else seemed okay. As June drew to a close, Marti and Wayne looked forward to still one more evening, relaxing, joking, and drinking over at the UpStairs Lounge.

Near Misses

Preston Davis was the organist for the weekly MCC services, and he and his lover enjoyed socializing with the other church members. They went every Sunday to the beer bust, having missed just one time. But they stayed up late Saturday evening, and Preston overslept while taking a nap Sunday afternoon. His lover didn't want to wake him and thought he'd go on to the bar alone. But he had a bit of a toothache. Maybe he ought to stay home, too. Preston and his lover missed only their second beer bust together and lost almost their entire circle of friends that evening.

When George was nineteen, he knew he was gay, but he didn't really know what to do about it. He'd like to start dating men, but he was too shy to approach anyone and too scared to let anyone approach him. He'd never been in a gay bar and didn't even know where they were, though he did figure there was *someplace* that men like him must meet.

Then one day while George was walking down the street, a streetcar passed. On board was Keith, who found George attractive enough that he decided to get off at the next stop and walk back toward George. They started talking, and Keith asked if George wanted to walk along the river with him. George was afraid this man was going to mug him and throw him in the river. But Keith was kind of cute, and God, he had to take a chance sometime.

"Well, how about if we go eat something?" George suggested. That ought to be safe enough.

"Would you like to go for a drink?"

A bar was probably reasonably safe, too, and it wouldn't hurt to find out where a gay bar was, so George agreed. They walked into the Quarter, but when Keith pointed out Wanda's, George shook his head. The place looked too seedy. They continued on, and Keith pointed to the UpStairs Lounge. George shrugged and they walked up into the bar, where they continued to talk.

Talking wasn't all that was on Keith's mind, though. He put his hand on George's knee, and George nervously pushed the hand aside. Then Keith put his hand on George's shoulder, and George squirmed away.

But soon the two men were lovers. They joined MCC around Easter of 1973, often but not always going to the UpStairs after church services were over. They became friends with Mitch and Horace and many of the other MCC members, going to the beach at Waveland with the group, and attending a wedding and reception at the UpStairs, at which Bill Larson officiated. It was George's first gay wedding, and he expected one of the men to be dressed perhaps as Scarlet O'Hara, but both men wore suits, and there were two grooms on top of the cake.

George and Keith continued to make the UpStairs their regular bar, and they enjoyed being with "the gang" on Sunday evenings. But on June 24th, Keith, who was working as a cook across the Causeway, returned home late. They missed church altogether and debated over whether to join their friends over at the UpStairs. They finally decided they were too tired and stayed home.

In 1998, George and Keith had been together for twenty-six years.

***

"Could you go see who that is?" Jason Guidry asked his lover as they relaxed in front of the TV set. His lover stood up and headed for the door.

"Thank God you're okay!" shouted a neighbor when Jason's lover opened the door. "The UpStairs is on fire!"

Jason and his lover rushed immediately to the scene, arriving after the fire was put out. As they walked from there to Charity hospital, Jason reflected on how close they'd come to being at the bar. Every Sunday morning, "morning" being whenever they woke up, even if it was early afternoon, Jason and his lover ate at the Ponchartrain Coffee Shop. Later in the afternoon, they'd go to the beer bust at the UpStairs Lounge.

This Sunday, Jason had eaten lunch with his boss's son, but afterward, Jason and his lover had still gone over for the beginning of the beer bust. Jason did want to spend some time alone with his lover, however, so they left after only a few minutes, promising their friends they'd be back shortly. But then Jason noticed a TV listing for a show about Indians, who had always fascinated him, and since their whole routine for the day had been messed up anyway, Jason decided to just stay home.

"But we told them we'd be back."

"Oh, they'll be so drunk they won't know if we're there or not."

Jason and his lover donated blood when they arrived at Charity, and they looked around for their friends. It was days before they knew for sure just who was dead, but in all, they lost almost two dozen friends and acquaintances, including most of the eight couples in their dinner circuit. Several lived on their street, just a few doors down, one even right next door.

Jason would miss soft-spoken Perry Waters, with whom he could always count on for a decent conversation. He'd miss Skip, too, and all the ideas they shared about Mardi Gras balls. Jason had been to thirty balls during the 1973 Carnival season, fifteen on consecutive nights, and Skip had never tired of hearing about any of it. Jason knew Fred and Earl, a nice-looking couple with an open relationship. Regina and Reggie made up another couple who came over regularly for dinner. Jason knew Luther as well, who used his wit to make people laugh, unlike Phil, who often used his wit to cut people down. But Phil could also be nice, like when he provided a huge buffet on holidays for the bar patrons to enjoy.

Jason had also known Mitch and Horace for years, since before they'd become lovers three years earlier. He watched as their parents came to town to settle Mitch and Horace's estate. Because Mitch had credit cards, it was decided that Mitch was the one who'd put more money into their estate, and because he had two sons while Horace had no children, most of the money after everything was sold went to them, almost nothing going to Horace's family, though Jason knew

Horace was contributing continually to the house and property with his income as a barber.

Jason was so upset about the settlement that he and his lover went out and made their wills. *They* would decide where their money went. At least as much as the law allowed in this state that relied heavily on the Napoleonic code.

Jason felt a deep emptiness for a long while after the fire. Making new friends over the years only partially filled the void. And making those friends was harder than before because he never did get back into the bar scene. Besides, no one could really replace the friends he'd lost, and it would take years before time could heal the shock of losing so many at one time.

***

There were many who claimed to have been on their way to the bar or who said they'd just left before the fire. Phil Esteve estimated that there would have been from 500 to 1000 people at the bar if all their stories were true. One man, who'd come to New Orleans for two days as a tourist, had gone to the UpStairs Saturday night. He'd already booked his return flight for Sunday morning, and even if he'd wanted to stay in town another day, he couldn't change his flight and so was already home in Chicago when he saw the news report. "Oh my God," he told friends. "I was almost there when it happened." So some near misses were nearer than others by a couple of thousand miles.

But as with most tragedies, there were a few people who'd just left the site and others who were approaching. And though their stories are useful in suggesting how narrowly some of those who were victims came to missing the fire as well, and suggesting perhaps how their lives may have evolved if they'd been able to survive, the lingering emotion many of these "near miss" survivors express is not so much excitement at "nearly" having lived an adventure, but rather sadness that more of their friends hadn't been able to do the same.

Jean Gosnell

Jean Ruth Cory Gosnell was a pretty, dark-haired woman of thirty-seven in June of 1973. She'd been born on May 26, 1936. Her husband, Johnny William Gosnell, was dead now, but their three children were doing fine and on their own. Danny Jay, nineteen, and Shelly Lynn, seventeen, lived in Houston, and twenty-year-old David Eugene was studying in Denver. Jean was a real estate agent for J. W. Strougher at 2125 Dryades Street and had been living in New Orleans for three years, in an apartment on Iberville just across from the UpStairs Lounge. She'd met Luther Boggs, and as they became friends, he took her along to the bar. She began making other friends there as well, attending regularly for two years.

After the fire, a ladder from a fire engine eventually led Jean down to the street from the third-floor landing of the fire escape. She sat in the street next to Luther on the curb as they waited for an ambulance. Because she was an Air Force dependent, she was brought to the U. S. Public Health Hospital in Uptown New Orleans, where she remained in intensive care for months with burns over anywhere from 40 to 60 to 80% of her body, depending on the report.

Whatever the percentage, the burns were severe, and Jean was in the hospital "two days short of six months," as she put it. During that time, her mother died, but no one told

Jean for fear of endangering her weak health. No one told her that her son, David, had disappeared in Colorado and still didn't even know of his mother's injuries. And no one had told her about Luther's death or the death of her other friends, either.

Most of her straight friends deserted her, some because they were surprised to learn she was a lesbian. But she wasn't a lesbian. "I'm straight—I can't help it—I was born that way," she would tell her gay friends, but her straight friends weren't convinced, since she'd been injured at a gay bar. And those who weren't uncomfortable about her doubtful sexuality were instead uncomfortable dealing with a seriously injured friend.

But her gay friends rallied around her. While not one straight friend offered to help with bills, her gay friends and the memorial fund helped her pay not only her hospital bills, an incredibly low $300 for six months because the government paid for all but $1.75 a day, but also helped her pay two assistants she needed before regaining the use of her hands. She received some Social Security and a government pension from her husband's death, which helped during this period, and she also received numerous cards and gifts from gays and lesbians across the country.

Jean underwent at least six skin grafts in those months, plus surgery on her fingers, having steel pins put in temporarily. She suffered some permanent disability in her left hand but after months of painful rehabilitation was able to regain most of the use of her right hand.

When she returned to her apartment six months after the fire, she looked out across the street onto a charred building with plywood boarding up the windows. She couldn't bear to look out every day on the scene of so much suffering and death and moved to another apartment in the rear of her building.

The gay community had followed her progress for months in *The Advocate* and paid her way to the Los Angeles Gay Pride Celebration in 1974, one year after the fire. She rode in the parade as an honored guest and spoke briefly to the crowd. Then she returned to New Orleans and, after working part-time as a real estate agent again, tried to get on with her world. Her daughter Shelly had married Jessie Robert Lewis on October 27, 1973, while Jean was still hospitalized, and now Shelly was pregnant. Jean missed the lives that were lost, but she also looked forward to the new life to come.

Stewart Butler

Though Stewart Butler was born in Mobile, Alabama in 1930, his family moved to New Orleans in 1932. His sister was born there a year later. Stewart's mother had been born in Mexico City to "Yankee" parents from Wisconsin. Her mother had died when she was born, and her father died six or seven years later of tuberculosis, so her grandparents from Wisconsin ended up raising her after moving to Citronelle, Alabama, near Mobile. She went to nursing school in Mobile and then joined the U. S. Public Health Service. In Key West, Florida, she met Stewart's father, from backwoods Mississippi, and they married in 1928

The family lived on the grounds of the New Orleans Adolescent Hospital in Uptown New Orleans. While Stewart's mother was a nurse, his father was a pharmacist, though he increasingly became involved with supplies. There was a serenity on the hospital grounds that Stewart liked, as he rarely felt that serenity at school or while playing with his friends. He always felt alienated from other children because they knew he wasn't a native and felt therefore that his parents' jobs could take them to another city at any time. He was temporary, kind of like a "military brat," and so while to him New Orleans was home, he never seemed to quite fit in as a child.

Stewart went to LaSalle school on Perrier Street, which would later become the New Orleans Center for Creative Arts. During the Depression years, he'd walk around the schoolyard, up and down the streets as well, looking for tax tokens. He could trade ten of them for a penny, and with five pennies, he could buy a huge ice cream cone. In addition to scavenging, Stewart also sold magazine subscriptions to make a little money.

Stewart often walked over to Kelly's, the corner grocery, which was one block in from Tchoupitoulas, a gravel road at that time. The back gate to the store was on Tchoupitoulas, and Stewart liked to climb over it when going to buy bread or other items from the store. He liked the little walk to the neighborhood grocery, even after being hit by a car once and cutting his scalp.

Stewart also loved Mardi Gras, enchanted by the flambeaux, the torches carried by black men, and by the parade floats drawn by mules. Carnival season was always a good time.

One of the unpleasant events of his childhood, though, took place at school. Several of the other boys got together to play a trick on the teacher. They were cub scouts and said they had to go somewhere that day because of their scouting. Though Stewart wasn't a cub scout, he knew they were lying and told the teacher. The other boys wanted revenge and captured him later, dragging him over to the steam radiator. They tried to force him up against it, wanting to burn him, but he fought for all he was worth to avoid the blistering metal. He got away.

In the Spring of 1942, shortly after the war started, Stewart's father found a new job, to oversee all supplies at Carville, an institution for people with Hansen's disease. Carville, which opened in 1894, was commonly known as "the leper colony" and was situated along the Mississippi River south of Baton Rouge. Stewart's father was not only in charge of buying medicines but also such things as cows, coffins, ladies' underwear—in short, everything that might be needed in the otherwise self-contained community.

Covering about 450 acres, Carville was for the most part self-sufficient. The residents had their own dairy farm. There was a water purification plant so they could take water out of the river. There were fields for corn and other vegetables, and there was a plant for generating electricity.

There were houses for married couples where both spouses had Hansen's disease. Also living on the grounds were about twenty or thirty families who made up the staff—doctors, electricians, plumbers, and so on. Not everyone who worked at Carville lived there, but most of those who were heads of the various departments did.

Stewart hadn't been too anxious to move to Carville because no dogs were allowed, and he didn't want to give his up. But he soon found he quite liked the place. It seemed to be a great big country club. An unmarked boundary divided the grounds into "staff" and "patient" sides, and both were well equipped with everything. There were tennis courts on both sides, a golf course on both sides, and a movie theater on both sides. But the divisions weren't set in stone. If you missed the movie when it played on your side, you could go on over to the other theater to watch it there. The movies were free, and Stewart was allowed to go once a week, on weekends.

The further one went into the grounds, the less defined the boundary seemed to be. There was a swimming pool on the staff side and a softball diamond on the patients' side. Outside softball teams came in regularly to play the patients. And there was horseback riding and walking through the woods. Stewart had liked the peacefulness of the hospital grounds in New Orleans, but here that feeling was magnified a hundredfold. Carville was like living in another world, and Stewart liked it.

Stewart never felt much of a stigma attached with Carville. None of the staff seemed overly worried about catching the disease. They washed their hands a lot and didn't touch patients where there were obvious markings of the disease, but even so, they realized they were probably taking more precautions than necessary. Thus, they weren't fanatical about trying to avoid what they knew was not a very contagious disease. Sulfa drugs were arresting the malady, providing the first relief in centuries, and patients probably had a more optimistic outlook at this time than ever before.

There were only two churches at Carville, so a resident could be either Catholic or Union Protestant. Stewart had been raised both as a Methodist and Presbyterian, so he went to the Protestant church at Carville, but religion was never much of an issue for him.

In the 7th grade, Stewart went to St. Gabriel, the country school at Carville, being one of only two boys in the class who wore shoes. There were few boys his age, most of them either a couple of years older or younger, so he again felt a certain amount of isolation. He was able, however, to play tag football with the others or play basketball in the wide area between the back of his house and the back of another, where he'd built a basketball court. Stewart also liked to shoot birds on the levee and in the woods, or hunt for thistles and gather pecans. He grew a Victory Garden during the war, as did many of the others, and he and his family also raised chickens.

Still a scavenger, Stewart continued to gather foil and newspaper and anything else he could sell. There was gas and food rationing, no one could buy tires, and after years of depression and war, it became natural for him to find a way to recycle and make money at the same time. Later as a teenager, Stewart sold Christmas cards and newspapers to earn money. He also had a bread route. And he magnanimously offered to drive his sister to music lessons because it gave him an opportunity to stop at the neighbor's homes to see if his neighbors wanted him to pick up any groceries. Stewart charged 10% of the cost for his services.

In 8th and 9th grade, Stewart attended the Gulf Coast Military Academy. When he was back at Carville for breaks or for summer, he took his turn along with the others as a lookout, standing in a tower on the levee and watching for enemy planes. Whenever he saw any plane at all, he called the Civil Defense and reported the plane and the direction it was heading.

After the war was over, Stewart left the military academy and finished high school in Baton Rouge. He then enrolled at Louisiana State University in 1947. It took him a while to decide on a major, but he finally settled on Government. He never did graduate, however, because even though he had enough hours, he didn't study much his last two years and was unable to maintain a C average in his major. Even so, he may have stuck it out and eventually completed the requirements for his degree, except for one small indiscretion.

Stewart stole a Civil Defense tape recorder from a campus building. Everyone else had tape recorders to help them with their studies, so he wanted one, too. He knew where one was stored and simply took the device. It wasn't until he brought it home that he realized it contained what appeared to be top secret tape about germ warfare.

Stewart was kicked out of LSU in 1951. But the incident didn't keep him from being accepted into the Officer Candidate School later that year. Stewart had decided he wanted to be a lieutenant in the army and spent the winter of 1951 in Fort Dix, New Jersey, in basic training. After this, he went to the OCS in Fort Riley, Kansas.

It was here Stewart met and fell in love with Max, a sweet, strong, all-American farm boy from Iowa. Max was Catholic, so Stewart began studying Catholicism in preparation to converting officially. He did well on the tests the priest gave him, but when he wrote his parents, who had moved to Long Island in 1949, to tell them of his plans, they drove from New York to Kansas to talk to him about it.

"We don't mind if you convert," his mother said, "but we just think you ought to wait a little while. Think it over some more."

He consented to wait, and his parents drove back to New York breathing a sigh of relief. What they didn't realize was that religion wasn't really the issue at all. Stewart was struggling with the possibility that he might be gay, and he wanted to accept that even less than his parents wanted to accept the idea of his converting to Catholicism.

Stewart even discussed the problem at length with a friend, and after becoming friends with Max, Stewart wrote his other friend that this experience with the Iowa farm boy had been good for him in clarifying his real feelings. "At least I know I'm not a homosexual," Stewart wrote, "because the idea of sex with a man is repulsive to me, unless of course it was with a man like Max, and someone like that wouldn't do it."

From Kansas, Stewart moved on to the Associate Field Medical Officers School in Fort Sam Houston in Texas. But he left the medical service corps to serve his last year as a basic training officer at Camp Pickett, Virginia, so even though his service was during the Korean War, he was never sent to Korea.

His closest call to a battle injury came while he was driving a weapons carrier. He was distracted by a cute guy walking along the sidewalk, and while ogling the man, Stewart didn't realize the car in front of him had stopped. He crashed right into it. But Stewart still didn't think he was gay.

When Stewart left the army in 1954, he bought a 1950 Chevrolet station wagon. He had $350 and nothing pressing to do. He'd wondered what it would be like to live in Alaska, so he figured if he was ever going to go, now was the time. He had no idea how long he'd stay or what he'd do when he arrived, but he wanted to try it out. He took off in his Chevy and ended up staying ten years.

Stewart attended the University of Alaska near Fairbanks for three of those years. He was elected president of the student body and became editor of the school newspaper. He studied geology, geological engineering, and mining engineering. He spent one summer working on the Alaska highway, and he did two stints of six weeks each working up on the Arctic coast.

A year after graduating with a dual degree in business administration and geological engineering, Stewart married Sophie Andola. Sophie was 7/8 Native American, but having been raised by foster parents, she was as westernized as he was. After a while, Sophie began asking Stewart some disturbing questions, such as, "How come you're always looking at guys?"

"What're you talking about?" Stewart would sputter in response. "Me? Not me."

Their marriage lasted barely a year, but even then, Stewart wasn't ready to deal with his gayness. He devoted most of his energy to his work as a draftsman at the Fairbanks City Engineers office. He also decided to play around some in the politics of the early statehood of Alaska. He worked during one legislative session in Juneau as a messenger for the legislature, and he ran for the state Senate and the House of Representatives. But a friend told him that if he was serious about politics, he needed to go down to Hastings College of Law in San Francisco.

Living in San Francisco did little to encourage Stewart to come out. Perhaps that was because he was there for so brief a period. But shortly after his arrival, he decided to pay a surprise visit to his parents, who were visiting his sister in Waterville, Maine, for Christmas. On the bus on the way there, he met Gregory, a seventeen-year-old boy who seduced Stewart, a thirty-three-year-old man. Dealing with all the feelings which were finally released within him took up so much of his time and energy that Stewart abandoned law school a year later and headed back to New Orleans.

The next couple of years were filled with chaos as Greg left, came back, left again, came back another time, and finally left once more. When Greg was around, Stewart would take him to functions at work, introducing him as his half-brother. Once, though, Stewart's parents had come down for a visit, and people from work stopped by to meet them. Greg had gone off, so he had to find a way to explain why Greg hadn't wanted to visit with their parents. Caught up in a mass of lies, and telling different lies to different people, he managed to get though without anyone calling him on things he'd told them.

In this two-year period, Stewart lived at three different addresses on Esplanade, three in the French Quarter, and one in the Mid-City area of New Orleans. He was working two jobs, saving enough money to go back to school, but he also needed time for sex, wanting to make up for lost years, becoming very promiscuous.

He finally settled down into his job as a surveyor draftsman, working in the Central Business District, but he wanted to go back to law school and so needed an apartment somewhere between the CBD and Loyola's Uptown campus. Looking through the paper, he saw an ad: "Cool, spacious apt. on fringe of Garden District, $70 a mo., including utilities." He went to see the place and fell instantly in love with it.

The landlady, Edna Connelly, showed him around the lower rear of the house at 2115 Prytania. It was furnished with beautiful wooden tables, cabinets of fine dishes, and bookcases filled with old hardcover books. The front hall was 55 feet long and 12 feet wide, with a 14-foot ceiling. There was a marble fireplace, fine moldings, and chandeliers.

Stewart had brought his dog, Jocko, a black, shaggy, mixed breed terrier, along with him to find out if pets were allowed. Most people found Jocko irresistible, and it didn't take much persuasion to have Mrs. Connelly accept the idea. She sighed, though, when Stewart mentioned a cat, but she accepted that as well. Stewart had planned to have air conditioning and a shower at the top of his list, feeling they were the only way to survive in New Orleans, but this apartment had neither and he realized he was still getting an incredible deal. He moved into the house in 1967, and before long, the house had become a part of him.

Stewart returned to law school and continued with his main job as a draftsman, but he also continued with his promiscuity. Lafitte's became his "security blanket." Often, he was there every night for weeks at a time. He'd feel ill at ease until he could get inside those doors.

Stewart attended law school for a year, but his savings were exhausted and he dropped out again. He had three brief relationships over the next couple of years, two for a couple of months each and one for a year. One of his ex-lovers described their relationship as "more than roommates and less than lovers." Stewart also had some sexual friends who were never boyfriends.

He partied constantly, discovering marijuana and then selling it. A few times he did some LSD. He tried Metropolitan Community Church but was disillusioned by religion and found solace in sex and drugs. Hedonism seemed the best religion to him.

One rainy, cold night at Lafitte's, a couple of weeks before Mardi Gras in 1973, Stewart saw a man who looked like Prince Valiant. At first, Stewart thought the guy was a young hustler but found out later he was thirty-six. The man came over, introduced himself as Alfred, and asked, "Why don't you take me home with you? You can fuck me and I'll suck you."

Stewart thought, "What the hell? Why not?" and left the bar with Alfred. He soon began to doubt his decision when, on the way to the car, Alfred added, "You'll probably kick me out tomorrow like everybody else."

But Stewart didn't kick him out. They didn't become lovers right away, but Alfred Doolittle became one more in Stewart's circle of "friends, tricks, and associates." Soon Alfred's money ran out, but he kept saying, "I'm supposed to be getting some money next week."

Stewart thought, "Yeah, right." He figured Alfred was hoping for some john to give him $25 or something.

But Stewart soon learned that Alfred received a $1300 check each month as part of the trust fund established to take care of him when his parents died. Alfred's grandmother in San Francisco also helped whenever Alfred needed her. On the social register, this gracious woman entertained dignitaries and foreign diplomats, especially in the first years of the UN's existence.

Alfred, as it turned out, had mental problems and was on medication. If he neglected the pills, it was likely he'd take off his clothes while at the opera or start talking about Russia, explaining that the reason Russia was acting as it did was because Alfred had refused to wear a red dress with his gold slippers. Most of the time, though, he was coherent, and when he was "normal," Stewart found him fun to have around. Stewart let him stay the rest of the month, and the next month, and the next. Their friendship grew, and they often went to the bars together.

Stewart had started going to the UpStairs not long after it opened. He went often, but it certainly wasn't his main bar. He'd pass by the UpStairs as one of his many stops in the Quarter, though other times it was the main destination. He went to the UpStairs for a Father's Day party, for instance. And he went to the Easter Bonnet contest. Sometimes, he brought his dog Jocko with him, serving him vodka and milk, once letting him drink too much and get drunk. "Barhound" Jocko wandered out of the bar and down the stairs before Stewart noticed. Stewart found him after a short search, bumbling along in nearby Exchange Alley.

Jocko didn't come along on the night of June 24. Stewart and Alfred didn't intend to spend all evening at the UpStairs, but they wanted to enjoy at least part of the beer bust and talk to some of their friends before heading to their other Sunday stops in the Quarter.

It seemed just like any other summer evening.

"After you," Stewart said, ushering Alfred in ahead of him, and they climbed the steps to join their friends inside.

Larry Raybourne and Leon Richard Maples

"See you at the UpStairs later." Larry Raybourne signed the note and slipped it under his friend's door. She wasn't a regular at the bar, never having gone more than a few times, and even Larry only went once a week or so. His place was at Wanda's down the block, naturally enough, since he tended bar there, but he did like the UpStairs. He always had a sense of "going home" when he went to the bar.

Larry's first Mardi Gras was back in 1964. He became instantly enchanted with New Orleans and made every Mardi Gras after that. He loved the city so much that he and his lover decorated their home in Cleveland, Ohio, to give it the flavor of an old New Orleans bordello. That red flocked velvet wallpaper with gold trim didn't impress every visitor to their home, but Larry loved it. When Larry discovered the UpStairs in 1972, he looked around at a bar decorated almost as he'd decorated his home back in Cleveland, and he kept coming back.

Most of the nostalgia, however, wasn't because he missed Cleveland. After all, he'd decorated the house to remind him of the trips he and his lover made to New Orleans. What he missed now was his lover of several years, and all the good times they'd shared, despite the problems caused by his lover's multiple sclerosis.

Larry made a point of enjoying life all around. He learned early about LSD in the '60's and used it regularly, only having good trips and hallucinations, even when one time he sat in his house and watched orange flames lick up the red wallpaper all around him. He felt no horror, only fascination. He wasn't sure if it was his positive attitude that made his LSD trips enjoyable, or if he was able to maintain a positive attitude because his trips and other things generally went well for him.

Back in 1961, when he'd posed for a photograph on a gay greeting card and had his picture sold across the country, things had been a little rough at work, but things always seemed to work out for the best eventually.

Then in 1968, things changed. Larry had just finished writing a gay book and was looking for a publisher. Suddenly, the FBI showed up, ransacked the house, and took his two copies of the manuscript. In the wake of the scandal that followed, Larry's lover committed suicide.

So when Larry went to the UpStairs Lounge, he liked to remember the good times before that tragedy, back when he and his lover were happy. Larry went on with his life, though, and by the time he moved to New Orleans in late 1971, he'd found another lover. Or a semi-lover, anyway. Larry was unable to provide for him since he only had a low-paying job, and his roommate, in addition to being a semi-lover, was also a semi-hustler and didn't seem to be looking too hard for any regular work.

But soon after Larry arrived in New Orleans, he met a guy named Glenn Green at Wanda's who said he could take care of the kid Larry had brought with him from Cleveland.

The kid promptly moved in with Glenn. A quiet guy, Glenn was a little hard to know. He apologized a few times to Larry for stealing the guy Larry had brought to town, but Larry had not been terribly set on the guy anyway and wasn't mad, so he and Glenn continued to talk when they ran into each other at Wanda's or the UpStairs.

Larry himself was not overly talkative, and while he eventually learned to recognize most of the regulars at the UpStairs, he didn't know many of them personally. He was a table hopper, never staying in any one place for very long, and somehow never quite fitting in with the different people at the various tables, which was probably why he ended up spending most of his time over at Wanda's.

He did think Luther Boggs looked distinguished and could tell he was well-liked, but he didn't know him any more than that. He began to know Mitch and Horace, though, after attending an anniversary party for them in the third room of the bar, so now he talked to them when he saw them. And the guy who always wore the big straw hat seemed nice.

But there was one other guy who started showing up at the bar around May of 1973, and he and Larry soon became friends. The guy was Leon Richard Maples, a lanky, thirty-two-year-old auto mechanic from Florida who liked to wear cowboy boots. Leon had been born on February 2, 1941, to Warren G. and Pearl M. Johnson Maples, and his last permanent address was at 6612 Pine Summit Drive in Jacksonville. He had two young sons but was divorced, and one of the reasons he'd come to New Orleans was to think about his life and where he was heading.

He didn't seem to get a whole lot of thinking done, however, as far as Larry could see. Leon was out almost every night, going home with a different guy each time. Leon thought it was a lot of fun, and besides, it saved on the hotel bill. One of those first nights, Leon came home with Larry.

Larry liked Leon's boyishness and clean-cut look. While it was clear Leon needed financial assistance since he was only visiting and not living in New Orleans, Leon never asked anyone for money. Guys just seemed to like him so well they wanted to buy him drinks, and could he help it if he was good-looking enough that they wanted to bring him home?

But somewhere amid all the partying and sleeping around, Leon did get to do some thinking and soul searching. At the UpStairs Lounge late Saturday night, or rather, early Sunday morning on June 24, Leon told Larry he was going back to Florida to be with his family. Larry couldn't be sure if Leon intended to go back to his ex-wife or just be near her and the kids. Perhaps Leon had been so promiscuous not only because he had nowhere to stay but also because he wanted to have his fill of sex with guys before going back to his family. But would he ever be able to give up guys after having so many? Whatever doubts Larry might have had, Leon apparently didn't harbor any and seemed quite happy about his decision to return to Florida.

Around 4:00 a.m., as Larry started to leave the bar, Leon gave him a hug. "I'll miss you. I guess I won't see you anymore." Larry wished him a happy life and left for home.

Larry would indeed miss him, he realized when he woke up again later that day. Perhaps the hope of seeing Leon one last time before he left was what prompted Larry to tell his girlfriend to meet him at the UpStairs rather than their usual rendezvous point at Wanda's. Even if Leon had already left, the UpStairs ought to be fun on a Sunday evening. As 8:00 approached, Larry left his apartment and headed for 604 Iberville.

Buddy Rasmussen

Douglas Rasmussen, later nicknamed Buddy, was born in Houston on December 18, 1940, the oldest of six children. His father died when Buddy was two, and his mother remarried when he was five. He was fifteen before he realized she'd been pregnant with her fourth child well before the marriage date.

Buddy's mother had been too poor after her first husband's death to raise all three of her children, so Buddy's two full brothers were adopted by an uncle, and Buddy rarely ever saw them again, getting to spend just one week with them every other summer. They never visited him in return. They had their own parents now and felt little connection to people they couldn't even remember.

For Buddy's first Christmas with his stepfather, the man decided to give Buddy a real treat. He dressed up as Santa and came into the third-story apartment up the fire escape. He brought Buddy a plastic chicken that laid marbles. Buddy was frightened by the odd gift.

Perhaps Buddy's lack of appreciation contributed to his stepfather's future treatment of him. Perhaps the man had every intention of treating Buddy like a son and only later realized he was incapable of it. Whatever the reasons, the fact was that Buddy's stepfather seemed to find it increasingly difficult over the years to tolerate him.

Not all of Buddy's childhood memories were negative, of course. Certainly the chicken pox and measles weren't pleasant, but his mother's care had let him feel a love that always seemed present. He also enjoyed listening to polka music as he sat at the kitchen table. And while he was rarely allowed outside to play with other children, he did occasionally find a way to play from a distance. Once, he went onto the balcony outside his bedroom and blew soap bubbles, watching the kids below break them with a stick as the bubbles slowly drifted downward.

Buddy's family lived in the projects while he was in grammar school. That was one of the reasons his folks didn't want him playing outside. The other was that since he was several years older than his half brothers and sister, he made a good, cheap, babysitter.

One day in second grade, Buddy sat inside reading, doing his homework. While he was thus occupied, his sister fell off the porch. She wasn't badly hurt, but Buddy's stepfather was furious. "Where the hell were you?" he demanded. "What was so God-damned important you couldn't watch your sister?"

"I-I was reading," Buddy replied.

"Reading!?" his stepfather shouted in fury before beating Buddy.

From that day until he graduated high school. Buddy never once brought another book home from school, finishing his homework at school during his spare time. At home, Buddy watched the other kids, washed, ironed, and did much of the cooking. The rest of the little free time he had he spent trying to stay away from his stepfather.

The man never physically abused Buddy's mother as far as Buddy could tell, but the kids were terrified of him. Once, Buddy's sister was sick and kept crying. Her father became so infuriated by the noise that he beat her so badly she had to be hospitalized. Maybe the man was treating Buddy like his own son, after all.

Buddy's stepfather never drank until he got off work. But he had at least six beers at home every night and started by 9:00 a.m. on Saturdays. One time, he came home so drunk that Buddy's mother had to help him up the stairs. Once he was in bed, she broke a broom handle across his behind. But this was the 1940's, not an easy time for a single mother, and she was afraid to leave him, even though he did often spend his entire paycheck on alcohol. Instead, she worked so there'd be enough money for groceries.

Not that there really was. Buddy's stepfather insisted on having meat at every meal. There certainly wasn't enough money for that, so the kids and their mother ate beans every evening throughout the week. Buddy's stepfather waited until the kids were in bed and then had a dinner of meat and potatoes. He ate with the family only on Sunday, when they were all able to eat chicken.

Buddy took on a paper route when he was eleven, but his stepfather whipped him when he bought a pair of skates with his money. After that, the man always went with him and collected Buddy's money for him, never allowing him to spend any of it on himself. Sometimes, Buddy had a couple of papers left over and was able to sell them on his own, making a few cents he didn't have to report to his father.

As Buddy grew older, he took an interest in sports. He got along well enough with the other kids at school, but he was never able to socialize since he always had to go right home after classes were over. Sports even reduced time for socializing because Buddy had to practice football or basketball during school hours. His folks wouldn't permit him to stay after school for practice. Buddy never was able to become very proficient at either sport.

He was never even able to attend any of the games. During his high school years, he was only allowed out for four activities. He attended one football game, went on one date, and was able to go to both his junior-senior prom and his senior prom. Other than that, he wasn't allowed to date, because he was the oldest and always needed at home.

Buddy never did terribly well in English, his reading time obviously limited, but he did do well in math and chemistry, and he found he was interested in art. He may have been just an average art student, but he had an exceptional teacher, Mrs. Neal, who helped him reach into himself. He did well with ceramics, and he was able to help decorate for the school play since Mrs. Neal was in charge of sets and staging. Buddy took her art class in both his junior and senior years, and despite never being able to do any "homework" at home, he earned a place on the honor roll in his senior year.

Doing all his studying at school was not his only obstacle, though. Buddy also had to be careful not to give himself away. He was attending Smiley High School illegally. It was a rural school, and during his junior year, Buddy gave a wrong address so he could continue to attend after his family moved. He'd walk each morning to a place within the school district and catch the bus to school.

Buddy also had to listen to the continual arguments between his mother and stepfather, listening to him accuse her of everything imaginable. His stepfather yelled at Buddy, too, and ran him out of the house several times. Buddy would head for his grandmother's house, determined to tell her everything, but then his stepfather would come along to take him back, and Buddy would decide to wait a little longer before burdening his grandmother with the truth about his stepfather.

Buddy's stepfather kept taking Buddy back because of the Social Security check he received each month for Buddy's dead father. What with the Social Security checks, Buddy's paper route, and Buddy mowing lawns to pay for his school clothes, his stepfather never had to put out too much money to support the boy.

Then the year Buddy was a junior, he passed by a 7-11 convenience store each day on his way to and from the school bus. Every day, Buddy went in to ask for a job. Every day, he was told there was no opening. Since he had to be home immediately after school, there wasn't much opportunity to apply anywhere else for a job. So even though it seemed hopeless, Buddy continued to stop in every day after school. "Got any work for me today?"

One day, a Thursday, the manager did have work for him. The guy who worked there regularly was sick, thirty boxes of groceries had just come in, and their contents needed to be priced and shelved. "Ever worked in a grocery store, kid?" the manager asked.

"No, but I learn quickly."

"Want to work today?"

"Yes, sir! But let me go home first to tell my mother where I am, and to grab a bite to eat."

"Okay. Can you be back around 5:00?"

When Buddy returned, the manager explained how to price the merchandise and shelve it and then went off to attend to other business. When Buddy walked up to the manager three hours later and asked if there was anything else for him to do, the manager grew upset.

"No, I want you to finish pricing and shelving first. You can't just switch to something else because you're tired of that."

"Well, I finished it."

The manager went to see for himself. Sure enough, what usually took the regular boy two days Buddy had done in a few hours. The manager asked Buddy next to stack returnable bottles, a huge binful of them. When Buddy finished that, the manager shook his head and had Buddy mop the floor.

The manager fired the other boy and hired Buddy, having Buddy work two days a week. The manager also told two other stores about Buddy, so Buddy worked two days at each of the three stores, six days a week. For the seventh day, the three stores bid for the opportunity to have Buddy on site.

Buddy would go to school each morning and then work each evening until midnight, week after week. He still did most of his studying at school, so his making the honor roll came during a year he was also working full-time.

Buddy's stepfather was pleased Buddy was working. The other kids were getting old enough not to need him as a babysitter, and now Buddy could start paying for room and board, even if he was only seventeen, even if the man was still receiving Social Security checks for his care.

Buddy continued working at the 7-11 after he graduated. His folks didn't want Buddy to leave the house for anything else, though. Buddy felt so oppressed at home he felt he just had to get away. He tried to join the Navy when he was seventeen, but his mother and stepfather wouldn't sign the papers. When he turned eighteen in December, he joined the Air Force without telling them.

"Wake me up at 7:00 in the morning, Mom," he said.

But he woke up on his own, finished packing a few things, and announced, "I'm leaving today." He went to Lackland for basic training and came back home on leave after he finished.

"When are you leaving?" Buddy's stepfather asked as soon as Buddy stepped through the door. Buddy returned to base before his leave was up.

Buddy was stationed in Fairbanks, Alaska, in the fire prevention division of the fire department. He did fire inspections, wrote a weekly paper on fire prevention, and was able to use his art by making floats for the parade on fire prevention day. In his spare time, he learned how to ski.

Becoming worldly in the military took a while. Buddy had played around with a couple of other boys when he was a kid, but for the most part, he never had time to deal with his sexuality. He suspected now he might be gay, but this was 1959. Buddy was afraid of being discharged and so never approached anyone with any questions. He saw a couple of other guys he suspected were gay, but they were bitchy and didn't fit in with the other guys, so Buddy avoided them.

He knew little of heterosexuality, either. His chief in the fire department, McFadden, once asked Buddy to do him a favor and buy him a package of condoms. Buddy didn't know what a condom was and so felt no embarrassment to ask the clerk for a box of them.

"A box? Do you mean a package of twelve, or a gross?"

Buddy didn't know, so he decided to go for the larger box, which contained twelve smaller boxes, each with twelve condoms. Buddy saw the raised eyebrows but didn't understand the reason for the snickers or the whispering.

After eighteen months in Alaska, Buddy was transferred to Japan. He was still in the fire department, serving as an E-3 fire chief, low in the hierarchy. He worked twenty-four hours on and twenty-four hours off, plus he had one extra day off each week, and one more day off once a month. It was an easy job, with not much work, and it gave Buddy time to pal around with his friend, Dalgren.

Buddy was only halfway admitting his gayness to himself, so he enjoyed for the most part running around with Dalgren, drinking and whoring together. This was the first time Buddy ever had sex with a woman. Running around with his friend didn't last very long, however, because Dalgren soon had a woman living with him.

But Buddy found another guy to hang around with, a Japanese youth who worked as a stock boy but who wanted to be an interpreter. The two would go on trips together, Buddy paying for food and transportation, the Japanese boy getting the chance to practice his English, and Buddy getting an interpreter and tour guide. If Buddy ever saw anything he liked, he'd tell his friend, who would in turn barter for it and get it at a better price than Buddy could have managed on his own.

The young man's mother made a kimono for Buddy, and Buddy joined his friend in the public bathhouse, the first American to go into that town's bathhouse. Going to bathhouses was against military regulations, but Buddy loved going. There were no private showers in the military dorms, so Buddy couldn't see what the big fuss was, anyway.

Buddy never did know if his Japanese friend was gay or not. He was still too nervous to ever bring up such a subject. But Dalgren was living with a woman, and another friend, Taurence, got married, and Buddy began to feel more pressure because he couldn't fit in. Then he was given a lower job driving the fire truck, and he didn't like the lower position. All of that added together created an unpleasant situation for Buddy. He was beginning to get ulcers as he worried about being gay, and with the language barrier, he didn't feel he'd ever be able to do anything about it while in Japan.

After a year in that country, Buddy requested a transfer to Iwo Jima. It was considered isolated duty and so counted as double time. Buddy could serve six months there and knock a year off his commitment to the Air Force.

In Iwo Jima, Buddy spent five days a week cleaning and polishing fire trucks. He also continued to do fire inspections and monitor the radio to listen for fire reports. In addition to his forty hours of work a week, he was also on call during his off time. There wasn't much else to do during his off hours. Iwo Jima was called isolated duty because it was, in fact, isolated. Buddy managed to climb Mt. Iwo Jima, for which he could have been court-martialed for endangering himself, and he went to see movies. The only other thing to do was drink.

Buddy had managed by this time to become just a little more worldly. It was after his first four months in Japan that he'd gone with twenty buddies to Hong Kong for four days. Everything was so cheap there they'd all ordered new suits and new shoes. Food was so inexpensive that they ordered everything on the hotel menu. It was the first real meal Buddy had ever eaten out in his life. He had a bacon-lettuce-and-tomato sandwich for his first time while in Hong Kong and liked it so much he had another every day. Buddy enjoyed how sophisticated it made him feel.

In Iwo Jima, he was able to become just a bit more experienced. He took his first job as a bartender in a club on the island. One of his duties as bartender was to build an elaborate stone wall out of white mortar and black lava to divide the NCO's club from the officers' club.

After six months on Iwo Jima, Buddy was sent back to the States to finish the his remaining time at Parrin Air Force base in Texas. During his service, he'd occasionally written to his two full brothers but never received a response. He wrote to his mother and stepfather as well, and to his grandmother, who sent loving but awful care packages. Still, it was nice to be remembered, though he did grow tired of all the Old Spice that everyone always sent.

Buddy had begun dealing internally with his sexuality but as yet had done nothing outwardly. Because becoming involved with men was going to be awkward, he'd decided to wait until he returned to America and could at least eliminate the language barrier. The wait would also give him time to think more about it.

Now in Texas, he no longer felt trapped by language. Still, he was nervous and afraid, and it wasn't until just before he was discharged, after almost four years in the service, that he finally had his first sexual experience with a man.

After leaving the Air Force, Buddy moved back to Houston, returning to work at the 7-11 and sharing half of a converted garage with his half-brother. Buddy bought a car, tried to avoid his stepfather, and tried to find other men like himself. He drove around and sometimes saw men hanging out on a corner. He talked to a few but was afraid to try picking anyone up because he didn't know how.

Buddy's half-brother married and moved out, and Buddy discovered gay bars. Before long, he met a man and they moved in together. Buddy was happy to have found someone to be with, so he didn't want to be too picky, but it seemed his lover never worked. It wasn't long before they began to have disagreements about money.

Buddy was managing a 7-11 outside of Houston and making good money, enough to buy a home. Still, he didn't much like being the only one to bring money home. It might be different if his lover knew how to handle it, but the guy always seemed to spend more than necessary, and Buddy worked too hard to want to see the money leave so quickly.

Then another problem arose, this one at work. There were sliding glass doors across the entire front of the store, so it was easy for people to steal. $50 a month in merchandise went missing. Buddy's boss wanted to retrain him how to deal with this.

The problem was that first of all, during the retraining, Buddy would be making less money, but more importantly, the retraining had nothing to do with stopping the theft. It only dealt with how to raise certain prices, while higher-ups from the store weren't around, to cover for the stealing. Buddy felt this would mean he was stealing from his customers, and he was afraid that if he did it, he'd never be able to pass a lie detector test. He refused to go through retraining and was fired.

He was able to collect unemployment for a while, and he and his lover moved to Nuevo Loredo on the Mexican border, living on the Mexican side. Buddy would go to the American side to pick up his unemployment checks and then go back to Mexico.

His lover did finally get a job, as a waiter at a drive-in restaurant. Buddy helped him at work and so got the tips. There were still problems, though, because his lover continued to spend more money than they brought in.

Eventually, Buddy even had to hock the cameras he'd bought while in Japan.

Buddy generalized the disillusionment he felt in his relationship to all gay relationships and decided he wanted to get over being gay. He felt that going back to the military would be the way to do it, getting out of a gay environment, so he joined the Navy.

Because he'd been inactive for two years, he had to go to boot camp again. He understood that the military was a dictatorship, that men had to be able to act on command, so he was made the chief petty officer in charge over his company in boot camp, being in charge at night after the commanding officer went home.

Buddy was a "bastard," but his company won awards. Being stern kept the other guys from liking him, which kept temptation out of his way, but my, what a nice-looking guy that kid from Florida was. And he looked to be about eleven inches long even flaccid, so long that he hung well below the bottom of his boxer shorts. Buddy hoped that military life would soon help him stop noticing such things.

After boot camp, Buddy went to Maryland, where he became a fire control technician, studying missiles and computers. He received a hash mark for his four years of prior military service and so became a petty officer 3rd class. He graduated with honors at the top of his class from A School and then went on to B School, where he was promoted to petty officer. As a ranking student, having been able to keep the rank from his previous service, Buddy was in charge of the other students. He also made more money than the others and soon bought a car.

He did start to have sex again, though, and realized he hadn't escaped his gayness as he'd hoped. He continued to study hard in C School, still studying missile control and computers. In the first phase of school, he was second in his class, the first being a college graduate. They became good friends, working and studying together, and even going to New York together. In the second phase of school, Buddy took a test and qualified for the naval academy's officer training school.

Meanwhile, Buddy had been going to New York regularly and tricking with a friend there. He'd bring a carload of Navy buddies with him, and by their chipping in for gas and the use of his car, Buddy was able to pay for his hotel room while in the city. His friends would go off whoring and Buddy would go see his friend.

One day, Buddy saw a sailor on the street. They cruised each other and then Buddy picked him up. After driving around for a while, they stopped at a refinery storage area. They talked a little more, fondled each other, and then Buddy went down on the sailor.

A moment later, a bright light shone on the car. A police car had pulled up and a police officer wanted to see what was up. The sailor was, and because he had an erection, the police suspected what was going on and arrested them.

The two men were brought to the police station, where they were interrogated separately for hours. They both stuck to their stories. The only problem was that they told two different stories. The sailor insisted that he had a hard on because they'd gone to the area with a third guy and a girl. The couple went off behind the storage area to have sex, and the sailor got excited thinking about it. The story might have worked except Buddy said they'd gone to the area alone.

"And why was only one of you sitting up when I turned the spotlight on the car?"

"Well, I dropped my cigarette. I'd just leaned down to pick it up when you came by."

The police knew someone was lying, and they confronted Buddy with the other's story. Buddy insisted he didn't know why the other guy was lying, that the truth was there were only the two of them there, and all they'd been doing was talking. Buddy then pulled a toll booth ticket out of his pocket, which showed that only two people had been in the car when it passed the booth on the toll road.

Unable to really prove anything, the police let them go but sent them to the shore patrol. The penalty for homosexual acts was five years in prison if they were caught, but Buddy was tired of the hassle and affirmed that he was gay. "I can't change it," he said, "and I can't pretend any longer."

He was not prosecuted but was discharged. The discharge came two months before Buddy would have been eligible for reenlistment and a large bonus.

Buddy left Maryland and visited his grandmother, telling her he was gay. Then he went to see his mother and stepfather, and he told them, too. "If you can't accept it," he said, "I won't come back." They weren't thrilled, particularly his stepfather, so the announcement only added problems to the already troubled relationship.

But being honest about the "dreadful secret" gave Buddy a freedom that was incredible, so he continued to be open about his orientation. He went back to 7-11 to apply again for a job, and he told his prospective employer right off that he was gay. He didn't want it to come out later and create problems. If it was going to cause trouble, he wanted to know right away.

It did cause trouble. 7-11 didn't hire him. Buddy next applied at IBM, coming out to another openly gay executive. The executive wouldn't hire Buddy, either, because while he felt one could be openly gay and still be reasonably discreet, he felt Buddy was *too* open.

For six months, Buddy applied for jobs but was never hired. He began wondering if he'd have to go back to accepting a double standard. The idea irked him, and he decided to keep trying just a little longer. Finally, he found a job where he could be openly gay without any hassles—as a waiter at a gay bar.

He ran into his ex-lover, and they got together again. They were so poor they took furniture from an abandoned house to have some furniture themselves. They lost what little they had when their house caught fire one night. All they had time to save was an armful of clothes.

Buddy became increasingly frustrated when his lover refused to get a job and continued to spend Buddy's money unwisely. He set a date and told his lover he'd better have a job by then, because if that date came and Buddy didn't have a check in his hand, that was it, their relationship was over. His lover would not only have to get a job, but he would also have to let Buddy manage all the money. It was the only way they could survive, Buddy insisted, and it *would* be this way, or else.

Several weeks passed before his lover even began looking for a job. Buddy didn't press the issue, but he would remind his lover of the deadline. "If I don't have a check in my hand by that date, we're through."

His lover finally did find a job, but he found it just before the deadline. Buddy said nothing, but he set his alarm for 11:55 the night of the deadline. When it went off, he sat up in bed and turned to his groggy lover. "Where's the check?" Buddy demanded.

"Wh-what? You know I don't get paid until tomorrow."

"Then we're through. You knew what was expected, and you waited too long."

Buddy decided to head for Florida, but since he had so little money, he was forced to hitchhike. Because he was tall, though, few people wanted to give him a ride. He was too intimidating. He walked long stretches, through the entire city of Orange, Texas, without being picked up.

While walking through the country, he was picked up by a preacher who could only take him a short distance because he was making his rounds to members of his congregation. Buddy thanked him for the lift and walked on. Twice more, the preacher picked Buddy up as he ran into him that day while making his rounds. No one else stopped for him.

After three days, Buddy made it to New Orleans. He was too tired to go directly on to Florida and decided to stop for a while. He remembered that when he lived at the house that burned down, he had two neighbors, lovers, who worked in a department store. They stole from the crystal and silver department, and when the police found their house full of stolen merchandise, the two men left town. Buddy remembered that one of them had come to New Orleans. He thought he remembered the address and so started knocking on doors in the neighborhood.

Buddy found him, and his former neighbor helped him find a job through Manpower. It was 1967, Buddy was twenty-six years old, and he decided to stay in New Orleans. He soon took a job as a bartender, and he began to feel at home in his new city.

Buddy tended bar at the Royal Orleans hotel and the Holiday Inn. Later, he had a job as a part-time bartender and janitor at the Caverns. The bar was made to look like a cave, with fake stalagmites included in the decor. When Buddy first began working there, the bar closed at 4:00 a.m., but Buddy kept it open while he cleaned up, and soon the bar was staying open twenty-four hours a day.

It was while working at the Caverns that Buddy met Phil Esteve, who hired him to work at his new bar, the UpStairs Lounge. By this time in late 1970, Buddy had been with his lover, Roland, for about a year. Roland was in general a quiet and private person, and he never talked much about his family.

When Buddy went to Ville Platte with Roland to visit family, he enjoyed the visits well enough, though he could never quite get used to the idea of the grease gravy Roland's mother poured over the rice. She tried to be a good hostess, though, getting up every fifteen minutes to serve tiny cups of coffee to everyone. She did this continually, all day long, hopping up to serve, then hopping up to collect and wash the cups, and then hopping up to serve again. Roland said very little. He just sat on the porch and rocked.

Roland liked to rock a lot, in Ville Platte, in New Orleans, or wherever he happened to be. He liked to rock so much that he would do so even while sitting in a stationary chair, which looked so odd Buddy sometimes wondered if Roland wasn't losing his grip on reality. He might have been on the spectrum, but at the time, few people understood anything about autism. When choosing a Christmas present for Roland one year, Buddy knew what would be appreciated and so bought Roland a rocking chair.

One day around the middle of 1971, while working at the UpStairs, Buddy noticed an attractive new customer walking in. Buddy could tell that the man was new to the gay scene. He liked to be friendly to his customers anyway, but there was something special about this guy, so Buddy made sure to introduce himself and learn the man's name. It was William Duncan. Buddy introduced Bill to several of the others sitting at a table nearby, hoping Bill would then feel comfortable enough to stick around for a while and maybe come back.

Two of the others at the table were other bartenders, Napoleon and Wayne. Wayne, sometimes called Weenie, was there with his lover, Lonnie. And Harry was with them, too. Harry, at 5'4" and 225 pounds, liked to do cartwheels in drag.

This was Bill's first time ever in a gay bar, however, and he didn't initially like the men Buddy introduced him to. He did like Buddy, though, and stayed until Buddy closed the bar that night.

Buddy and Bill fast became good friends, Bill coming to the bar regularly every Friday or Saturday night. He rarely came to the beer bust on Sunday because Buddy would be too busy to talk, but he sometimes came after the beer bust, without staying late because he had to work the next morning.

Bill not only liked Buddy, but he wanted to be his lover, too. He knew Roland, or Adam as he was known at the bar, and knew that Buddy wasn't pleased with Adam's drinking. Bill tried for the next two years to get Buddy to leave Adam, but Buddy refused.

"I won't do it," Buddy said. "If I did, you'd always wonder when I was going to dump *you.*"

So Buddy and Bill remained good friends, and Buddy also made friends with many of the other customers, though Bill remained in a category different from the others, not just a friend and not really a boyfriend, but something in between.

When Buddy first began working at the UpStairs, he tried hard to learn everyone's name, but the customers would change seats when his back was turned to deliberately confuse him, and eventually Buddy just started calling everyone "sweetheart" or "honey." Still, as regular as many of the customers were, he couldn't help but learn their names. There was J.P., who was bartender Mike Wolf's lover, Bill Bailey, always friendly, outgoing, and vivacious, Sid Espinache, a good-looking man, and Frank Dufrene, with his high-pitched voice, effeminate mannerisms, big nose, and sweet personality.

Buddy was good friends with Bob and Bettye McAnear up until the time they moved to McAllister, Texas. And there was Jean Gosnell and J.C. Carrier and Wayne Barras and Raymond and John Bleechner and Ricky "Mother" Cross. Mother Cross, who had a brace on one leg from an accident, was tall and slim and did drag. Phil Esteve, with his vicious tongue, once drove Mother Cross to tears at a party at a friend's house, and Buddy was glad the bar was doing well enough that Phil didn't need to come around too often. Buddy knew Dave Gary, too, the piano player, who sometimes brought a friend to practice with or to take turns playing throughout the evening.

But whether Buddy could remember everyone's name, he could always remember what they were drinking, up to fifty or more customers at a time, and he knew when they needed a refill. On June 24, Buddy pulled on the pink, tie-dyed jumpsuit he'd made himself, joking about how he'd match the wallpaper at the bar. He went to work as usual at the UpStairs, taking Adam along with him to unlock the gate to the stairwell at noon.

"Boy, it's going to be a hot one," he said, looking up briefly at the summer sun before wiping off the sweat. And it was just past the summer equinox. The sun wouldn't even set until 8:00.

The Fund

Almost immediately after the fire, the Reverend Troy Perry announced the need for funds to help bury the dead and aid the injured survivors in paying medical bills, and in assisting them with rent and other bills until they had recovered enough to work full-time again. The National New Orleans Memorial Fund was established three days after the fire, and the trustees were Troy Perry, Los Angeles gay activist Morris Kight, New York activist Morty Manford, Reverend John Gill, Lucien Baril, who was later excluded, Chris Gamble of New Orleans, Reverend J. Paul Breton, and the publisher of the *Advocate,* Dick Michaels.

Ken Bartley was named treasurer and Joel Monroe, a CPA, was named auditor. The *Advocate* acted as custodian of the fund and ran reports on its progress throughout the next several issues. Eventually over $17,300 was raised from across the U.S. and Canada, though at a slightly earlier date, $17,900 was listed as the total. Individuals, religious groups, and bars all held fundraisers to contribute what they could. Among the donors were:

The Advocate-$500

Agape MCC-$30

Anik Homophile Association, Toronto-$42

B.J.'s bar, Los Angeles, fundraiser-$257.28

Bonfire Lounge, Anchorage-$140

Boulder (CO) Gay Liberation-$69.36

Chicago benefit, sponsored by Free Spirit Fellowship and the Trip Lounge-$252

Club Miami Baths-$500

Congregation Beth Chayim Chadashim, MCT-$52.28

Detroit benefit, sponsored by Don's Beef 'n' Ale, Motor City Alliance for Gays, and *Gayzette*-$188

Dignity-$50

Dignity/Chicago-$119.15

Four Poster bar, Los Angeles, fundraiser-$372.75

Friends of Smokey's Den, Springfield, IL-$310

Frolic Room, Los Angeles, benefit, sponsored by the Helping Hands Center-$400

Gay Activist Alliance of Morris County, NJ-$70

Gay Activists Alliance of New Jersey-$110

Gay Alliance of Queens County-$10

Gay Awareness, Washington State University-$10

Gay Community Center, Montreal-$9.80

Gay Liberation Arizona Desert, Phoenix and Tempe-$6.50

Gay Liberation of Westchester-$25

Gay People at Columbia-$10

Gay People's Union, Milwaukee-$75

Homophile Union of Boston-$54.65

Illinois State University Gay People's Alliance-$9

From individuals-$3377.86

Integrity/Houston-$25

Kent Gay Liberation Front-$100

Krewe of Zeus, Lake Charles, LA-$35

Long Beach Homophile Community (Vicky Awards)-$314.40

Metropolitan Community Church/Atlanta-$372

MCC/Baltimore-$23.75

MCC/Boston-$40

MCC/Chicago-$50

MCC/Dallas-$98.90

MCC/Detroit-$166.20

MCC/Jacksonville Study Group-$405 (including $100.62 from patrons of the Commodore Lounge, $35 from patrons and owners of the Little Dude tavern, $61.43 from the study group, and $192.46 from a benefit

MCC/Long Beach-$146

MCC/Los Angeles-$443.58

MCC/NewYork-$137

MCC/Oklahoma City-$30.80

MCC/Philadelphia-$121.81

MCC/Salt Lake City-$189

MCC/San Fernando-$28

MCC/San Francisco-$550

MCC/San Jose-$276

MCC/Santa Barbara-$19.68

MCC/Tampa-$384

MCC/Toronto-$7.30

MCC/Washington, DC-$207

MCC/Washington, DC, in memory of Ray Street-$28

Montrose Gaze Community Center, Houston-$117

Paul's M & K Tavern, Asbury Park, NJ, benefit-$713

Radicalqueens and Gay Activists Alliance of Philadelphia-$98

Selectmen of Detroit-$25

Syracuse (NY) Gay Freedom League-$30

Tantalus, Boston-$25

Temporary fund in New Orleans, transferred later to main fund-$1109.48

United MCC/Tulsa-$100

United States Mission-$5

Up North bar, Chicago, benefit-$1500 (originally listed as Up Front bar)

Warehouse VIII, Miami, benefit-$1370; early reports estimated the donation as $2500, breaking this down by listing $1900 worth of the contributions as follows: $500 from Jack Campbell of nationwide Club Baths chain, $200 from Miami Gay Activists Alliance, $100 from Ron of Bachelors II and Bachelors West, $50 from the Femme Jesters, $50 from Malcolm of the Nook bar, and $1000 from Warehouse VIII and the show's cast

West Side Discussion Group, New York-$25

Winter Palace, Anchorage, benefit--$80

The total through December 13, 1973 was $16,516.53, leaving $70 unaccounted for in this list, which only adds up to $16,446.53.

A later donor was Zero to Success, Los Angeles-$250.

An additional $534 was collected from various donors over the next several weeks, for a total of over $17,300.

Not everyone was impressed by the fundraising, however. The Reverend Ray Broshears, a San Francisco street minister, denounced the fund as a "rip-off of the gay community," claiming he didn't trust Perry, Kight, or Michaels, and saying he believed the treasurer, Bartley, had "sticky fingers." He was also afraid that the money would go to the MCC, the *Advocate,* or some other group and not reach the victims. It doesn't appear he had any evidence to back up his suspicions.

Rather than donate to the fund, Broshears said he'd raise money and distribute it in New Orleans directly by himself, hoping to sponsor some of the victims, even helping them relocate to another city if they needed to leave the town where they'd suffered. He later relented and donated the $400 his group raised to the fund.

Broshears, though, was not the only person to suspect the money wasn't reaching the victims, several people in New Orleans continuing to murmur over the next two decades about how Troy Perry had skipped town with the money, even though the money was not even in his custody. None of them offered evidence to back up their suspicions, either. It's possible the accusations were based on nothing more than personality differences.

There were, however, some who did take advantage of the situation to make a few bucks. There were isolated reports of several men making their way through the French Quarter asking for donations, before any fund was officially set up, and whether this money ever made it to the victims or was ever really intended to go to them is unknown.

Even in cases where there was some official sanction, the money didn't always reach its destination. David Schwartz was living in Phoenix, Arizona, at the time and recalled attending a fundraiser at the Valley Review for victims of the fire. There was an elaborate drag show, and a hat was passed around twice during the evening. At the end of the show, however, one of the performers ran off with the money.

What made one of the fund's abuses bizarre was that it apparently came through Lucien Baril, who'd been Bill Larson's lover. Jason Guidry had known both Bill and Lucien, together maybe two and a half years. Only it later turned out that Lucien's real name was Richard, and he skipped town sometime after the fire, apparently after embezzling an undetermined amount of money, either from MCC or the local memorial fund for the victims. He was immediately removed from his position of trustee.

So just how was the money in the fund spent? $1000 went toward expenses incurred before the fund was set up, mostly by those who then set up the fund. $700 of this thousand went to various gay leaders, to pay their hotel bills when they arrived in New Orleans after the fire. Troy Perry said his hotel bill was paid by MCC's Miami congregation. Morris Kight said, "I used my airline ticket, which had been contributed by friends...to bring me and Morty Manford to New Orleans. We had $6 left when we got there."

$200 went to establish a petty cash fund in New Orleans for day-to-day expenses. $223.35 was spent for phone calls, to locate insurance coverage, to find available public relief, and to contact families and companions or others who could offer financial support. $125 went for printing informative, educational, and historical materials about the fire. $15 was spent for a plate in memory of Reverend Bill Larson, and $250 was spent for a bronze plaque in memory of all the victims. Jerry Lee Juong donated another plaque, which he handcrafted of Hawaiian wood and which contained a poem written for the victims. These expenses totaled $813.35.

On December 13, 1973, the trustees of the fund agreed to send Morris Kight to New Orleans to assess the needs of the survivors. On January 21, 1974, Kight announced ten grants to help several of the victims and their families. They were:

1. $300 to a woman for her brother's funeral, half of the $600 she'd requested.

2. $500 to a burn victim. His hospital bills to date were $1800 but were partly paid through a personal loan. The trustees also agreed to negotiate with the doctor to try lowering the bill.

3. $360 to the widow of one of the deceased. She said that her twelve-year-old son had been harassed at school when his father's name had been publicized, so she'd had to transfer the boy to a private school. $360 was the cost of tuition for one year.

4. $885 to a badly burned man who could only work part-time to support his burned lover. Insurance covered most of his $2700 bills.

5. $918 to the lover of the recipient of grant #4. His bills came to $718, and the additional money was for "personal needs."

6. $771 to a non-gay woman to pay $171 of her $300 medical bills and $200 every month for three months to pay for the help of two roommates and a larger apartment where the helpers could live with her while she recovered.

7. $400 to a seriously burned man. His bills were $1962 to date, but the trustees hoped to negotiate with the doctors to lower the bill.

8. $500 to a "disabled merchantman living in the care of a sister in Massachusetts," though his hospital bill was paid by the government.

9. $300 to a man living in Arkansas. He claimed to have $4900 in medical bills and was presently living on $200 from Social Security disability each month. Why was his grant so small? He was reported to be living with a "male companion," so perhaps it was felt the companion was in a position to pay a portion of the bills, but as this was one of the larger bills and yet one of the smaller grants, it's curious.

10. $100 to a man not burned but who was "helpful" to the group who flew immediately to New Orleans after the fire. The $100 was for "pocket money" to help the man when he was released after a four-month prison term for an unmentioned offense. There's a lack of transparency here since this is a full third of what the burn victim above received.

No names are mentioned in connection with the grants, but the identities of some of these recipients can be guessed. The men from grants #4 and 5 could be Eugene (Earl) Thomas and Fred Scharohway. #6 is undoubtedly Jean Gosnell. Roger Dunn or Sidney Espinache could both be either #2 or #7. #8 is almost surely Edward B. Gillis, and #9 is probably Michael Wayne Scarborough.

Morris Kight said that seventeen people were known to have had hospital stays of more than two days, and they were all eligible for grants, but only nine of them had been located by the time the first grants were distributed. The total money spent from the grants and the previous expenses is $4929.35. Perhaps Kight felt he had to hold back until he located all of those who were hospitalized, but clearly he'd located those with the most serious injuries, who were the most likely to need the money.

Further breakdowns of how the money was spent are less clear. $350 went to fly Jean Gosnell out to Los Angeles for Gay Pride one year after the fire, but other than this one specific, the other expenses are vague. In July of 1974, Kight gave an unofficial breakdown as follows:

$7503 to survivors for medical bills, which included individual grants of $1500, $1385, $1418, $1900, and $1300; $1213 for hospital costs and a stipend to a survivor; $360 for private school tuition for a child of one of the deceased; $550 for burial costs for two of the victims; $500 for board, care, and living needs of a survivor; $100 for the legal expenses of a survivor; and $600 in travel expenses for two trustees, one for a trip to New Orleans, and one to attend a trustee meeting.

Kight's breakdown a year after the fire only totals $10,826, but thirteen months after the fund was established, about the same time as Kight's estimate, the *Advocate* reported that $4200 of the more than $17,000 was still in the fund, a discrepancy of roughly $3000. The trustees at this time were considering offering stipends of $100 a month from August 1974 to December of that year for two men who'd been burned and whose income was still below subsistence levels. They were also discussing the possibility of using the remaining funds toward the acquisition of a memorial gay community center in New Orleans, but this plan was never realized.

The last reports, then, still leave almost $6000 unaccounted for. Perhaps eventually the money was divided again among the families of the victims and among the survivors, but a specific report stating such was not available from the *Advocate*.

So was there any mishandling of the money? It's impossible to say with certainty. Clearly, some of the victims could have used more, since they did not initially receive all they requested. Since there was a significant amount left, it's unclear why these survivors didn't receive enough to fully pay more of their bills. If they did later receive their full requests, there's apparently no record of it, and that distribution occurred quite a while after the request.

One wonders why no one in New Orleans was considered capable of determining needs, why trustees had to use a significant part of the money to be flown in for the purpose. In any case, at least a sizeable portion of the fund did reach the victims and helped them pay varying portions of their bills.

Money wasn't the only contribution, however. Many people went to Charity Hospital in New Orleans to donate blood. Groups in other cities went to their local hospitals to give blood and have it credited to the injured in New Orleans. Gays and lesbians in Denver donated blood, and people in

Inglewood, California donated twenty-three pints of blood by July 19.

Bartender Eddie Storcz of the Brass Rail in San Diego organized a blood drive which would last three weeks and during which he hoped to get 600 pints of blood donated, an estimate surely a bit high. Buddy, manager of Ken's River Club, helped organize a massive blood drive in Los Angeles. By July 26, thirty-four bars in the city agreed to give a free drink to anyone with a receipt for having donated blood and designating it for MCC/Los Angeles, which would then credit it to the injured in New Orleans.

Burials were also donated. So many bodies remained unclaimed in Charity Hospital's morgue even after they were identified that several funeral homes about New Orleans, Bultman, Lamano-Panno-Fallo, Tharp-Sontheimer, and others, volunteered to take two, three, or even four bodies each. Jim Roberts, the mortician who'd embalmed and prepared Jayne Mansfield's body several years earlier, worked at Bultman and said that the various funeral homes donated their time and services for many of the unclaimed bodies, embalming them, then donating coffins and burial plots for those whose families refused to claim them.

When Bill Larson's family refused to accept his cremated remains, those remains were put in an urn at the New Orleans MCC. But a friend of a church member owned a burial plot at St. Roch Cemetery #1 and donated that for the burial of the ashes.

Morris Kight said the fire created a situation where the gay community in America for the first time was asked to work together in an emergency. This, of course, would be a circumstance they'd find themselves in full-time only a decade later.

While the AIDS crisis in the U.S. involved tens of thousands of victims, the UpStairs Lounge emergency was a local, singular event, and with Stonewall only four years in the past, much of the gay community in America was in fact not a community at all. Being able to organize across the nation to any degree was an accomplishment of at least some merit.

But as with most local emergencies, the country soon forgot about the fire. The survivors, obviously, would never forget, but their suffering was eased just a little by the financial help given to them by thousands of strangers, strangers who, although they might frequent "disreputable" bars or might love someone of the same sex, knew what it meant to be compassionate.

And the survivors never forgot that, either.

Robert Lumpkin

A bitter, cold wind blew steadily that January night in 1973, but David Crumley wanted to go out anyway. It was Friday, and he'd been working hard all week as a timekeeper at a French Quarter hotel and studying hard for his classes in architectural history at Tulane University. Tonight, he wanted to relax and have some fun. And he knew that the place to find some fun, even on a cold, January night, was Lafitte's.

He'd hardly walked in the door when another man walked up and offered him a drink. The guy was cute enough, no model, but trim, with eyes and a smile that promised a spirit to make up for any small lack in his body. By the time David and Bobby had finished their first drink, they were both hot enough to brave the cold outside as they rushed to their cars and hurried to Bobby's upstairs apartment on Magazine Street to rip off one another's clothes.

Robert Keith Lumpkin was twenty-nine years old, born on July 19, 1943, to Earl Keith and Lena Stone Lumpkin. David was several years younger, about twenty, a junior in college. That first night in Bobby's bedroom, as Bobby and David began exploring each other's bodies passionately, Bobby told David he'd just gotten over an STI, what was then called a case of VD, but he assured David he was fine now, and he certainly looked fine, about 5' 10", with light brown, slightly reddish hair, and a hairy chest. David himself was decent enough looking, with a slim 28" waist and a sweet smile. The two men spent the rest of the night fully enjoying and sharing their bodies.

They spent several nights a week for the next few weeks repeating the experience. Bobby liked being "top," but David wasn't much into being fucked. "You've got such a great ass," Bobby moaned. "I've just got to have it." He persuaded, and David relented. Bobby fucked away to his heart's desire, and David found that the well-endowed Bobby did a good job. They both enjoyed their sex.

One other thing they liked to do was have David rim Bobby. But a month after they met, just a week before Mardi Gras, Bobby called him from the hospital. He had hepatitis.

David had just returned from a mainstream Mardi Gras ball with his family, which he'd attended with a female date. He'd also kissed probably fifty women during the evening. So he spent the next day calling everyone to tell them to get shots, and by Saturday, four days before Mardi Gras, he was yellow. David's family nursed him through the next month, most of which time Bobby remained in the hospital. Both were critically ill, and David suffered permanent liver damage as a result.

But once they were well enough to get up and out, they were back together again. Though they continued to see each other regularly, a few nights each week, they made no special commitment. David loved Bobby, but Bobby liked his freedom. He went out alone at times for an occasional trick, and sometimes he even went up to Baton Rouge for a night out. Some of his roving was for fun or to keep up with friends and acquaintances, but some of it was to bring in a couple of extra bucks.

Though Bobby Lumpkin was born in Jacksonville, Florida, his family had lived in Jackson, Mississippi for years, and his father was an executive for the Bell telephone company there. He was a soft, gentle man who smiled and laughed easily, while his mother was a very active, demanding woman, a little self-centered at times.

His father liked to play golf but was otherwise not very energetic. Bobby, too, was not overly active physically as a child. He did play with his dog, and certainly, he loved amusement parks, but most of his time was spent indoors, reading comic books and putting together model cars and airplanes, a hobby he thoroughly enjoyed.

For two weeks each summer, Bobby went to Birmingham to visit his maternal grandparents and cousins. His grandfather had been a coal miner and his grandmother a homemaker. Bobby was close in age to one of his cousins, Terry Stone, so they became good friends as they played together each summer, until Bobby's family stopped visiting when Bobby was about eleven.

Terry and Bobby still kept in touch a little, though, enough for Bobby to tell him about dating a girl he really liked in high school, and about the Studebaker Avanti he bought which he dearly loved, and to tell him, too, of his close high school friend who was killed in a car accident during Bobby's senior year.

After high school, Bobby went to Oxford to attend Ole Miss, where he joined a fraternity and majored in business.

He never graduated and eventually decided to take a job with Bell telephone in New Orleans. His coroner's report lists his occupation as a switchman for a local railroad. Though he had a steady income, Bobby still liked to hustle a little on the side, more for the thrill of it than for the money, but money was nice, too.

David was never quite sure what Bobby did with the phone company. All he knew was that when they'd meet for dinner at a restaurant on Burgundy in the Quarter after work, Bobby looked tired and would say, "Don't bother me for an hour or so." He'd get a drink and relax, and by the time the dinner was over, Bobby had unwound enough to be friendly again. He and David would go back to Bobby's apartment and spend the next several hours having sex.

The following morning, Bobby would pull himself groggily out of bed, having gotten little sleep, and trudge off to work exhausted. He never ate breakfast, but David finally convinced him that a good meal in the morning would help him feel better. Bobby tried it, and it worked.

Bobby was a neat dresser, wearing a striped or solid color button-down shirt, starched and ironed, with his blue jeans. He was clean-cut and cared about his personal appearance. His apartment, however, was a mess, with pieces of leftover pizza on the table and dishes piled in the sink. What with work, having sex, and going out, there just wasn't time to do everything.

One of Bobby's other pastimes was dancing, which he did whenever he went up to Baton Rouge. Though it was illegal, he and David sometimes went to the Grog on Rampart to dance. When Bobby went out without David, he'd talk to other friends like Wayne McAlpine or Brobson Lutz, who met Bobby when Brobson began medical school in 1968. Bobby also had several friends who'd moved down from Mississippi, so he liked to talk to them regularly, too.

None of his friends remembered if Bobby had ever come out to his family, but his cousin Terry, who himself learned of Bobby's homosexuality at his death, said he later learned Bobby had in fact told his parents, and they'd chosen not to tell anyone else in the family. Bobby was reasonably close to his family, visiting often, but he never talked about them to his friends or even to David. His father was deceased now, but Bobby wouldn't give out much more information than that.

He didn't talk about much besides what was going on right then and there. He did mention once that a friend of his from Mississippi, Sherman, had committed suicide, but Bobby preferred dwelling on the positive, or at least on the lively and fun. Sometimes, when he and David would walk together through the Quarter, David would point out various buildings, telling Bobby when it was built and in what architectural style, giving some of the building's history over the years since.

Bobby could only take so much before he'd say, "Get off that fucking tour guide bit." He wasn't into anything "cultural," and he and David never even went to a movie together. Instead, he was serious and practical. Other than work, the only things that really interested him were dancing and sex. The most cultural thing he might mention was to suggest which kind of pants David should wear to show off his butt.

In early 1973, after recovering from his case of hepatitis, Bobby returned to Lafitte's but was kicked out for hustling. He needed to pick another bar, and though the UpStairs also forbid hustling, it was in the right neighborhood and offered opportunities nearby. He and David both began going more often, and David even tried to get a job as bartender but was turned down for lack of experience.

David continued with his job as timekeeper at a nearby hotel. He met Bobby early Sunday evening at the UpStairs on June 24 and then went on to work. It was on his shift at the hotel that David heard the sirens, not knowing their destination.

But the news eventually trickled down, and by the time David ran over to the bar, the fire was extinguished, the stench of burned flesh hanging in the air. "Maybe he left. Maybe he left," David told himself, staring at the bar in disbelief. "Maybe he left."

But Bobby was the 12th body identified. Fragments of blue jeans were found on his legs. He received extensive 3rd and 4th degree burns over 80% of his body, with much loss of skin and fat from his body, and his face destroyed. The first eleven identifications had been confirmed through fingerprints. Bobby, who had no fingertips left, was identified through dental plates.

Courtney Craighead and
MCC-New Orleans

Sex and religion. They just didn't seem to go together very well. And yet Courtney Craighead had been interested in both for as long as he could remember, at least since he was nine, shortly after he moved to El Dorado, Arkansas, from Magnolia. He missed his Sunday School friends and school friends from Magnolia, but Courtney soon made a lot of friends in the 3rd grade and in his neighborhood, adjusting quickly to the new town.

As an only child, he knew he needed to make friends fast or go without. Since he liked school anyway, it was easier for him to be happy and therefore friendly with the other kids. Courtney made friends at Sunday School, too, and in the Cub Scouts.

At the age of nine, Courtney made his first sexual advance to another boy, which was accepted. The advances and subsequent fooling around continued steadily from then on as Courtney progressed through childhood and adolescence. A bathroom and hall separated his bedroom from that of his parents, so when he had a friend sleep over, they could stay quiet enough not to be heard.

Courtney would pretend he was asleep and let his hand wander to the crotch of the boy sleeping beside him. If the boy was interested, he'd turn toward Courtney. If not, he wouldn't. From his first contact with one of his third-grade pals in 1948, up through the early 1970's, Courtney and that pal continued to have sex regularly, even after the other guy married and had children.

In Boy Scouts, Courtney and a few of the other scouts would set up their tent and all have sex together inside. Most of them only seemed to be experimenting and so quit after a while, but Courtney continued to seek sex with other boys. He dated girls maybe two or three times in high school, more like going to a movie with a friend who was a girl than really going on a date. He knew what he wanted, and it wasn't girls.

After high school, Courtney went to Centenary College in Shreveport, Louisiana. He'd never been forced to go to church and attended because he wanted to. He had perfect attendance in his Young Adult choir in high school, his name was embossed on a hymnal as a reward. In Centenary, Courtney studied pre-theology for a year, intending to become a Methodist minister, having always taken as much interest in religion as he had in sex.

He'd felt vaguely uneasy about the combination of being gay and Christian but figured he'd resolve it all eventually. While studying theology, however, he realized he wasn't going to be able to reconcile it. How could he bring others to Christ if he was an abomination in God's sight? He knew he couldn't change being gay, so he changed what he *could* change, his major.

The following three years, Courtney took social science courses—psychology, history, government, and sociology. He planned to become a teacher but started worrying about being accused of molesting the boys in his class and so eventually gave up that career as well. As always, though, Courtney remained sexually active. He hung around with a group of seven guys and seven girls in college, and of that group, Courtney eventually had sex with four of the guys, the other two becoming Methodist ministers.

As much as Courtney liked college, he liked being social even more. He often went to the Piccadilly Pizza Palace near campus, once going three times in one night with different friends. He talked with friends in his dormitory rather than study, and he'd fool around with one of the guys in the shower or his bedroom. Other times, he'd go to the bars in Bossier City, which were crawling with cute military men. As a result, his grades weren't very high, so in 1961, after four years at Centenary, Courtney left before graduating and moved to Little Rock, the town where he'd been born back in 1939.

In Little Rock, Courtney worked on getting his radio technician/engineer license. He also worked on Don, his roommate for three years. Don insisted he was straight and acted disgusted at any talk of homosexuality. He dated women regularly, and Courtney would often see Don and his girlfriend curled up on the couch together when he returned home from work.

None of that stopped Don from enjoying sex with Courtney. When Don's girlfriend wasn't over, and Courtney came home from work around 1:30 a.m., he'd go into Don's bedroom and climb into bed with him. They'd take turns doing oral and anal sex to each other. Then Courtney was required to get up and sleep in his own room. Don wouldn't stand for two men sleeping together. Only faggots did that. He also wouldn't stand for any verbal display of affection.

If Courtney told Don he loved him, Courtney could forget about sex for the next two or three weeks. Otherwise, they had sex regularly, a couple of times a week the whole time they lived together. Then Don joined the Army, married a woman, and had kids, but even that didn't stop him from having sex with Courtney any time they got together over the following years.

Being "straight" also didn't prevent Don from enjoying a gift Courtney sent him while Don was stationed in Korea. Courtney, who was working at a radio station, made a reel-to-reel tape of love songs arranged in such a way that their titles told an additional love story. Don, who was also working on a radio transmitter, played the tape in Korea and thanked Courtney for the tape, though he said nothing about noticing any other message on the tape.

Being gay soon brought a larger hassle to Courtney's life than just a long-distance relationship. The associate pastor of Courtney's church in Little Rock found out that Courtney was gay and began calling him on the phone, asking him repeatedly to come in for counseling, while suggesting that Courtney see a psychiatrist he knew as well.

"Please come in," the man urged. "We need to talk. This will be our secret." Courtney put off talking to the man, and two weeks later, it seemed that suddenly everyone in the adult Sunday School had learned he was gay. They weren't happy. Neither was he. Courtney left the church in 1967.

In 1968, Courtney went down to New Orleans for Mardi Gras. That was where he met Paul, only sixteen, ten years younger than Courtney. When Courtney went back to Little Rock, Paul went along. They stayed together for the next two and a half years. Then Paul joined the Marines, but as before with other relationships, Courtney kept in touch, and whenever they were able to meet, they continued to have sex.

Courtney moved to New Orleans in April of 1970. He'd met Buddy Rasmussen at the Caverns during Mardi Gras of 1968, so when the UpStairs opened in the Fall of 1970, Courtney went to see what the new bar was like. He became a regular right from the beginning, enjoying the core group that always came, made up mostly of waiters or other people in the area who'd stop by the bar after work.

Courtney had worked from April to August but then found himself unemployed, so when the UpStairs opened, he worked occasionally in the bar for tips. Like Buddy, he soon began to know people by what they drank, or who they came in with, or who else was likely to come in the door ten minutes after they arrived.

Courtney was not much of a performer, so he rarely participated in dancing at the bar, and he didn't take part in the drag shows or plays, either. He did enjoy watching, though. One guy, Tom Woods, did a skit where he played Madame Wudda, a psychic. Because he had a beard, he wore a veil over his face. For part of the skit, Madame Wudda had to ride a bicycle. The bike was set up off the floor, and he was backlit, so all the audience could see was the silhouette pedaling away against the screen in the background, his veil fluttering in the breeze created by a fan.

Another regular performer was Wayne, the Alaskan Native American who tended bar at the UpStairs. He and his lover, Lonnie, did a scene where Wayne played a Canadian Mountie singing "When I'm Calling You" to Lonnie, who was drifting demurely back and forth on a swing. Those two continued performing up until the time the government made a settlement with Wayne's tribe, offering a certain amount of money if the tribe's members would homestead the land. So Wayne and Lonnie moved to Alaska.

While Courtney didn't like participating in the shows, he did enjoy participating in Mardi Gras. He'd go out on the landing of the fire escape at the UpStairs and take pictures of the crowd passing below, or of bartender Buddy dressed as a genie, in a flimsy, see-through blue outfit, and his lover Adam dressed as an artist, with a large French artist's hat.

These were the days when parades still went through the Quarter, and the crowd was so thick it took an hour and a half to get from the UpStairs to the Caverns. Courtney would grope his way through the crowd. He especially enjoyed places like Lafitte's, where up to three hundred people would squeeze inside the bar for a mass orgy, packed so tightly that people could hardly move.

Well, certain body parts could still move.

But Courtney liked the Quarter even during regular times. It was fun talking to friends. It was fun picking people up. And it was fun watching other people. Once, as he passed the Finale, a gay bar on Royal and Ursulines, he saw two lesbians getting into a cab. A sailor walking by made a pass at one of the women, and the other woman decked him.

Some of the violence was harsher, however. One night, Courtney met a guy at the UpStairs, and they spent a good while talking. It finally became clear that the guy wanted to go home with Courtney, but Courtney had someone staying with him and couldn't invite the guy home. He'd remember who he was, though, and if Courtney ran into him again when he was free, he'd see if they could get together.

The man seemed a little disappointed, but these things happened. Courtney gave him a peck good-bye and then left. The next day, Courtney learned that the man had been killed during the night, cut up by the guy he did end up going home with.

Still, there were more good memories than bad from the UpStairs. Like the time Courtney's ex-lover, Paul, was in town on a pass from the military. Courtney had told Paul to meet him at the UpStairs, that Courtney would come right after work at 4:00. Paul, still only nineteen at the time, was a typically hunky Marine, so Buddy and a couple of other guys, who didn't know he was waiting for Courtney, plied him with drinks, trying to entice Paul to go home with them. By the time Courtney finally walked in, Paul was feeling a little drunk. "Hey, I'm tired," he told Courtney. "Let's go home." And he took Courtney and left. The others were so jealous they wouldn't let him forget the incident for weeks.

And there was the time they held a birthday party for Buddy in the third room of the bar. Buddy, who'd never had a birthday party because he was born on December 18, decided he finally wanted to have one like everybody else. For the party, they had three big, K & B purple garbage cans, each filled with a different drink. One garbage can held a mixture of screwdrivers. Another was filled with bourbon and Coke, and the last held gin and tonic. Beside the garbage cans was a huge pile of presents for Buddy, who was enjoying himself perhaps a bit too much and was soon so drunk he fell right into his pile of gifts.

It was at about this time, around 11:00 or so, that the manager on duty began coughing up blood because of an ulcer. He came into the back and announced he was going home. Because someone with a manager's license was required to be on duty, and Buddy was the only other one there with a license, Buddy was now on duty. The only problem was that he'd passed out.

Courtney and some of the others dragged him to the front room and propped him at a corner table near the piano. Then they went behind the bar and took over, Courtney the only one with any bar experience. They kept the bar open until the regular closing time of 4:00 a.m. and then went on home.

It was in 1971 that Courtney began to attend church again. A branch of the Metropolitan Community Church was organizing in New Orleans, and Courtney felt comfortable at the early meetings since they were held at the UpStairs. Through MCC, Courtney was finally able to reconcile himself with God. He could finally believe that God truly did love him and that God would accept his love in return. As a result, Courtney felt a desire to serve, and he was ordained a deacon by Troy Perry in April of 1972.

Striving to be close to God helped Courtney in 1973 to deal with the news his mother had been diagnosed with breast cancer. His mother, a dedicated schoolteacher forced to retire at the age of sixty-five, had loved teaching so much that instead of accepting retirement, she'd signed on as a substitute teacher, working three and four days every week, as often as she could. Courtney admired his mother's efforts, and though intellectually and even spiritually he knew that everyone had to die, facing the reality of her death was difficult. Prayer, meditation, and the company of other church members helped him through.

Courtney met another deacon, Bill Larson, through the MCC. A carpenter by trade, Bill worked at the Richardson Center and was a quiet, earnest man who'd been born into a poor family and learned quickly how to work hard. He now did house painting and remodeling, so when Bill saw a house a few doors down from where he lived at 1375 Magazine that he felt would be just right for meetings, MCC bought the house. Bill got right to work on the building, adapting it to fit the needs of the congregation.

The house was a double, but Bill cut a doorway upstairs so a person could go from one apartment to the next. They bought an altar made of Norwegian fir from a junk dealer and installed it. Courtney and many of the other church members helped with all the work, holding work parties where they tore down a wall to enlarge the worship area, then cleaning and painting and whatever else was necessary to get the place in shape.

While Bill Larson was the interim worship coordinator, MCC chartered a tiny riverboat so the church members could have a party. The ones who'd chartered the boat didn't tell the boat's owner the MCC was a gay group and there'd be men dancing with men at the party, and women dancing with women. Many of the church members were upset, feeling the church was being deceitful to the boat's owner. Others felt that since there was nothing wrong with gays dancing together, it was no different for gays to be renting the boat for a party than for straight folks, who wouldn't go out of their way to say they'd have men dancing with women, and women dancing with men.

Several of the members couldn't be convinced, past personality conflicts playing into their feelings, and they left the congregation. After the pastor left as well, Bill was appointed the temporary pastor in the fall of 1972. Church services were at 3:00, and afterward, many of the members headed over to the UpStairs for the beer bust. Bill went. Mitch, the associate pastor, went with his lover, Horace. Richard "Mother" Cross, the clerk at the church, went. Robert Lumpkin, Glenn Green, Reginald Adams, and Skip Getchell also went. John Golding, on the church board of elders, went, as did Hubert Cooley, who'd previously been with MCC in Long Beach, California. And Courtney went, too, along with still more members.

Being involved in church again didn't keep Courtney from being promiscuous, of course. He enjoyed sex, and he enjoyed enjoying it. On a visit to New York, he discovered bathhouses and loved being "trashy" there. The UpStairs wasn't the place back home where Courtney usually tried to fulfill his sexual needs, though he certainly picked up a few guys there. Often, however, he went to the UpStairs simply to enjoy the company of his friends.

On June 24, he went with the rest of the MCC gang over to the bar, there being a little extra reason to party since someone had just donated an air conditioner to the church.

Besides, many of the church members had attended the funeral of seventeen-year-old Ronnie Leingang that weekend, who'd drowned while diving off a pole in Lake Ponchartrain, so a little partying sounded like a good idea, to get their minds back on life and living. Courtney even brought a straight friend of his, Theo Ancelet, from near Lake Charles in southwest Louisiana.

Courtney had met Theo at Charity hospital when Courtney had gone to visit a sick friend. While walking down the hall to his friend's room, Courtney ran into Theo, who had broken a leg and needed a place to stay for a few days after he got out of the hospital. The two men hit it off well, so Courtney offered his apartment. Then after Theo was back on his feet, they kept in touch, and occasionally Theo would go to the UpStairs with Courtney for the beer bust.

This was one of those nights. Not that Courtney would be drinking much, having just been released from the hospital in April because of infectious hepatitis. He wouldn't be able to drink for a year. But he could still talk to his friends and have fun. Courtney and Theo paid their deposit on the beer mug and went to sit at a table in the second room of the UpStairs. That's where they were sitting when a huge orange fireball and thick clouds of black smoke burst into the bar.

John and Jane Golding

John and Jane Golding lived a peaceful, quiet existence in their New Orleans home. Married in 1947, they celebrated their 25th anniversary in December of 1972. John, Jane, their two daughters, and one son went to church together regularly. Once, they took the bus to Rochester to visit John's mother, and another time they took a bus to Knoxville to visit Jane's brother, enjoying their family ties but feeling limited by the distance and lack of personal transportation. They had little money but refused to live beyond their means and had so far managed to avoid going into debt except for the monthly notes they paid on their home. All in all, they were an average family except for one thing. John was gay.

Born in 1924, John was put up for adoption at six months and quickly adopted. His father went south and his mother went north, and John was raised during the Depression without any knowledge of his birth parents. When he was thirteen, his "stepsister" sent him up north to stay with a woman. With the family as poor as it was, this was an understandable if somewhat odd move to make. It wasn't until he arrived that John discovered that the woman he'd be staying with was his birth mother.

John reached manhood just as World War II was raging, and he spent a long while in the service. After the war, he met

Jane, they courted, and then they married on December 29, 1947. Within a year, their first daughter was born, followed five years later by another daughter and eight years after that by a son.

As the kids grew, their parents took them to the movies when they could afford it, went on picnics together, and headed to the beach, stopping anywhere interesting that lay along the bus routes, since they couldn't afford a car. John, a hard worker, never seemed to have the knack it took to make money. He was pushed by his mother to go to a salesman school but didn't have the heart for selling.

He tried working in a furniture store office, but that only lasted a couple of years. Then there was New Orleans Public Service Incorporated, or NOPSI, for almost five years and some work with the Department of Sanitation for a few more years, but no job seemed to last. John either became too bored or discovered something else he wanted to try.

John felt guilty when he heard Jane sigh. He knew she felt he was wasting his life. She'd told him she knew he had a good mind, but she grew to accept he wasn't a go-getter. He'd tell her, "If you don't have it, then you don't need it." She disagreed, but what was there to do? At least the house notes were always paid, and they always had enough money for clothes and food. They might not have the most comfortable existence, but John did provide enough that Jane was able to stay home and raise their children.

Over the years, Jane found herself pushed more and more toward them. John loved his kids and did spend time with them, and John and Jane got along well enough, too, but there was something missing. John knew he was being distant, but he didn't want to hurt Jane, yet how could he talk to her about what he was feeling and thinking without hurting her? He could tell she was hurt by his emotional distance, but there were degrees of hurt, and he chose the one he felt was less painful. It wasn't as if he ignored her, after all. There were plenty of other things to talk about, even if they weren't the things he really needed to be talking about.

Another problem was that John knew Jane felt he was a little too strict with the kids. As a child, he'd always had to eat whatever was on his plate. If he didn't, he went hungry. But when their kids didn't like something, Jane would prepare something else for them. John felt she was spoiling them, but then she spoiled him just as much, and he never seemed to mind that. She only cooked what she knew he'd like. That was different, though. Because of his upbringing, he'd learned how to be appreciative. Hardly a day went by that he didn't compliment Jane on her meals.

John and Jane talked often, and Jane marveled at how close they were as friends, despite the wall she often felt between them. John was no dancer, so they rarely went to parties, but they did go to movies together and occasionally to see stage plays when they could scrape the money together. Yes, they were closer than some couples she knew, but there was something...something...

Jane was shocked when her husband told her he was gay. At first, she didn't believe him, but as he began to go out more and more with his "friends" in the late '60's and early '70's, she became convinced. His friends would call on the phone, and Jane soon learned to dislike and distrust the word "friend."

John asked if she thought she'd be better off without him, but with three children and no work experience, what was she going to do? She needed his financial support, and she still loved him despite his being gay. He was still kind and generous, still gentle and mild. He was still the kind of guy everyone loved. People often said, "To know John is to like him." Well, she liked him, too. And besides, he needed her. He couldn't even pick out clothes without going up to her and asking, "Does this match?" More often, she'd set out his clothes for him. Why, without her, he'd be in the gutter within two years. So they stayed together.

Soon, John was living two lives, a quiet one at home, and another with his friends. Jane would often hear John on the phone talking to his gay friends. She didn't like it, but at least he wasn't lying to her. The big wall that had existed between them now was gone, but in its place was a moat. Sometimes, the drawbridge was let down and they were able to meet on the bridge for brief periods and communicate.

June 24th was one of those days. That Sunday afternoon, John and Jane had a long talk about their situation, and while the talk didn't really solve their problems, Jane felt better than she had in a long time. She smiled and went about her afternoon housework and dinner preparation, making spaghetti and meatballs, one of John's favorite meals. As she worked, she overheard John on the phone, talking to some friends about meeting later at the UpStairs. Whatever that was. Jane had heard him mention the UpStairs before but never asked what it was. She didn't really want to know.

The two other women who meant a lot to John had died recently, and Jane felt more than ever how much John needed her. Jane's mother had treated John like her own son. She knew he was gay and didn't understand it, but she didn't let that get in the way of her love for him. Her death in September of 1972 left both Jane and John shaken. Then only a few months later, John's stepsister died of a heart attack in John's home. She, too, had known John was gay, and she was disgusted by the idea, but she and John found other things to talk about and remained friendly.

Jane was still recovering from these two deaths and was grateful that John had opened up a little more that afternoon. He wasn't really what she'd prefer in a husband in some ways, but when he really talked to her, she felt loved and knew she'd made the right decision to stay with him. And he always came home to *her,* didn't he? Surely, that proved something, too.

As John finished his spaghetti that evening, he stood up from the table. "Lady," he said, calling Jane by his pet name for her, "that's so good. That's so delicious." They smiled and then she began washing dishes as he finished getting ready to go out.

Not a perfect life, she thought. Certainly not a perfect life. But she knew she was still better off with him than without.

"See you later," John said as he headed for the door. Jane couldn't quite bring herself to say, "Have a good time," but she managed another smile in response and watched as her husband left to join his friends over at the UpStairs Lounge.

The Homophobic Response

"[There has been] an anonymous phone call to Channel 8 news," reported Alec Gifford, a newscaster for WVUE, the ABC affiliate in New Orleans, "saying the bar was fire-bombed by a vigilante group that has declared war on homosexuals in New Orleans. The caller, a woman, said the group calls itself 'Black Momma, White Momma' after a movie by that name, that it is made up of several women, as well as five men who have been sexually attacked by homosexuals. The caller said the group is planning more attacks and has maps outlining their future targets."

Though this turned out to be a crank call, the fact that the newscaster would accept this claim without checking it out, and then broadcast it across the city the evening after the fire, shows the climate that then existed for gays. Later in 1973, the bestseller *Everything You Always Wanted to Know About Sex—But Were Afraid to Ask,* by David Reuben, would classify gay men for years to come as cold, selfish, promiscuous, and eternally searching for the perfect penis.

Just a month before the fire, in May, the American Psychological Association met in Honolulu, the Board of Trustees voting unanimously to abolish homosexuality from the category of mental disorders. Those results were not released until December of 1973, however, so during the time of the fire and its aftermath, most people still officially claimed that being gay meant a person was mentally ill.

Of course, the majority of the population formed its opinions without the help of the APA. Religion played a major role in developing attitudes. One woman in New Orleans was overheard saying, "The Lord had something to do with this. He caught them and punished them." As harsh as this may sound, this is not an uncommon attitude toward victims of disaster, whether those victims are gay or not.

A Southern Baptist preacher, commenting on the sin of dancing, pointed to the Cocoanut Grove fire, which killed hundreds, to show how the Lord dealt with sinners. Preachers and priests through the years have insisted that plagues, earthquakes, and other disasters were the result of sin. Blaming the victim is probably not so much done out of hate as to try pacifying the speaker's mind that he or she will escape such a horrible fate him or herself.

But it can hardly be denied that the fact that the victims at the UpStairs were at a gay bar did affect how they were treated. When mourners placed flowers at the entrance to the bar, some even arriving from other cities, people began stealing them shortly after they'd been left. Finally, someone, an old man who worked on a shrimp boat, according to Morris Kight, set himself up as an unofficial guard to protect the flowers.

The political response was also less than satisfying. On June 27, the group of "fairy carpetbaggers," as they were called by some, the out-of-state gay activists who stayed in New Orleans immediately after the fire, sent a telegram to Governor Edwin Edwards, asking him to declare July 1 a statewide day of mourning. The telegram was hand-delivered to the governor's office, but when Morty Manford called to ask about the governor's response, he was told that the telegram had never arrived.

Even after the telegram was found, the governor never did make any kind of response whatsoever. Mayor Moon Landrieu of New Orleans apparently felt much the same way as the governor, and while saying he didn't value gay life any less than straight life, he did say he was "not aware of any lack of concern in this community." Perhaps he wasn't aware of witnesses at the scene of the fire overhearing a firefighter saying, "That's good enough for them. That's what they deserve," and a police officer saying, "Burn, fruit, burn."

There was, however, one political group in the state which did offer its sympathy, also sending a bulletin supporting the national day of mourning. This group was the Young Democrats at Louisiana State University in Baton Rouge.

Naturally, the reason many steered clear of any association with the fire victims was because of that sticky word "gay." Many people, both gay and straight, were afraid in 1973 even to say the word "gay." It was almost as if saying the word for straight people were an admission of some kind, it was giving in, it was using the word that "those people" *wanted* people to use.

WVUE, for one, was not going to do it any more than necessary. On its morning news show for June 26, the newscaster talked about "The Lounge, a well known gathering place for homosexuals." A gathering place for homosexuals? What was that? It sounded like a trough for horses. Maybe it was something like flypaper, something that mysteriously attracted homosexuals and kept them there. A gathering place for homosexuals. Was there any way to say that in a shorter fashion? On a thirty-minute news show, wasn't brevity an important issue? Instead of a "gathering place for homosexuals," how about that other term occasionally used, "gay bar"?

In fact, the original transcript for that morning's show *does* read, "The Lounge, a well known gay bar." But "gay bar" is scratched out, and handwritten over it is the longer "euphemistic" phrase.

The homophobia of some of the investigators makes one wonder just how much they cared about finding the arsonist. Presumably, solving a case is a good career move regardless of personal feelings, and the investigators with the State Fire Marshal's Office, Edward S. Hyde, William M. Roth, Jr., and John M. Fischer, did seem to be honestly searching for the arsonist, but their attitude toward the victims did at times come to the surface in the questioning. When Allen Guidry was interviewed, the direction of the questions for a moment seemed to veer away from anything remotely pertinent to the investigation.

"Who do you hustle?"

"Men."

"You hustle queers."

"Yes."

"You like to fool with these queer people."

"They're nice people."

"Degenerates?" As it had already been established that Allen was a hustler, the point of these questions isn't clear, and in the questioning of Ralph Forest, this same tone crops up.

"Have you ever committed any sexual acts with Rodger?"

"Yes, I have."

"In what way? What I mean, who was the man and who..."

"Fifty-fifty proposition."

In addition to being an ignorant question, it also seems to have little to do with the investigation. Moments like these in the transcript suggest a lack of understanding or compassion not only toward the witnesses but also toward the victims. Yet despite this, the investigators did continue to question and search for the arsonist. The fact that they apparently gave up the search several months before the prime suspect's suicide could mean a loss of interest or simply having run up against a wall, unable to proceed further.

But there was another aspect to the cool way the general public as well as city and state officials reacted to the tragedy, and that's how their reaction affected the reaction of friends and relatives of the victims. "Did you hear about the weenie roast in the French Quarter?" someone overheard a police officer say. "Sorry y'all missed the company barbecue," another heard his boss say.

"The most difficult thing for me," recounted one man fifteen years later, "was the fact that I had to go to work the next day, and I had to shield the grief because I wasn't out of the closet at work." Many mourners not only had to hide their feelings from coworkers but from family members as well. The grief anyone might feel after the death of one or more friends was painful enough, but these mourners had the additional pain of isolation and alienation, of feeling not only that nobody else cared about their loss but also that many people were downright *glad* so many gay people had been neatly disposed of.

But perhaps the harshest result of the homophobia was the reaction of family members. Bill Larson's mother, apparently upset over seeing her son referred to as homosexual in the news, said she didn't want her son returned to her hometown, for fear of the scandal it would raise if her neighbors connected her to the Larson killed in the fire. His remains were cremated, and since Bill's mother didn't want the ashes either, they were kept at the MCC in New Orleans for the next several years. Bodies of two of the others who had been identified were never claimed by anyone at all.

Gays were, of course, used to this kind of reaction. Going to a bar in the '60's had always been a risk. There were periodic raids, and all those arrested for simply being in a gay bar had their names printed in the newspaper the following day. One woman told of a friend who was arrested in a raid. After her bail was paid that evening, she went home, packed what she could, and left New Orleans before the newspaper came out in the morning.

Her whole life had to change now, simply because she had been in a building where other gay people met. She wasn't arrested for intoxication or for performing any indecent or sexual acts. She was arrested solely for being on the premises of a gay establishment.

Many gays and lesbians lived in constant fear of being discovered. Often, gay men had regular lesbian dates they brought to office parties, and vice versa. But gay people also developed a sense of resiliency in adapting to the pressures of the times. One incident which stayed in the minds of the community for years occurred back in 1962, eleven years before the fire. Police raided the Krewe of Yuba ball in Metairie, a suburb of New Orleans. People ran in all directions. One man, in drag, escaped out a back exit. But now here he was, in a dress, in a suburb, with no way to get back to his home in New Orleans.

He knocked on the door of a house nearby. A woman answered.

"Oh, can you please help me?" the man asked in falsetto. "I've just had an argument with my boyfriend, and he dumped me here right on the street! Could I please call a friend to come pick me up?"

"Oh, certainly, you poor thing." She opened her door.

"Thank you so much. Men can be such beasts sometimes! You're such a dear!"

But beneath the humor was a layer of fear. The next day, people could see women's clothing strewn in trails along the road as the items had been discarded from moving cars while the men quickly changed and tried to get rid of the evidence.

Even for people living "on the edge," for people used to harassment, sometimes it was all just a little too much to bear. Raids diminished over the following decade, but they still occurred, and for many folks, a certain level of fear remained.

The fear was also sometimes accompanied by a sense of inferiority. Any time people are forced to deny their true feelings and personality, they diminish themselves just a bit in their own eyes. When a person must deny herself or himself every day of his or her life, five times a day, ten times a day, twenty times a day in various, little ways, day after day for years, it's virtually impossible not to feel inferior to some extent.

This is probably part of the reason the Stonewall riots were so surprising not only to mainstream society but to gays as well. The riots, which began on June 28, 1969 and continued for several days, changed the face of the gay rights movement. Though there'd been a few pioneering gay organizations struggling for decades, after Stonewall, several new organizations sprang up, and a stronger sense of "gay pride" began to enter the consciousness of gays and lesbians across the country.

Each year, on or just before June 28, gays in the larger cities began marching to celebrate Stonewall, to celebrate gay pride or rather to acknowledge their own acceptance of their orientation. They gathered to publicly acknowledge the "terrible secret," to demand their rights, to enjoy the fellowship of others, and to experience the fulfillment of that unique desire not to be invisible any longer. With each passing year, the last week of June came to bring a larger and larger celebration. In 1973, the weekend of June 23 and 24 was chosen as the time to celebrate since the 28th was a Thursday. On the 24th, the largest crowd yet for Gay Pride, a group of over 17,000 gays and lesbians, gathered to march in the streets of New York City.

New Orleans had no organized celebration yet. But some of those at the UpStairs for the beer bust that evening raised their glasses in memory of Stonewall and the beginning of "gay liberation." The need for that liberation was to become all too apparent a few short hours later when a man who'd just escaped the bar overheard two firefighters talking.

"We can't get up there," the first said in frustration.

"Oh, fuck it," said the other. "It's only faggots. Let 'em burn."

The Warrens

Willie Inez Whatley Warren, a fifty-nine-year-old housekeeper from Monroeville, Alabama, lived at 3506 Washington Avenue in New Orleans, as did twenty-six-year-old James Curtis Warren. Her twenty-four-year-old son Eddie Hose lived at 462 Westwood Drive in Marrero, on the Westbank of the Mississippi. Inez, whose parents were Isaac Bush and Gay Brille Matheny Whatley, was born on August 29, 1913. She'd been married to Jimmy Curtis Warren and lived with him in Pensacola, Florida, but she was now divorced. One friend remembered her jaw being broken once when she was beaten by a male lover.

Eddie, born on April 16, 1949, was divorced and living as a cook. James was married to a woman named Fay, and they had a son, Michael. James worked as a carpenter. Some said that both Eddie and James worked part-time as hustlers, and that Inez encouraged this. Others insisted that while they may have been "low-class" in some ways, they were honest enough, and when Inez would tell men, "Oh, take my son home. He's a nice, sweet boy," it was out of a desire for her sons to be happy rather than a desire for their wages. But there was nothing dishonorable about sex work in any event, if that were the case.

The three stopped by Paul Veret's house a couple of times on their way to the Quarter, as Paul knew them from the bars, but he was one acquaintance who didn't much like them. "They were seedy, predatory slobs," he described them. "And it was the mother who set the tone."

Individual opinions, of course, might have been influenced by personal grudges, and aren't necessarily reliable.

Inez, who had false teeth, was obese. She, James, and Eddie arrived at the UpStairs on the 24th in time for the beer bust and stayed afterwards. Inez received 3rd and 4n degree burns over 35% of her body. Her back was burned, her face and the front of her legs charred. She died of carbon monoxide asphyxiation and was identified through fingerprints.

James received 3rd and 4th degree burns over 85% of his body. Only the right anterior chest and his abdomen had any skin left intact. He, too, was identified through fingerprints.

Eddie received 3rd and 4th degree burns over 95% of his body. He lost several fingers and his face was destroyed. His body was recovered in a similar condition to that of his brother, with only the right lateral chest and the anterior of his abdomen having any skin left intact. As with his brother and mother, he was also identified through fingerprints.

Wayne Barras

Wayne Barras was born into a poor family in 1940, poor enough that they had to move into the Iberville housing project just beyond the French Quarter when he was seven. But they were a religious family and sacrificed whatever was necessary to be sure Wayne received a good, Catholic education at parochial schools. Going to Catholic schools shielded him somewhat from a few of the realities of life in the projects. As a teenager, he'd see a police car, with its lights flashing, parked almost every night on Marais Street in the project. It was years before he realized there were drugs in his neighborhood.

Wayne belonged to the Catholic Youth Organization and hung around with other kids in the CYO. They were "goody-goodies," and he liked being a good boy. When he was fourteen, Wayne went on his first date, with thirteen-year-old Barbara Champagne. As they walked down the street together, Wayne's friends followed behind, urging him to hold Barbara's hand. It took everything he had to do it, but he finally managed. That was about all he did, though. Both he and his friends were virgins and wanted to stay that way until marriage.

Wayne liked sports, but being skinny, he didn't have the build to do well. He'd drop the pass in football or strike out in baseball. He wanted to excel because he thought the other kids would accept him then. As it was, none of the other guys on the football team would even talk to him. He was too nelly, and they thought he was queer, even though they knew he was dating girls.

Early in his senior year, however, Wayne was approached by Herman, the water boy for the track team, as Wayne was training for a track event. "Hey, Wayne," Herman said, "want to suck my dick?"

Wayne was shocked at the suggestion. Yes, come to think of it, he probably *would* like it, but he wasn't about to let anyone else know.

"No."

"Come on, Wayne. I want you to suck my dick."

"No, I'm not like that, and if you ask me one more time, I'll clobber you."

Wayne thought this would be the end of it, but for some reason, soon the guys on the football team all started talking to him and accepting him into their friendships. Had the water boy just been a test? Thank God he'd said no!

When Wayne was twenty-one and attending college, he stopped at Sidney's bookstore and glanced through the magazine racks. There, he saw a few magazines with pictures of cute, young, naked men. He became aroused and finally realized that those feelings he'd occasionally wondered about were real, that he was probably one of those queers. The idea wasn't a pleasant one, and Wayne tried to deny it to himself for the next few years.

After college, Wayne began working at D. H. Holmes on Canal Street. One of his coworkers, Linda, seemed interested, and though he'd wanted to wait until marriage before having sex, he began thinking it might not be a bad idea to see if this sex stuff was really going to work. Wayne called Linda "Pizza" because she always brought pizza over, and he finally accepted a date with her. She later told him he was her 41st sexual encounter. For twenty-six-year-old virgin Wayne Barras, the idea was shocking, but soon he began to see that one could have sex and still be a good person.

Wayne had sex just a few times with women that year, but it wasn't until he was twenty-seven that he had any encounters with men. There was another gay salesperson at Holmes named Duke. During Mardi Gras, Duke met Courtney Craighead, and through Duke, Wayne met Courtney. Wayne and Duke took off for Little Rock one weekend to see Courtney, and during that weekend, Courtney made his move, and Wayne was introduced to gay sex.

He liked it and began going to the bars. In Lafitte's one night, Wayne approached another man for the first time. He turned out to be a doctor, and they went home and had great sex. After this, Wayne began going out more and more, and soon enough he began to catch up with Linda's tally.

Wayne went to almost all the bars. In one, he saw a drag queen named Royena performing. The guy looked vaguely familiar, like someone Wayne had been friends with back in 9th grade. After the show, Wayne introduced himself and found out that his old pal Roy now had breast implants.

Wayne preferred sleazier bars such as the Midship on Iberville. He liked being a "Mother Hen," helping the unfortunates, the "leftovers of the leftovers." What he really liked, though, was "helping" them to bed.

But he did take people in and let them live with him for months on end. Courtney Craighead lived with him a while as he tried to get on his feet, and Bill Larson lived with him for a time as well. Bill was a nice guy, someone Wayne could always feel comfortable around. When Bill was feeling down, he might express what he was feeling, but he'd do it in a way that didn't try to seek sympathy or pity.

Bill was also good with kids. Some young teenage boys sometimes came over, looking for John, a friend of Wayne's. John had money, the vice president of an insurance underwriter firm, and he liked teenagers. Some of them liked John, too, and would come over hoping to find him. At times, they'd get rowdy, but Bill could quiet them down easily. He got along well with the teens, though he himself wasn't into chicken. The youngest man Wayne ever saw Bill going with was an eighteen- or nineteen-year-old black guy he dated for a brief period.

Another roommate Wayne had was Bob Babb, who moved in after Courtney and Bill moved out. Bob was an artist for *Westbank Guide* and spent his days reading *Time,* occasional books, or drawing. Wayne was into sports, which Bob disliked, and it seemed the only thing the two men had in common was barhopping. Well, they also sometimes had various men in common. Wayne would bring someone home, and Bob would become interested and claim the man as his.

One of the many bars Wayne and Bob frequented regularly was the UpStairs Lounge, almost never missing the beer bust on Sunday evenings. They took part in the first

Mardi Gras costume contest there, with Bob winning first place for an elaborate, outrageous headdress, and Wayne placing second for his green swamp monster outfit.

Wayne enjoyed going to the bar with Bob because it gave him someone to talk to if he didn't know anyone else, but really, there was rarely any danger of that. If someone new came to the bar, Buddy would often find out his name and announce it to the crowd, letting everyone know that a newcomer had arrived, and encouraging everyone to say hi and talk to him. The new arrival usually didn't stay a stranger for long.

And of course, Wayne knew Courtney and Bill, who were also regulars, and Wayne became friends with another Bill, the one Buddy was dating. John, the chicken hawk, sometimes showed up, and Tad Turner was always friendly. There was Al, who looked so much like Wayne that Wayne would call Al "Wayne" and Al would call Wayne "Al." Then there was Herb, who tried to go out with macho guys in their early twenties. Every time Herb would find a new boyfriend, he'd tell Wayne, "Oh, this is the one. I'm really in love this time." A few months later, Wayne would see him with someone else, saying the same thing yet again.

And there was Jay, who worked at Skeffington's. He'd plant a big kiss on Wayne every time he walked in the bar. First, he'd make a major production out of it, saying, "Oh, there he is. Let me get prepared. Let me get prepared." Then he'd gather all his energy together and wrap his arms around Wayne, plastering a big kiss on him. Most of Wayne's friends at the UpStairs greeted him with a hug or a kiss, but no one made the show out of it that Jay did.

As far as real shows went, Wayne didn't participate much in the plays at the UpStairs, but Bob did to some extent. One of his roles was "Dakota Strange." But Wayne didn't even attend the performances often enough to know what other roles his roommate might play.

One thing he knew Bob liked, though, was the name Michael. It seemed that almost every guy Bob dated was named Michael. Bob even started referring to them as Michael One, Michael Two, and Michael Three when discussing them, just so everyone could keep them straight. Bob went off with one of the Michaels to St. Thomas Island for several months, during which time Wayne found a roommate who paid rent, but when Bob came back to the States, Wayne took him in again.

Supporting another person finally started to take its toll, and Wayne announced that he was planning to move, alone. Wayne worked as a lab technician at Union Carbide in Taft, so he made plans to move to Destrehan, where a quick hop across the river on the ferry would put him only another half hour from work.

Just because he no longer wanted to live with Bob, though, didn't mean Wayne didn't still like him. In the meantime, they still went barhopping together, including their regular Sunday trip to the beer bust. On June 24, Wayne and Bob started making plans to leave for the Quarter as usual. But for some reason, though Wayne had missed only about three beer busts since he'd started attending, he decided he really didn't want to go tonight. He felt too lazy. He just wanted to relax.

But Bob wanted to go and begged, "Oh, come on. Everyone's going to be there. They'll be expecting us."

"That's just it. It's too predictable. It's the same thing every week. I'm bored with it."

"Aw, you're just in a mood. It won't be boring once we get there. Come on."

Wayne knew that Bob was probably right. He felt torn over the minor decision, debating with himself over what to do. Sheesh, he finally thought. What was the big deal? Go or stay? He just needed to make up his mind and do it. He looked toward Bob one more time and made his decision.

The Unidentified

Since the known dead included people from multiple states, the number of possible identities of the remaining corpses was large. Many people whose husband or son or brother or lover was missing or on an unannounced trip began to wonder if it was just possible their loved one was among the dead. The coroner's office was inundated with names of men suspected to be one of those as yet unidentified. Comparing all the medical and dental charts with the remains was not an easy job, but from among the numerous charts sent in from across the country as well as Canada and Mexico, there were a few that matched the remains, and one by one the dead were named.

But there were still a few unnamed bodies. Were these men who had no one to miss them? Loners? Men whose parents had disowned them for being gay and so didn't care to know if their son was missing or not? Were two lovers dead, with no one else to miss them? Had all their closest friends who might be able to identify them perhaps died along with them at the bar?

One woman, short and gray-haired, had no real reason to suspect her missing son might have been in a gay bar. Her son wasn't gay. He'd show up, and she'd tell him firmly not to go so long without contacting her. Then things would be all right.

But he didn't show up. And while she knew her son well enough to know he couldn't be gay, it was true he was thirty-eight and unmarried. "At first," she said, two and a half weeks after the fire, "I just wouldn't think about him being one of those poor souls, but now...Lord help me if he is. He's all I had."

Irby Landreneau's parents in False River, Louisiana, knew their oldest son was gay, but homosexuality was a touchy subject and so rarely discussed. Irby's mother, however, was convinced her son had been at the bar and tried desperately to get in touch. Irby was, in fact, an occasional customer at the UpStairs, though his parents probably didn't know the names of the bars he frequented. But Irby didn't call Sunday night to say he was okay. And he didn't call the next day, or the day after.

Irby's mother, of course, called him, but there was no answer, not even after three days of calling. This was long before answering machines became common, so reaching someone could be hit or miss in the best of times. But why didn't *he* call?

Oh, God, should she send his dental charts? What would happen if the neighbors learned her son was gay? If he was identified as one of the dead, that was one thing, but if he wasn't even at the bar, and it got around that his dental charts were in New Orleans at the coroner's office, the neighbors would *know*. What should she do? She called again. There was no answer.

Little by little, the bodies were identified, this one by fingerprints, that one by a friend, this other by dental charts. With the dental charts, the coroners tried to find as many as twelve to fourteen points of similarity between the charts and the victim before they were willing to make a positive I.D., so the more mouth work that had been done, the easier it was to cancel out coincidence.

Clothes were often burned away and of little help in identifying the victims. Wallets were sometimes lying beside a pile of bodies with no way to determine to which person the wallet belonged. Even when there might have been a possibility of identifying a body through identification carried on the person, the chief of detectives, Major Henry Morris, doubted it would be helpful. "We don't even know these papers belonged to people we found them on," he said. "Some thieves hung out there and you know this was a queer bar."

When Morris Kight heard the remark, he replied that there was absolutely no justification to believe gay people carried around false identification. Of course, there'd been a case when a man visiting New Orleans disappeared, and when his family couldn't contact him, they had the police looking all over the city. The one place they didn't look was jail, where the man had been since being arrested by a vice cop his first day in town. The gay man had given a false name, hoping to avoid ruining his reputation. It turned out, however, that each name found on the victims at the UpStairs did in fact belong to someone who was missing, and often fingerprints were used to verify the identities.

One problem today in connecting the remains at the bar to possible I.D.'s is that different departments had different numbers for the same bodies, which is made evident when a number listed as an overweight female by one group is listed as a slender male on another list. There is apparently little documentation for which bodies were found where in the bar, which might have offered slight clues. Some lovers and friends may have heard at the time, however, as they often have clear ideas as to where their loved one was found.

Early in the identification process, the state fire marshal's records show how the meagerness of the remains made the work difficult.

Body #2 had a white metal chain around its neck, with two doves.

Body #4 had blue pants with gray stripes, a blue button-up shirt, black boots, purple socks, a white metal wedding band on the left ring finger, a brown leather change purse with two quarters and a $1 bill in the right front pants pocket.

Body #5 also had blue pants and a blue shirt, a white belt with a silver button, blue and tan shoes that had a two-inch heel, gray socks, and a white metal bracelet on the left hand.

Body #6 had a yellow metal ring on the left index finger.

Body #7 had black leather shoes, green socks, brown pants, a black belt, a large metal buckle with antique flowered designs, and a pink and white checked shirt.

Body #13 had a white metal neck chain with a religious medal.

Body #17 had a ring with the initials H. (G.?).

Body #19 had a yellow wedding band.

Body #20 had a ring with the initials G. M. and a yellow neck chain.

Body #21 had a white chain and a religious medal.

Body #24 had a Country Club Motel key.

Body #26 had a yellow wedding band.

Body #28 had an address, that of Tina Terrell, 300 Ponce de Leon St., the word "Son," and then the rest of an address, P.O. Box 417, Scottsdale, GA.

Body #29 had a belt buckle containing a silver dollar.

But this same list describes all twenty-nine bodies found in the bar as white males, which is not accurate, neglecting the one woman and one black male. Found not on a body but near the second Chartres Street window was a buckle with the names Leon and Lynn, and a wallet with pictures and the names Leon and Kenneth.

With no skin remaining on the fingers of some victims, neither fingerprinting nor the sometimes burned wallets provided any help in identification. One man was finally identified by that motel key. Another was identified by a ring. Eventually, all but three of the bodies were identified. People suspected who a couple of these might be, but there was no way to make a positive I.D.

Several years after the fire, a man walked into a bar in Baton Rouge and gasped. "Don! My God! I thought you were dead! I haven't seen you since the night of the fire! What happened to you?"

Don Sherry had been at the UpStairs and escaped out the back exit physically unharmed. Mentally, however, he was so traumatized by the horror of that evening he could no longer bear to remain in the same city. He left without contacting anyone. It was only after several years that he could go out again, and only when one of his former friends happened to run into him was the friend able to let others know that Don was not one of the corpses left still unidentified.

Irby Landreneau's mother eventually found her son as well, also unharmed. He'd gone to see a movie that Sunday evening and then headed over to the UpStairs, seeing the bar in flames as he arrived. Desperate to track down friends, he'd just never gotten around to contacting his mother until a few days after the fire.

MCC members turned over a list of names of men they thought might be the victims. Among the possibilities were Norman LaVergne, James Paige, Reginald Tubbs, Byron Tanner, Larry Frost, Bobbie (an ex-lover of Napoleon), and Adlai S. "Tad" Turner, Jr.

Despite various suspicions about who the last bodies might be, those three remained unidentified, and eventually no more efforts were made to discover their names. Among the coroner's reports and autopsies, these three are listed as:

Body #18, No. 173-6-284

This was an adult white male who had extensive 2nd, 3rd, and 4th degree burns over 70% of his body. He was wearing brown shoes, and there were fragments of his pants remaining. His fingers were wrinkled and partially charred, and his facial features showed edematous swelling and reddish, irregular black discoloration.

Body #23, No. 173-6-285, police I. D. tag #1849

The body was that of an adult, slender white male, with extensive 3rd and 4th degree burns over 90% of his body. He was wearing brown shoes and black socks. The man's fingers were destroyed as well as his facial configurations.

Body #28, No. 173-6-286, police I. D. tag #1848

This was an adult male with extensive 2nd, 3rd, and 4th degree burns over 60% of his body. The skin beneath the pants and the lower part of the undershirt showed a preserved white skin, but there was extensive charring of the upper thoracic area, of the facial region, of the upper extremities, and of the feet also.

There were no visible tattoos or scars on any of these three bodies, though they may have existed on parts of the body where the skin was burned away. No more is known about these men other than the condition of their bodies at death. The members of the New Orleans congregation of the Metropolitan Community Church offered to pay for a decent burial for the men, but since there was no provable kinship, the MCC members had no legal claim to the bodies. They were buried finally in an indigent cemetery originally listed as 527 City Park Avenue but which turned out to be a remote graveyard in New Orleans East called Resthaven.

One the men was tentatively identified in 2018 as Larry Norman Frost but would need to be exhumed for confirmation, and the specific burial plot is unknown.

Guy Andersen

Guy Andersen (sometimes spelled Anderson) was in New Orleans for a visit. Born in Illinois on November 17, 1931, to Roy and Mildred Frye Anderson, he presently lived at 225 North Plum Grove Road in Palatine, Illinois. Forty-one-years-old, Guy had never married and made his living as a research investigator. He had upper dentures.

Guy received extensive 3rd and 4th degree burns over 90% of his body. His fingertips were badly charred, as was much of his upper body, including his head, arms, and abdomen. He was identified by a hotel key.

Adolph Medina

Adolph Medina grew up in downtown San Antonio near the YMCA. His father, a printer, was from Mexico, and his mother was an American-born Mexican-American who actually spoke Spanish more often than his Mexican father. Adolph, the seventh child in the family, was born on January 29, 1941, and grew up speaking both Spanish and English.

Adolph enjoyed being the baby of the family, but his mother had one last child when Adolph was ten, so now there were three girls and five boys in the family. Fortunately, the newcomer turned out to be a nice kid, so it wasn't so bad having a baby brother. Adolph's parents and grandparents on both sides were Protestants, rare for their Mexican-American Catholic community, but there was a Baptist church in the neighborhood, and the family attended regularly.

Adolph studied at the San Antonio Vocational and Technical School rather than at a typical high school and learned printing as his father had, working on the school newspaper and yearbook. He also enjoyed drama class. He was small and didn't participate in sports, but he would sometimes go to football games with his best friend, Rudy.

Afterward, if they were in a particularly festive mood, they might even play around a little, but Adolph didn't think much about it. They were just "getting off." It would be several more years before Adolph would come out, not because he had trouble accepting himself, but because he really had no idea there might be more beyond what he and Rudy had done.

In his late teens and early twenties, Adolph attended "record hops" held in nightclubs during the day, or in churches or ballrooms. He liked dancing and had a good time. Joe, the DJ working the dances, was two or three years older than Adolph and always nice to him, saying hi or giving him a free pass to the next dance or, as Adolph was leaving, even giving him a 45 record of one of the songs he'd played that day.

Life was carefree and fun until November of 1963. The day the rest of the country would remember as the day Kennedy was assassinated, Adolph would remember as the day he received his draft notice. Being drafted wasn't terrible, but it did force him to face a different level of responsibility. He didn't need to report immediately, however, and so had time to move a few things out to California where he'd be stationed.

After making one trip out, he returned to San Antonio and called Rudy so they could go driving around. While they were out, they ran into Joe, the disk jockey, who was a friend of Rudy's now, and Joe asked for Adolph's phone number. Adolph figured he was okay and gave him the number but then was surprised to see how often Joe kept calling his mother's house. Adolph, out another time with Rudy, asked what was going on.

"Adolph, stop the car by that phone booth and call Joe at the radio station right now."

"What? Why?"

"You're my sister and I want what's best for you."

"Huh?"

"I couldn't figure you out for the longest time, but you're gay, just like me. Now give Joe a call and do whatever he wants."

Adolph called Joe, who asked him to come over later that evening. After he hung up, Adolph reported back to Rudy. "Good. Now you go over there tonight and do whatever he tells you to do."

He did. It was the first time Adolph had ever actually undressed and climbed in bed with another man, and he was scared, but he liked it, too. After going out to California for a while, he was stationed back in San Antonio, and Adolph continued seeing Joe occasionally, but Joe had too many boyfriends and Adolph didn't like it.

In the Army for two years, from January 1964 to January 1966, Adolph trained to be a medical corpsman and was stationed in a medical battalion, but he served mostly as a company clerk, acting as a secretary to a cute company commander. He had to be careful while in the Army, but in 1965, a gay bar twelve miles outside of town opened. Called "The Country," it was a dance bar, open on Wednesday, Friday, Saturday, and Sunday evenings.

When MP's came in or someone from the liquor control board, someone would flash a light, and the gays and lesbians would immediately switch to start dancing with each other. After Adolph left the service, he was arrested several times for dancing and sometimes taken down to jail for no reason, but he wasn't about to let harassment keep him from doing what he wanted to do.

Shortly after he left the Army in 1966, while at a straight bar one evening, Adolph saw a tremendously cute man, and being aggressive, he struck up a conversation and got the man in bed. Chuck, who'd also recently left the Army after being stationed in Germany, insisted he was straight, but that didn't keep them from seeing each other again. And again. And again.

They eventually moved in together, but Chuck, now in a civil service job, was so terrified of being accused of homosexuality—"And I'm *not* gay!"—that they fought often. They decided to live apart and simply date each other regularly. Chuck exuded masculinity, rode a motorcycle, and Adolph found himself not only enjoying the sex but also falling deeply in love for the first time. They went out in the country together, and Chuck would entice Adolph to dive into the Sun River with all his clothes on.

They'd swim and play and eat and enjoy each other's company. When Chuck bought a boat, they'd go boating on the lake together. They rarely went to bars, both because Adolph didn't like the way other gays, even knowing they were a couple, would make moves on Chuck, and because Chuck simply didn't feel comfortable around gay men. "Because I'm not gay." Despite Chuck's heterosexuality, however, he and Adolph managed to remain lovers over the next several years.

Adolph worked for a wig company with stores all over Texas. The company frequently asked him to go to different cities and open a salon, managing it until it was operating smoothly. Then he'd move on to another assignment. In 1972, the company asked Adolph to manage a new salon just opening in New Orleans. That was asking a lot, but he'd been to the Quarter a couple of years earlier and liked it, even though by that time gays were dancing in bars in downtown San Antonio and still couldn't in New Orleans. Nevertheless, it seemed like a fun city, and sometimes, Chuck, with his "I love you like a brother" routine, could get a bit old, so maybe a little distance would be a good thing for a while.

Adolph moved to an apartment on the edge of the French Quarter, on Esplanade near Burgundy. Even though this was at the far diagonal end of the Quarter away from the UpStairs, the Lounge soon became his "home bar." He made friends in the city, and he kept in touch with Chuck, going back to visit him once and having Chuck come visit twice in the year after he arrived.

But that didn't mean he wasn't going to play around a little, too. After all, he wasn't married, as Chuck himself pointed out. And there was a nice guy he'd met at the UpStairs he wanted to get to know better.

So he did. He and Bob met several times at the bar, yet they took things slowly and didn't jump right into bed. But on June 24, when his group of friends decided to leave the UpStairs and head somewhere else, Adolph and Bob stayed behind. This was going to be the night, they decided. They'd stay at the UpStairs just a little while longer and then rather than head to another bar, they'd go home together for the first time.

Nervous, Adolph had wanted to stay completely sober this evening as he and Bob talked, though he usually liked to have several drinks at the beer bust. Now that his other friends had left, though, he thought he'd go ahead and have just one drink. Adolph sipped as he and Bob continued to talk. They were just deciding whose apartment they were going to head toward when suddenly flames exploded into the bar.

Richard Everett

"What would the Lord want me to do?" That was the question Ricky Everett always tried to ask himself whenever he had to make a decision, large or small. "Which choice will help me to best serve God?" He always asked himself these questions, then always asked God, too, and for the most part, he usually seemed to make the right choices, as far as he could tell.

Born in Crowley, Louisiana, on December 12, 1947, Richard Frank Everett had moved with his family to Yazoo City, Mississippi, by the time he started grammar school. His maternal grandmother was the music director at First Presbyterian Church in Yazoo City, so Ricky was raised Presbyterian, though from a very young age he seemed inclined toward a more "spirit centered" religion. Even as a child, he believed firmly in prayer not as a means of appealing to or pacifying God but as a means of communication. He felt God's love for him but sometimes felt that churches neglected that aspect of God, the aspect of love.

Of course, during his few years in Yazoo City, these feelings and ideas were just forming. While religion was important, Ricky also enjoyed running up and down the rolling hills predominant in the area. The family lived first in a white, two-story house in town but then moved to a family estate three miles outside city limits. They had stables, horses, every pet imaginable, and lots of hills. The Natchez Trace even cut across their land. Ricky and his brother, two years older, found several Civil War artifacts there, including old flintlock guns and even a cannon. They also found lots of arrowheads on other parts of their land and some Indian pottery, some of it with hardly a scratch, though the majority was broken.

In addition to all the history, the estate also offered some innovation. Ricky's grandfather took tracks for logs from a sawmill and built a roller coaster on the property, up and down the hills, for the private use of his grandchildren, making the estate a source of continual adventure.

Ricky and his brother usually got along well enough, but Ricky also knew he was the faster runner, so at times he'd provoke his brother. Whenever his brother came after him, Ricky would take off, and his brother would eventually tire of the chase and collapse onto the ground laughing. Ricky would then collapse as well, and together they'd laugh until they weren't angry anymore.

One time Ricky didn't laugh, though, was when he and his brother were mowing the lawn together and Ricky reached down to pull something away from the machine. He reached too close to the blades, and the tips of his index finger and ring finger on his left hand were chopped off.

But most of his childhood was reasonably happy. He played Little League baseball and admired from afar a cousin who pitched for the Pittsburg Pirates. He learned from his mother's genealogy stories that someone on her side of the family had introduced rugby to England, but neither rugby nor football ever interested Ricky.

The family history stories held minimal interest for him but great interest for his mother. The family traced their line back through England and Scotland into Scandinavia and 7th century Germany. On Ricky's maternal grandmother's side, one group, the Hooks, came over on the Mayflower. From England came some dukes and squires, while from Scotland came some thieves and murderers offered the choice of prison or going to America. What brought the two sides together in America the family could never learn, though Ricky thought perhaps the family didn't really want to find out.

Both Ricky's mother and grandmother belonged to the Daughters of the American Revolution, and his grandmother was a leader in the Masons for both the Rainbow Girls, a group for young girls, and Eastern Star, for women, for the state of Mississippi. His grandmother had married at fourteen and been given dated Civil War silver as a wedding gift. She fell in love with it and collected silver forever after. Members of the groups she led often gave her more silver on special occasions because they knew she liked it. Some of her music students also chipped in to buy her silver. In her kitchen, three walls were lined with silver items.

Ricky's paternal grandmother, "Little Grandma," lived outside of Port Barry, near Opelousas, in Louisiana. She used palmetto leaves for the roof of her cabin and drank rainwater from a cistern. Little Grandma liked to fish, and she hunted with double-barreled shotgun. Tired of neighbors crossing over her land, she fenced off a section and chased away anyone who trespassed. Once a cousin came up to the fence and yelled for her to call off her dog so he could cross through. Out came Little Grandma with her shotgun, saying, "If you cross that fence, I'll blow your brains out." The cousin walked around her property instead.

On his mother's side, the whole family seemed musically inclined except for Ricky. His grandmother both taught and directed music. His mother had been a singer and dancer before she married, and his brother wrote and sang songs. Because of his mother's early career and because his dad's side of the family was involved in politics, Ricky's parents and grandparents socialized often among the upper crust in the Yazoo City-Vicksburg area. His parents knew storyteller Jerry Clower and other prominent figures in the region.

In 1957, when Ricky was in the 3rd grade, his father bought a new, pink, 1957 Chevy. Shortly after, the family moved to Baton Rouge, Louisiana, where Ricky's father took a job as the head of the engineering department for Allied Chemical. A few years later, Ricky's parents divorced, and his mother's brother called to tell the divorced mother that she and her two sons were going to move to Buras to be near him. She said she wasn't moving, but the next morning her brother showed up with a van and several men to move furniture, and soon Ricky was living in Buras.

After only a few years there, however, Ricky moved with his mother and brother to the Westbank of New Orleans, starting his sophomore year at West Jefferson High School. He wasn't terribly good in school, never caring much for it and studying as little as possible to receive steady C's on his report card. Of the gang of six that Ricky hung out with in high school, all but one eventually turned out to be gay, though none of them knew about the others during their high school years.

Ricky was laid back in high school, rarely doing anything terribly rebellious. Once, though, he did something he considered brazen. His brother had a musical group called the Spades, and the members all tattooed an ace of spades on the fleshy part of their left hand between the thumb and index finger. Ricky got a needle and began tattooing himself, but about halfway through, he realized the design was not looking much like a spade. Frustrated at first, he finally turned the design into a capital R and added a period after it. At least this way he could pretend the initial was what he'd intended all along.

Right after high school, Ricky tried something else daring. He joined the Navy. He went to San Diego for basic training and instantly regretted his decision. Even when his parents were breaking up, they'd never argued in front of him, so to be screamed at constantly now was a shock. He was forced to march in torrential rains, and despite being used to damp weather, he caught pneumonia and spent a week in the hospital. At that point, he felt he couldn't take any more, and so, feeling like a spoiled Mama's boy, he went to his commanding officer and told him he was gay.

Ricky next went to computer school and graduated with a B average, the best he'd done so far, but he never found a job he cared for. He worked for a while as a computer technician, then for a while as a computer operator, but none of it really meant much to him. Church was still the only organization where he enjoyed working.

When the Metropolitan Community Church formed its group in New Orleans, Ricky was the seventh person to join. He felt the meetings were a bit too casual at times, like when a member was allowed to bring his dog and let it run around the room throughout the meeting, but he still enjoyed the services. He also enjoyed the company of the other MCC members, Courtney Craighead, Mitch and Horace, Bill Larson, "Mother" Cross, and others.

He liked the socializing, such as the district conference party held on a small riverboat, and he liked even more the ability to be around Christians who didn't condemn him but let him worship as best he could. He'd never felt that being gay was wrong, but he'd often felt alone, and it was nice not to be alone anymore.

Ricky believed in true love, in finding a man and living with him happily ever after in a permanent, monogamous relationship. But Ricky's first lover was Lenny. They'd met when Ricky was the tobacco manager at a Schwegmann's grocery and Lenny was a manager trainee in another department. While Ricky was grateful they hadn't had to meet in a bar, their relationship somehow didn't measure up to his dreams. First of all, Ricky was still living with his mom, and Lenny had another roommate, but there was also a lack of communication, and when Ricky felt low, he found he was confiding in either Buddy Rasmussen over at the UpStairs or to Bill Larson, his minister.

More and more, he found himself confiding in Bill, and they had many long talks together. Bill also had a lover, so though Ricky wished things could be different between himself and the minister, he respected the way things were, and he never had sex with Bill. They became good friends, though, and Ricky often went with Bill when Bill wanted to discuss religious matters with Bill Richardson at St. George's. He also admired Bill's work with children and the homeless. Ricky wanted to find ways to help Bill with his projects.

Bill, in his turn, liked Ricky and respected Ricky's feelings for him. He sent Ricky a special letter one Christmas, telling him of his feelings, and another time, he gave Ricky a small gift. The gift was a live alligator. Ricky was delighted and put it in Lenny's bathtub. He couldn't tell Lenny who gave him the gift, but he did name it Alligator Bill. He wasn't quite sure what he'd do with the baby creature when it grew larger, but he'd enjoy it for now.

However, his enjoyment was to last only a few more hours. When Lenny's roommate came home in the middle of the night and decided to take a shower before going to bed, he didn't think to check the tub for reptiles. A minute into his shower, he let out a bloodcurdling scream and ripped off half the shower curtain in his escape. Alligator Bill was banished in the morning.

Since Bill and many other MCC members hung out at the UpStairs, Ricky enjoyed going to the bar regularly. He never left his mother's house on the Westbank without letting her know where he was heading, but he didn't want to tell her everything, so he'd just say, "I'm going out to the UpStairs." That's where she could reach him if she needed to get in touch for any reason. Sometimes, Ricky would be barhopping and run into someone at Lafitte's who'd say, "Your mom left a message for you at the UpStairs." So he'd go over later to pick it up. But he never told his mom it was a gay bar.

In addition to the MCC members at the UpStairs, there were other regulars Ricky enjoyed talking to. There was Luther Boggs, milkman Fat Harry "Harriet," and Napoleon and Stanley. Ricky had gone to high school with Stanley Plaisance. They'd done their homework together and even slept over at each other's house a few times, in separate beds, but neither knew at the time the other was gay. Stanley's lover Napoleon was the kind of guy who'd probably show up in sandals at a formal function, but Ricky found him sweet and could see he always seemed full of love for Stanley.

Napoleon and Stanley were two of several regulars who performed in the plays produced by Bettye and her husband. Ricky also took part. The cast would perform a play twice each weekend and do the same play week after week until the audience, who intentionally came back to see the same performance, knew the lines so well they'd start reciting them along with the actors. Then the performers would try to ad lib, just to throw the audience off.

And sometimes, they'd change roles. Michael West, for example, was usually the "Infamous Memphis Queen," but one night Ricky played the part instead. The point of the plays was to have a good time and do something a little different. It also gave the performers a chance to socialize further while rehearsing on stage, dressing frantically in the stairwell leading to the third-floor storage room, or waiting together behind the set next to the fire door which led out onto the roof of the neighboring building.

After Bettye and her husband moved away, the plays stopped, but the cast couldn't bear to stop performing, so they began preparing drag shows. The "Scummy and Scare" show, with Ricky starring as Cher's counterpart, went well enough. So did "An Evening with the Stars," with Ricky as Connie Francis. They also did other variety shows, with Mitch usually dressed as Kate Smith, singing "God Bless America." Ricky would sing different songs, such as "I Want to Be Loved by You" or any other song sung by a woman he could manage to make himself look like for the show, finally able to use some of that "family musical talent" he thought he'd missed out on.

Ricky didn't like groping or being groped by others, and the UpStairs always felt like a decent and friendly place, at least in contrast with most of the other bars. He noticed that even when Buddy was feeling down, the bartender did his best not to let on, to try cheering Ricky up instead. Ricky also liked Adam, who tried hard to disguise his Cajun accent by faking a cultured English one, but when he was drunk, as he often seemed to be, the Cajun started slipping out.

Ricky spent more time with Buddy than with Adam, and together they tried to outbitch Phil, but Phil had a quick tongue and usually won any bitch contests.

Mostly, though, Ricky visited with his MCC friends, going over to Mitch and Horace's house or talking to Bill. About a week before the fire, Ricky had a strange feeling and turned to Bill. "I have a feeling you won't be in the pulpit much longer. Either you'll be moving away or stepping down."

A week later, on June 24, Ricky went with Bill and another friend, Ronnie Rosenthal, to the Fatted Calf for dinner. As they ate, Ricky experienced the strange feeling again and said, "Bill, something bad is going to happen to you."

"I know it," Bill replied.

Ronnie just looked at both of them.

By the end of the meal, they'd all apparently shaken off the feeling and headed over to the UpStairs. If something bad was going to happen, it certainly wouldn't be there. The UpStairs was where they had fun, for goodness' sake. It was where their friends were. So, as they did every Sunday evening, they climbed the stairs to join the others for some gossip, some beer, and a good, good time.

Their good time ended that evening shortly before 8:00.

Mitch and Horace

Louis Horace Broussard was a hustler when Buddy Rasmussen first met him. Born on October 7, 1946, to Oniel and Lillian Broussard, in Kaplan, Louisiana, in the southwest part of the state, Horace used to work out of Wanda's, picking up johns and then bringing them over to the UpStairs. He lived a day-to-day kind of existence, counting the number of drinks he could get out of people as his salary. His success as a hustler, or at least his satisfaction with his job, was due partly to the fact that he liked obese men.

In a culture that claimed to thrive on diversity, it was still true that being gay was not the only deviation from the norm that society didn't accept. Being overweight wasn't acceptable, and while the obsession for being thin was not as pronounced in mainstream culture for men as for women, in the gay community, just the opposite was the case.

Horace, however, liked not only fat men but those who were downright obese. And since these were often those seeking the services of a hustler, Horace had perhaps found an occupation to which he was appropriately suited. He seemed content enough with his life, but then one day in 1971 he met Mitch.

Duane George Mitchell was born in Tennessee on September 14, 1941, the son of George and Mildred Campbell Mitchell. He'd been married to a woman named

Vicki Tane for a few years and had two sons, Duane Jr., who was eleven in 1973, and Stephen, ten that year. The boys lived with their mother in Fort Payne, Alabama. Mitch and Vicki had divorced when Mitch eventually accepted his orientation. They remained on good enough terms, however, that Vicki allowed the boys to visit their father in New Orleans for holidays or summer vacation.

Mitch, a salesman for Danos Beauty Supply Company in Harvey on the Westbank, was already heavyset when he met Horace, but after he and Horace moved in together, he began to gain even more weight. Horace stopped hustling when they became lovers and worked instead as a barber, at Chap's Barber Shop on Poydras and St. Charles. But he spent a lot of time at home cooking, cleaning, and fattening Mitch up. Mitch, about six feet tall, eventually grew to 300 pounds. Even Horace, only 5'6", went from 150 to 200 pounds.

But the weight gain wasn't only a sign of contented married life. It also signaled serious problems for Mitch, who was diabetic and who despite the urgency was still unable to manage his eating habits. He continued to drink as well, also an unhealthy habit for diabetics. Mitch would simply test his blood sugar level regularly and administer extra insulin when he needed it.

Though Mitch had a serious problem with his weight, his personality seemed just fine. He was always happy, smiling and joking, and he always seemed thoughtful of others. Feeling that religion offered a way to serve, he joined Metropolitan Community Church along with Horace and became the associate pastor for the New Orleans congregation.

Mitch and Horace were regulars at the UpStairs, coming one or two nights every week. They lived in a two-story double at 1426 Polymnia Street, though Horace's address was also listed at 1405 Terpsichore, so it wasn't as if a casual stroll would take them to the bar, as it might for some of the other regulars. To go was a conscious decision, made because they enjoyed the company of the others they met there. They especially enjoyed the beer bust, rarely if ever missing a Sunday afternoon at the UpStairs, wanting to socialize with the other MCC members who attended the beer bust almost as faithfully as they attended church services.

Buddy for one enjoyed having them at the bar. They never caused any trouble, never fussed, never argued with each other or anyone else. They were fun-loving and liked taking part in the shows. 300-pound Mitch enjoyed playing the dainty little girl in distress. For Mardi Gras, he might dress up as Queen Victoria.

He joined in the tricycle race wholeheartedly, though he ended up accidentally tearing the handlebars off the tricycle. After fastening them back on, they continued the race. Whenever someone would look disbelievingly at the small toy and say, "I'm not getting on that," Mitch would encourage further participation. "If I can get my big ass on there," he said, "you can, too." And so more customers tried.

Each anniversary that Mitch and Horace celebrated was a major occasion. As a hustler, Horace had not been sure he'd ever love one man enough to stay with him. And Mitch had not been at all convinced he'd ever find anyone willing to put up with his weight, let alone someone he liked. What the two men discovered was that they did truly love each other.

Horace didn't want to be taken care of. He was quite willing to pay his way. And Mitch didn't take in Horace simply because no one else might want his large body. He wanted Horace because he loved Horace.

"Promise me you'll never leave me," Mitch asked him one day as their relationship developed.

"I don't have to promise," Horace told him. "I won't ever want to leave you. You just be sure you never leave me."

"Never," Mitch promised.

Mitch's sons, Duane and Steve, had come to stay with the couple at the end of the school year, so by June 24, they'd been in New Orleans almost a month. Mitch and Horace weren't "out" to the boys, but they behaved naturally in front of them. Sometimes, they acted so much like an old married couple it must have been obvious even to kids raised in small-town Alabama the two were especially close.

One day, for instance, Mitch needed a new pair of slacks, so the four of them went shopping together. When Mitch found a pair he liked and tried them on, he asked Horace for his opinion. "What do you think?"

Horace shrugged dismissively. "They make you look fat." Apparently, even he had limits to his appreciation.

Mitch wasn't pleased by the answer. "Well, *I* like them," he insisted.

Horace shrugged again. "Fine," he said. "Go ahead and buy them if you don't mind looking fat."

Duane and Steve listened to the bickering, exchanging glances and trying not to snicker. But Mitch didn't care. They were all out spending time together, and that was a good thing.

Mitch and Horace didn't want to stop going to the beer bust, so each Sunday evening they'd bring the kids to the movie theater. They'd drop Duane and Steve off and then go on to the UpStairs, picking the boys up afterwards. On the 24th, the routine was the same. Disney's *The World's Greatest Athlete* was playing, and both boys were excited to see it.

"We'll pick you up in a couple of hours," Mitch told the boys as they started for the lobby doors. Then the men went on to meet their friends at the bar.

The Lawsuit

Thirty-two people were dead. One was a mother, and the others were fathers, husbands, sons, or brothers. Some of these were the sole providers for their families. What were those families going to do now? And what about those who were burned? Some of them would never fully recover, and even those who could deserved something for the months of agony they endured, didn't they? Somebody was at fault in this, and somebody was going to have to pay.

Perhaps it was the property owner, Anthony Guarino, who was at fault for having allowed the bar to operate in his building. But of course it must be more Philip Esteve's fault, since he was the operator of the bar, and he was the one who'd allowed the flammable carpeting and wallpaper in the bar as well as the false ceiling which fed oxygen to the fire. He'd permitted the bars on the windows and built the stage which blocked the roof exit from view.

But as Esteve had complied with the latest fire inspection, it must be the fire department at fault for not inspecting more often, or fire marshal Raymond B. Oliver's fault, or the fault of the city or fire department for accepting a fire code that was obviously unsatisfactory.

Or perhaps it was the insurance companies, the Oregon Automobile Insurance Company and the Northwestern

National Insurance Company, trying to get out of their responsibilities, who should be sued.

The problem wasn't only in deciding who might be liable but also in learning who could pay. What good would it do to hold Phil Esteve liable and have the court award a large settlement, when Esteve would then simply have to declare bankruptcy? The judgment in favor of the plaintiffs would then be meaningless. And the insurance companies were not going to pay for more than the insurance coverage, not enough to satisfy even one of the claims made by the plaintiffs. Clearly, the only way to get any money out of the settlement was to sue either the fire department or the city.

The attorneys for the complainants included George N. Papale, Robert E. Winn, James Ryan III, Gerald Thomas LaBorde, Vincent Glorioso Jr., Walter F. Gemeinhardt, George C. Stringer Jr., Max Zelden, Jane M. and Frederick J. Gisevius Jr., Dorothy R. Cowen, Charles R. Maloney, Albert S. Dittman Jr., Bernard J. Tortomasi Jr., Gilbert V. Andry III, Lowell Dye, Ed Pillault, and C. Monk Simons III.

The attorneys for the defendants included Philip J. Foto, Benjamin E. Loup, Philip S. Brooks, Philip D. Lorio III, Donald B. Ensenat, Lawrence D. Wiedemann, Caryl H. Vesy, Plauche F. Villere Jr., Robert E. Winn, Michael H. Bagot, Henry C. Klein, Robert M. Johnston, Dan C. Garner, William A. Porteous III, Paul B. Deal, Jerome B. Steen, and Jerry A. Kirby.

Not everyone sued, but many did. Edward B. Gillis, with 2nd and 3rd degree burns on his back, chest, face, arms, and legs, claimed permanent scarring and disfigurement and sued for $1,000,000. Jean Gosnell, with burns over 60-80% of her body, claimed she was disabled and had also acquired a nervous condition. She sued for $1,500,000. Michael Wayne Scarborough, who'd suffered severe burns over almost his entire body, sued for $4,200,000. Francis Dufrene, less seriously burned, also sued.

From San Mateo, Florida, Beatrice McKuen Burke, the mother of Donald Walter Dunbar, sued for $400,000 for her son's death. The sisters of the deceased Joseph H. Adams Jr., Jean Adams Jordan of Miami, Marilyn Adams West of Coral Gables, and Nancy Ann Adams of New York City, each asked for $100,000. Becky and Elwyn R. Gary of Greensboro, North Carolina, the parents of piano player David Gary, sued for $150,000 each. And Pamela Matyi, divorced wife of George Steven Matyi, and mother of their two children, Tina, born in 1968, and Todd, born in 1969, living in Soquel Canyon in Chino, California, sued for $500,000 for each child.

Jane Golding, the widow of John T. Golding and mother of their three children, sued for $2,000,000. The five sisters of Louis Horace Broussard, Vivian De Abate, Thelma Simon, Sedia Hollier, Delta Broussard, and Mary Nell Broussard, sued for a total of $625,000. The siblings of James Hambrick also sued, for $100,000 each. They were Agnes Noel, Raymond V. Hambrick, and Benjamin F. Hambrick Jr., all of Lexington, and Bennie Hambrick Shatz of Milwaukee, John M. Hambrick of Dallas, and Joseph C. Hambrick of Aurora, Indiana.

The Warrens sued for a total of $13,900,000. Robert Warren, one of Inez's sons, asked for $6,350,000, and the other sons and daughters asked for a total of $2,450,000. Fay

Warren asked for $3,000,000 for the loss of her husband James Curtis, and for another $2,100,000 on behalf of their son, Michael C. Warren.

Others who filed suits were Mrs. James Jones, guardian *ad litem* of Murray Paul Gordon; John D. Nixon, guardian *ad litem* of Clifford Mark Gordon; Lena Lumpkin; Beatrice Moyer; Ruth and Victor V. Bailey; Clarence McCloskey, Sr.; Ada V. Harrington; Horace Getchell, Sr.; and Helen Woodworm Bettis Stratton, guardian of Kenny Dean Stratton.

The suit lists Helen Stratton's late husband's name as James Stratton, where Larry's autopsy lists his father's name as Jesse. Mrs. Rita Barfield Williams, administrator of the estate of Douglas Maxwell Williams and "natural tutrix" of minor Sheri Adele Williams, also sued. In all, the amount of the combined lawsuits reached $28,000,000, and the fourteen individual lawsuits were eventually consolidated.

What the complainants received, however, was not $28,000,000 but $80,000 to be divided up among them, and this was a settlement not decided upon by the courts. There was $50,000 in liability insurance, and the insurance company put in an extra $5,000 as a goodwill gesture. Anthony Guarino, the owner of the building, came up with the remaining $25,000.

Two and a half years after the fire, Civil District Judge Gerald P. Fedoroff decided that the plaintiffs had no legal cause of action against the city. Just over a year later, on January 12, 1977, the Fourth Circuit Court of Appeal supported Fedoroff's decision. Judge Edward J. Stoulig wrote the majority opinion held by the three-judge appeal panel. Judge John C. Boutall concurred, and Judge Ernest N. Morial, who would soon become mayor of New Orleans, agreed in part but also dissented in part. Stoulig declared that the plaintiffs were "incorrect in assuming either failure to inspect or negligent inspection created a cause for action against the city to every patron injured in a fire in the premises."

The ruling didn't say that the city was *not* negligent (or, for that matter, that it *was*), only that even if the city were negligent, the patrons of the bar couldn't sue because the city had not been negligent to them as individuals but was only negligent toward the public in general. For example, in another case, a police officer directing traffic motioned the drivers of two different cars to move forward at the same time, and the cars collided.

It was determined that the city was responsible in that case because the officer was not negligent to the "public" but to those two specific drivers. At the UpStairs, however, even if there was negligence regarding inspections, the negligence was not toward specific individuals and therefore these specific people could not sue.

No one else had enough money to pay, so at this point the case was finally dropped. After three and a half years of battle, the relatives and victims had received the final word on their case—they'd lost, and the fact that a total of four prominent judges disagreed with them was somehow neither convincing nor satisfying, but it was what they'd have to accept.

The person at fault was the person who'd started the fire, and by the time the lawsuit was settled, he was long since dead himself. The end of the legal battle allowed for a new phase to begin regarding the fire, one of resignation and acceptance, which would eventually help many of the living to finally put the fire behind them.

Marcy Marcell, Clarence McCloskey, and Bill Bailey

Marcy was born on Orleans Street on November 27, 1947, presenting as male, and raised on St. Peter, so when she came out in 1965 at the age of eighteen, the transition to the Quarter was not very dramatic. She simply had to go a little further down the streets that had always been a part of her neighborhood. She liked Mid-City, though, where she grew up, and continued to live there and commute the short distance to the Quarter.

She'd gone to grammar school at McDonough 31 and began high school at S. J. Peters High. She enjoyed school well enough, though she played around a bit too much and was held back two years. Despite a certain effeminacy and being a "pretty boy," Marcy was rarely teased in school, perhaps because someone in her large family was often nearby to offer support, or perhaps simply because she got along well with others and was therefore well liked.

As a child, Marcy told her sister, "I'm going to live like a woman one day." Her sister thought it an odd remark, but Marcy was always clowning around, so she didn't think much of it. Marcy felt close to women but never attracted to them. By the age of eleven, she knew she felt an attraction toward masculine men, but it wasn't until she was fifteen that she really confronted the issue, going through a rough period during which she saw a psychiatrist. By the time she was seventeen or eighteen, however, she felt comfortable with her sexuality.

At fifteen, Marcy began working at Schwegmann's supermarket. Later, she ran the elevator at the Criminal Court Building in the afternoons after school. About this time, her father died and Marcy dropped out of school altogether to work full-time, or at least work two part-time jobs. She continued working at the Criminal Court Building, stationed in her elevator during the Clay Shaw trial, but also began tending bar part-time at Wanda's in the Quarter.

Marcy's sister's husband had a gay brother named Clarence, and in the late '60's, Marcy and Clarence became friends. Clarence Joseph McCloskey, Jr. was significantly older than Marcy, born on March 13, 1925, to Clarence Sr. and Francis Duchmann McCloskey, but the two were still able to relate. Clarence was also a native of New Orleans, so that was something else they had in common.

Marcy didn't spend a lot of time with Clarence's family, his brothers, Bernard and Henry, and his sisters, Rose Mary Little and Joyce Pitcher, but she did know that one of Clarence's brothers was a firefighter. His brothers weren't overly pleased Clarence was gay, but they tolerated it grudgingly.

In Lafitte's one night, Marcy met a man from Chicago who asked her to come up north with him. Marcy was just wild enough to do it, and Clarence, who'd been to the city before, told Marcy what to expect. Marcy arrived the day before Martin Luther King Jr. was killed in Tennessee and stayed through the Democratic Convention and the riots associated with that. She worked as a dancer at an underground club, doing her first female impersonating, but then Marcy returned to New Orleans in July of 1969 and worked at City Hall with the Sewerage and Water Board, still also tending bar part-time.

A little over a year later, Marcy began going to a new bar that had just opened on Iberville called the UpStairs Lounge. She developed the drag name Marcy Marcell, dancing every Sunday evening at the bar, though when she danced at the UpStairs, she often danced as a man, Marco. Even fifty years later, people often conflate drag queens and trans women, and the confusion was often rampant even in the LGBTQ community of the early 1970's.

Marcy had such energy and loved dancing so much that when she went to a bar, she could dance in front of the jukebox for hours while customers threw nickels and quarters at her. She'd often go home with $20 in change. As the shows became more popular, customers could be sure of seeing Marcy there each Sunday. In fact, she never missed one Sunday evening since she began working there during the beer bust.

In 1971, Marcy met Terry, a gorgeous construction worker, at Wanda's. They hit it off and soon became lovers. Terry was nineteen and worked part-time running the projector at the Pussycat Theater on Canal Street or working in adult bookstores when construction jobs were scarce.

Soon Marcy's brother-in-law's brother, Clarence, also found a lover. Clarence had lived with his mother for years at 816 North Gayoso Street, caring for her as her health deteriorated. But after her death, he was able to move out and was soon sharing an apartment at 1232 St. Andrew Street with Joseph William Bailey.

Bill Bailey, of Dadeville, Alabama, had been born to Victor and Ruth Lee Calloway Bailey on December 3, 1943. He had brown hair, a medium build, and worked as a waiter.

For a while, Clarence was a clerk at a printing company in town and later became the branch manager at Pick's Plywood and Building Supermart.

Clarence and Bill were both regulars at the UpStairs. Often, there'd be a crowd that would get together Sunday afternoon for a late lunch or early dinner at the Fatted Calf, then head over to the UpStairs for the beer bust, and afterwards go across the street to Mother Cross's apartment for a party or down to the Burgundy House for a sing-along. At the UpStairs, Marcy could always depend on running into Mitch and Horace, or Jean, or Rusty, or Regina and Reggie, Buddy and Adam, and of course, Clarence and Bill.

Clarence and Bill were monogamous, though Bill enjoyed flirting. Clarence, who collected porcelain objects, was sensitive, but he didn't mind Bill's flirting, realizing it was done innocently. Clarence's sensitivity, rather, ran more along the lines of sensing when someone needed a kind word or a pat on the shoulder.

One of his friends, Daniel Romero, also a regular at the UpStairs, would sometimes grow depressed. Three different times when Clarence came into the bar and saw Dan with that depressed look on his face, he walked back out and returned a few moments later with a rose to cheer him up.

In February of 1973, while Marcy was living at 1113 Burgundy, she saw a vision of a woman dressed in a white wedding gown, whom she felt was trying to warn her of something. She went to a pyschic, who told Marcy the spirit was that of a woman who'd had an unhappy marriage, and the warning was that something unhappy was about to happen in Marcy's relationship with Terry.

In June of 1973, Clarence and Bill made a short trip to Alabama to visit Bill's family. When they returned, they stopped at Marcy's on Friday to talk about how things had gone there. As they left, Marcy said, "Well, let's talk more on Sunday."

"Okay. See you at the UpStairs."

But on Sunday morning, as Marcy woke up, she had a strange feeling. It was almost as if a voice were telling her, "Don't go to work tonight." Of course, there was nothing terribly mysterious about it. Today was Terry's birthday. Terry was twenty-one now and knowing they hadn't seen each other in two weeks because of a big argument they'd had and wouldn't be able to celebrate Terry's birthday together unless one of them swallowed their pride was a depressing thought.

Marcy remembered the woman in white's warning and thought about how unhappy she felt over being apart from Terry. She debated whether to call Terry but didn't do it. By afternoon, Marcy knew Terry would be over at the Pussycat Theater and unavailable, so she began piddling around, trying to get ready for her show at the UpStairs.

She was usually at the bar by 5:00. She had still never missed a single beer bust and wasn't about to start now, because the money was so good. But soon it was 6:00, and then 6:30, and then 7:00, and Marcy still hadn't left for work.

She finally dressed and was all ready to leave her apartment in Mid-City, but then she switched on the TV and was caught up in a Bette Davis movie.

"Okay," she told herself. "I'll leave at the next commercial." She kept glancing at the clock, knowing she had to be ready to start dancing at 8:00, and she didn't want to just burst through the door and start dancing. She'd need to be there by at least 7:45. Okay. Five more minutes and she'd leave. And after work, maybe, just maybe, she'd call Terry and wish him a Happy Birthday.

Doug Williams

Douglas Maxwell Williams, Jr., twenty years old, of #4 Halle Place, Waggaman, Louisiana, was a truck driver for the Norbell Company and married to Rita Barfield. Another source has him married to a woman named Mary and living at 2341 Gordon Street. Born on December 27, 1952, to Douglas Sr. and Rita O'Donnell Williams, Doug, a Catholic, was survived by two sisters, Geraldine Maria Williams and Mrs. Richard Davidson, and by his grandparents, Mr. and Mrs. M. S. Williams. Doug had two tattoos, one about eight centimeters long of a panther or cat, on the back of his right forearm, and one on his left leg with "MOM" in capital letters. Doug received 2nd, 3rd, and 4th degree burns over 85% of his body. There was extensive charring and cracking of the skin of the abdominal area, head, and upper extremities. He was identified through fingerprints.

Reggie and Regina

Reginald Eugene Adams grew up in Dallas, Texas, in a nice, Catholic home. He was the eldest of three children, having both a younger brother and a younger sister. Reggie was born on May 31, 1949, to Millard and Florine Clark Adams and grew up with a deep sensitivity and a yearning for a higher, possibly religious life. Reggie's black-framed glasses gave him a bookish look, which Reggie didn't altogether dislike. His parents sent him first to St. Peter's Academy and later to Jesuit College Prep for his junior and senior year of high school, hoping to give him a good education.

In addition to his academic studies, Reggie also sang with the Good News Singers, his school's Glee Club, and performed at various parishes in Dallas and Ft. Worth. He also played the oboe in the band and was leader of his section. Reggie enjoyed these extracurricular activities because while he did enjoy studying, he didn't want to confine himself only to books. His parents were pleased, however, when their son voiced his desire to continue his education after graduating from high school in 1968. Education was important to them not only for the value of knowledge itself but also because it was necessary for black people to rise above their oppression.

Reggie decided to continue his studies with the Jesuits and moved to New Orleans to attend Loyola University, specializing in Black History. He began going to the UpStairs Lounge regularly, and one day, he met Regina there.

Regina Adams was born at Mercy Hospital in the Mid-City section of New Orleans, but though New Orleans is a largely Catholic city, she grew up Mormon. And presenting as male. She attended two different schools in Orleans Parish, but after her mother remarried when Regina was ten, the family moved to the Green Acres subdivision in the suburb of Metairie.

She attended three schools there, including T. J. Harris junior high and East Jefferson high school, none of these schools being integrated yet. At church, blacks had not yet been "allowed" the priesthood, which was one of the reasons there were few blacks anywhere in the Mormon Church. Regina's circle of friends, therefore, was almost exclusively white.

Throughout her high school years, Regina attended early morning seminary classes for an hour at church before heading on to school. She also helped build the church structure on Cleveland Place in Metairie, as most of the active members pitched in to help. Attending seminary classes was a typical youth activity for Mormon teens, as there was no official seminary, there being no professional clergy in the Church. Regina would be expected to serve two years as a full-time volunteer missionary as an "elder" when she turned nineteen, and she did consider going, though she wasn't sure yet.

Regina had four brothers and grew up playing football and baseball, but she knew she was different somehow. She was active in the Boy Scouts, a fundamental youth program for the Latter-day Saint Church. One of her scouting leaders, Jim Brooks, remembers always finding Regina with her hatchet, chopping away at wood. She would sit and chop and chop and chop.

In addition to school and church and scouting, Regina also worked at Westgate Drive-In theater and at Lakeside Cinema when it opened its first theaters, Lakeside the first modern shopping center built in Metairie. After graduating high school in 1970, Regina studied food service management at Jefferson Vo-Tech and began working at La Boucherie restaurant in the 300 block of Chartres in the Quarter, first as a busboy and then as a waiter, a block and a half from Iberville.

Regina didn't know anything about homosexuality or transgender issues, but as she made friends with the other waiters at work, she realized many of them were gay. One evening in 1971, they convinced her to come along to a nearby bar, the UpStairs Lounge. It was there that Regina met Reggie.

They hit it off right away, and Reggie actively began courting Regina, frequently taking her out to dinner. Reggie never figured out, and Regina never volunteered the information, that La Boucherie gave a free meal to each of the waiters, so Regina was never hungry after work. She enjoyed Reggie's company, however, and so continued to accept his invitations, though she usually ate very little for her second dinner. Regina enjoyed the cozy, candlelit cafes that Reggie would bring her to, but more than that, she enjoyed just talking with him. They often talked of religion, but they found they could talk on a variety of other subjects as well.

After six weeks, Regina and Reggie knew they loved each other and decided to move in together. Reggie had been living in the novitiate house at Loyola, but the two moved to a one-room apartment in the Castle Hotel on Julia Street. The area was in the Warehouse District and considered the city's Skid Row. Their place was one large room with a bathroom at the end. The bathroom had two doors, one leading to their room and one to the adjacent apartment. Whoever was using the bathroom would make sure the door to the other apartment was locked on the bathroom side and remember to unlock it when finishing up.

There was a sunken tub in the bathroom, and Regina and Reggie took turns washing one another. They had plants in the bedroom window in their second-story apartment and pushed their bed up against the window so they could lie together and look up at the stars while holding each other as they fell asleep.

Reggie began calling Regina by the name she soon adopted, telling her she was his queen.

After three months on Julia Street, the two moved to a larger apartment at 1017 Conti in the French Quarter. The bigger apartment brought bigger bills, and since Reggie now knew he could no longer become a priest, he wasn't sure just what he did want to do as a career. He dropped out of school to pay for the apartment, taking a job as a furniture salesman at Kirschman's.

Regina began working as a cashier in the parking garage at the Marriott, just across the street from the UpStairs, when the hotel opened in 1972. Later, both found jobs at the Saratoga Garage, Reggie working there at night after first spending the day working at Kirschman's. Through the combined income of the various jobs, they were able to pay not only for the apartment but also for a nice used car.

Because so much energy went into their jobs. Regina and Reggie didn't spend much time going out. Regina did visit his mother regularly to play canasta, and Reggie either came along or went to visit one of his Jesuit friends. The two lovers went grocery shopping together on Saturday and then planned whatever else they might do together that weekend. They fed the ducks at the park, took walks, and rode the paddleboats together. If a friend's birthday was coming up, they'd go out together to look for a gift. And together in bed, they either read, watched TV, or just discussed the news or anything else on their mind.

On Sunday evenings, though, they went regularly to the beer bust at the UpStairs Lounge, often going out afterwards to eat with friends. They knew Jimmy Demoll, who worked for Uddo Bleach Company, Roger "Tony Jean" Perrone, Bill Bailey, and many of the other regulars. It was nice to have just that one evening to relax with friends. Reggie was articulate and witty and enjoyed chatting and joking with his friends, and they enjoyed hearing the stories he could tell.

Regina and Reggie's weekday lives were fairly regimented, as they woke at the same time each morning and went to bed at the same time each evening. Regina woke up first and laid out Reggie's clothes. Then, after drawing

Reggie's bath water, Regina prepared breakfast for them both. After seeing Reggie off to work with a kiss, Regina finished getting ready herself and went off to her own job. Regina also took Reggie's clothes to the laundry once a week, which she'd started doing after they'd been together six months.

Regina enjoyed taking care of Reggie, and Reggie appreciated Regina's efforts to please him. Though Regina did many of the domestic things around the house, the two did not see each other as husband and wife, but as two equals, best friends who were also lovers.

Despite the homophobic religious backgrounds of their families, Regina and Reggie both found themselves reasonably well accepted. They spent Christmas with Regina's family in Metairie and visited Dallas for a week in the summer of 1972, spending a few days there with Reggie's friends but also a few days with his parents, who never said one negative word about Regina and Reggie's relationship, at least not in their presence. Regina felt well treated, and the two mothers had each other's phone numbers.

Three months after they met, Regina gave Reggie her high school ring, which Reggie always wore from then on. For their first Christmas together, Reggie gave Regina a necklace featuring an Italian fisherman, a good luck charm, which Regina always wore from that moment on. They couldn't really have wedding rings, but it did somehow feel reassuring to always wear a piece of jewelry that had been given by someone they loved, to always feel a tangible symbol of that love as it touched their skin. They were both wearing these tokens of their commitment on June 24th as they climbed the steps to the UpStairs Lounge.

The Injured

When J.C. Carrier reached the street after escaping, he saw that the bar was almost totally engulfed. A few last people made it through the windows, but that was it. He saw one of them running down the street, his clothes on fire.

He turned. There was Fred Scharohway. He seemed okay, but there was his lover, Earl, lying face down in the street, his back one solid blister.

"Let me help you," J.C. said, moving toward his friend.

Two police officers stepped in front of him. "I told you to move!" one of them shouted.

J.C. tried again to reach his friend but was not permitted to assist him in any way. "The mother fucking cops were bastards!" he said, still feeling bitter sixteen years later. The man was in pain, J.C. thought. Why couldn't they let J.C. comfort him?

About this time, Ronnie LeBoeuf arrived on the scene. The photographer was new on the staff of *The Times-Picayune*. One of the young photographer's first assignments had been to cover the Howard Johnson fire earlier that year that left nine people dead. He'd get an assignment and rush to the scene, often with little information other than the address. In January, he'd been told only, "The Howard

Johnson's on fire. Get over there." Not until he was taking pictures and had bullets flying past did he realize there was a sniper involved.

On June 24th, Ronnie was told there was a fire in the French Quarter. He sped on over, but as he looked at the scene, he was again faced with the unexpected. "Those aren't bodies in the windows, are they?" he thought. "Those can't be *bodies.*"

Behind those bodies, Ronnie could see a slim, dark figure with closed eyes. His hair and face were all the same color, and the hair looked odd, matted or covered with mud, but also perfectly in place. The man looked like a clay figure. Steeling himself to do his job, Ronnie began snapping pictures.

Pat Burke was a freelance photographer who had a friend, Skip, in the fire department. If Skip wasn't called to a fire himself but knew of it, he'd call Pat so Pat could go to the scene. Pat mostly sold to the *Daily Record* as it struggled unsuccessfully to compete with the *Times-Picayune.* Skip told him on the 24th that there was a big fire, already four-alarm, so Pat was on the scene in fifteen minutes after the call.

By the time he arrived, some of the injured had already been taken away. He found a friend, photographer Gerry Arnold, and surveyed the scene. "It's not as bad as it could have been," Pat noted. "At least it's only a mannequin factory." He could see that a lot of the inventory was damaged, of course, but...

"Those aren't mannequins," Gerry told him. Like looking at an optical illusion that suddenly changes as one sees the hidden picture, Pat's vision shifted instantly and became a defining moment in his life as he realized the horror he was witnessing. Working automatically, he focused on faces and feet and arms, taking snapshot after snapshot of every ghastly sight of the multitude plainly visible from the street below.

Paul Villien had graduated from LSU Medical School in April of 1973 and worked the following month at a Charity clinic in the Desire Housing Projects. A mentor encouraged him to do his residency in Emergency Medicine, a new specialty at the time. The only other cities in the U.S. with a residency in Emergency Medicine were Chicago and Los Angeles, and since Paul had grown up in Abbeville, Louisiana, he wanted to stay close to home.

He began his internship in June of 1973 and was sitting at the triage desk in the emergency room one Sunday evening when the doors opened and a young man stood there looking distraught.

"Can I help you?" Paul asked.

"I've been burned!" the young man cried out.

Paul wasn't sure what to think. The man looked fine, his hair perfectly combed. Could he really be hurt?

A moment later, a flood of other patients surged into the room, and the next several hours were at best controlled chaos. The first patients arrived in private vehicles, the ambulances arriving later. The emergency room staff treated fifteen to twenty burn patients altogether, some of them with relatively mild injuries and others critically injured.

Though the first patients to arrive looked "normal," the instant Paul or any of the other staff touched them, their hair crumbled into ash. Trying to insert an IV was next to impossible because though there'd been no apparent swelling at first, now patients were "swelling up like balloons."

It didn't take long for Paul to realize that most of the burn victims were gay.

Paul had been married to a woman for five years despite knowing from childhood that he was "different." During his junior year in medical school, a married friend invited him to a bar in the French Quarter. The bar turned out to be Lafitte's, Paul began making friends in the gay community, and before long, Paul met a pre-med student named Brock Bravo.

Paul and Brock began a relationship, Paul and his wife divorced, and the two men officially became a couple on August 25, 1972. They'd been together almost a year when the UpStairs Lounge was set on fire.

Paul worked through the night mostly helping burned men, but one patient was a dark-haired woman around thirty with a prosthetic leg. She'd been wearing a polyester outfit that had melted onto her skin and prosthesis. "It was horrifying," he recalled.

Paul recognized one of the burned men as the uncle of a former classmate in medical school. He called his friend, Matt, who rushed over to help treat his uncle. He and Paul spent hours debriding the uncle's wounds, giving him morphine to ease the pain.

Clancy DuBos had recently covered the drowning of a fifteen-year-old boy only three years younger than he was, but at the UpStairs, he was watching people die right before his eyes. He went to Charity and stationed himself in the trauma room, recording the misery he was witnessing, blocking out his own feelings to get the story as he was trained to do.

Clancy watched as one doctor cut dead skin from the chest of a middle-aged man who moaned steadily, rocking on his side. As the doctor worked, another ambulance arrived at the hospital, and more stretchers carrying more patients filed into the room. Some of the injured had broken fingers. Others had multiple fractures, including broken ankles, from having jumped to the pavement. Others had suffered second degree burns, and some were covered with third degree burns. A nurse's aide mopped blood from the floor. An intern drew more blood from one of the burned patients.

One man, about nineteen, slim and about 5'7", made the sign of the cross as he watched the confusion about him. He walked over to a pay phone, but his fingers were too badly burned for him to pull a nickel from his pocket. He asked someone to dial the number for him, and he waited for his friend to pick up the receiver.

"Hello, David?" he said a moment later, tears suddenly released, sliding down his face at the relief of finding a strong, compassionate friend. "Listen, I've had an accident. Yes, I'm at Charity Hospital. Please come quick. Please come...I hurt...a fire..."

Clancy stayed and watched the suffering for half the night and had his story out in the paper on Monday. It wasn't until that afternoon when he went to his girlfriend's house that he began to process his own feelings. "What was it like?" his girlfriend asked. Clancy walked out into the front yard, sat down, and cried.

Twenty-five years later, he said that of all the stories he'd ever covered, this one had the strongest impact on him. It was also the first time he ever saw gays as real people. He'd later write columns in favor of passing a gay rights ordinance in New Orleans.

Nick Banner was a police officer on the scene who'd seen a lot of gruesome things during his career. Once he entered a house where a man had been dead long enough to bloat and burst. His eyes had been flung up against the ceiling by the explosion of gases. But even scenes like that couldn't compare to the horror he witnessed at the UpStairs, a scene he couldn't talk about even twenty-five years later. When his wife Edie pressed for an account of his personal experience, all he could say was, "You pick someone up by the arm and have it come off in your hand and tell me you want to relive it."

If those who simply witnessed the scene were this traumatized, those who both witnessed and experienced it were far more profoundly affected. Three of the most seriously burned were Luther Boggs, Larry Stratton, and Jim Hambrick. When they were admitted, Dr. Isidore Brickman, director of Charity, ordered the hospital to open its new burn unit. The unit hadn't been scheduled to open for several weeks yet but was considered one of the best in the nation at the time and possibly the best in the South.

The other injured included:

Adolph Medina, thirty-two, of San Antonio

Francis Dufrene, twenty-one

Linn "Rusty" Quinton, twenty-five

Philip Byrd

Bob Vann (likely a safe "bar name" used by Bob Vanlangendonck)

Roger Dunn, twenty-six, in guarded condition at West Jefferson. Roger, a public school teacher, lived at 4306 Prytania.

Jimmy Demoll, whose back was burned. In 1990, he was living in Bay St. Louis, Mississippi, with Roger Perrone.

Michael Wayne Scarborough, twenty-seven, who was sent to West Jefferson Hospital in fair condition and then to Our Lady of the Lake in Baton Rouge to be closer to his family.

Sidney Espinache, fifty, who was in serious condition at Baptist Hospital, where he faced many months of painful treatment. Friends described him as a handsome man before the fire, one of his friends always prodding him to take a nude photograph of himself, which Sid never did. His burns left major scars over large portions of his body.

His lover, Joe Adams, who had never married and who lived at 2116 Athena Avenue, died in the fire, with extensive

4th degree burns over 95% of his body. There was extensive charring and cracking of the entire body surface except for a patch six centimeters long on his left leg which showed he had white skin. He was identified through dental charts. The memories of Joe's death and of his own suffering were so painful that even seventeen years later, Sid couldn't talk about anything even remotely associated with the fire.

Edward B. Gillis, fifty-two, in poor condition at the VA hospital. Gillis, born on November 5, 1920, was originally from Boston but had lived in New Orleans for fifteen years. He was a merchantman, a member of the National Maritime Union, and a military veteran. He'd only been to the UpStairs three or four times. Eddie was transferred to the Veteran's hospital in Boston, where he faced major long-term treatment. In 1990, he said he was still receiving periodic skin grafts.

Jean Gosnell, thirty-six, in fair condition at the U. S. Public Health Service Hospital.

Eugene Earl Thomas, forty-two, in fair condition at Touro, with 3rd degree burns over 90% of his back.

Fred Scharohway (also reported as either Ohway or Scarborough), twenty-two, also in Touro with 3rd degree burns over 90% of one arm. Fred and Earl were lovers, lived at 2301 Houma Boulevard in Biloxi, and were both later transferred to Gulfport Memorial Hospital in Mississippi, since Earl's family lived in the area.

Though permanently scarred, both physically and emotionally, most of these people survived, enduring months of skin grafts and endless hours of therapy. But the three most seriously injured died slowly, one by one, within the next few weeks. Benjamin Hambrick came down from Lexington to sit by his brother's bedside. Jim and the friend he'd gone to the bar with had both been injured, but Jim had been much more seriously burned. And Jim's heart, weakened by his earlier illness, wasn't making the battle for survival any easier.

Benjamin looked over to see the man in the next bed. His name was Larry Stratton, and his face, chest, arms, and hands had been badly burned, one hand hanging suspended in a hammock. The only thing the man ever said was, "Oh, oh, oh, oh." "Oh, oh, oh, oh." "Oh, oh, oh, oh."

Benjamin watched as the man's wife tried to come into the room. The doctor kept her in the hall, telling her that her husband was not going to live, and it would be better for her not to see him. Benjamin listened as the woman talked of how she and her husband had had an argument and how he'd taken off for New Orleans, leaving her alone with their nine-month-old baby. The doctor asked for her address so he'd know how to make arrangements after her husband died. Then he sent her home.

Benjamin went back in the room and looked at the young man. "Oh, oh, oh, oh," he said again. Then Benjamin looked at his brother, lying silent and motionless, too injured even to moan, and he sat down, preparing himself for the evening vigil by his brother's side.

Jim Hambrick died four days after the fire, on June 28. He'd received 2nd and 3rd degree burns over 50% of his body. His eyebrows and half of his moustache had been burned off, as well as some of the hair on his scalp. Jim died of cardiorespiratory arrest at 6:15 p.m. Thursday evening.

Luther Boggs lived for over two weeks, though he'd received 3rd degree burns over 50% of his body, on his face, head, his back, and the backs of his legs. Luther died on July 10 of bilateral confluent bronchopneumonia and cerebral edema.

Twenty-five-year-old Larry Dean Stratton, reaching only 5'7" and weighing just 115 pounds, had been small enough to easily slip through the barred windows. The painter from East St. Louis, Illinois, simply hadn't been close enough to get to the windows before the flames reached him. He received 3rd degree burns over 80-85% of his body. Only his abdomen and part of his chest escaped the flames.

Larry had escharotomies and a tracheostomy performed, but on the morning of July 12, two and a half weeks after being burned, Larry also succumbed to the physical trauma of losing almost all of the largest vital organ of his body. He developed bilateral confluent bronchopneumonia, as had Luther, and because there wasn't enough skin to keep fluids inside his body, not enough fluid went to his kidneys. They shut down, and Larry experienced sepsis and renal failure. His wife, as well as his parents, Jesse and Helen Bettis Stratton, had to be notified of his death.

The suffering of the thirty-two dead had ended, but the grief and misery of their loved ones and the other injured was still only just beginning.

Gerald Gordon

Thirty-seven-year-old Gerald Hoyt Gordon, of Cornersville, Tennessee, had lived at 2705 West Main Street, Unit #5, in Houma, Louisiana, before moving to 238 St. Charles in New Orleans. Gerry, a divorced shipping clerk who worked at Century Printing Corporation, had been born on February 21, 1936, to William Carl and Dorothy Wilson Gordon.

Gerry had a young lover named J. P. who had not gone to the UpStairs that evening and who even in 1991 could not bear to talk about Gerry. The night of June 24th, Gerry was wearing a blue, jumper style suit when he went to the bar. He received 2nd and 3rd degree burns over 30% of his body, including the upper chest, shoulders, and face, but he died of carbon monoxide asphyxia. He was identified both by a friend, Mike Shoundorn, and by fingerprints taken when he was in the Air Force.

Ferris LeBlanc

Ferris Jerome LeBlanc was born on June 22, 1923 in Sheboygan, Michigan, the ninth child of thirteen, seven boys and six girls. The family soon moved to San Bernardino, California and then on to Stockton. From there, the family moved to a small town in Oregon and then back down to San Jose.

Ferris's father was in construction and so overworked he sometimes slept on the ground at the job site with just a pillow. This did little for his health, and Ferris was ten when his father died of pneumonia. Even at such a young age, he willingly took over many of his father's household responsibilities. Several of his older siblings were already married and gone, so he helped bathe his three youngest siblings. Marilyn, the eleventh child, had been born seven years after Ferris, with Mary Lou and Bernard following.

It was just as well he enjoyed helping as their mother wasn't terribly interested in the kids. She was interested mostly in Hollywood and movie stars. The day Marilyn was born, she wrote in her diary, "Marilyn born cranky." The next day, her entry read, "Marilyn still cranky." And that was the last she wrote about the child for some time.

Ferris was good-natured and happy. He helped dress the kids for school, helped the younger kids cross busy intersections to get them safely to kindergarten. While in Oregon, Ferris urged the younger girls to take part in a local talent show, teaching them to tap dance. As the girls grew older, he helped them with their hair and make-up. Stylish himself, he taught the girls how to dress well.

In Stockton, Ferris attended the same high school as Jeanette Morrison, though he was a few years older than the young woman who would soon become known as Janet Leigh.

When Ferris and one of his brothers went off to fight in WWII, the family worried they'd lose one or both brothers, but fortunately they returned safely, even with Ferris fighting at the Battle of the Bulge. An uncle, however, was killed in the war.

In San Francisco, Ferris frequented the Purple Onion and saw Phyllis Diller perform before she made it big in stand-up comedy. He told family members that a talent scout had seen him dancing and wanted to do a screen test but that he felt suspicious and turned the man down. Ferris still had his art, though. He enjoyed painting with oils.

It had never been a secret in the family that Ferris was homosexual, and no one seemed to have any trouble with it, during a time when many families did. His homosexuality was never the slightest issue, not even for his mother, who could sometimes write scathing things about family in her diary.

Ferris had two long-term partners and brought both to meet the family. They were included in group photos, included in every activity, and fully considered family members. As his sister Marilyn often said, "We're French. We didn't care."

The first of Ferris's partners was Robert Guillaume and pronounced his name "Row-Bear." The two men were together over twenty years. They owned a salon in San Francisco and lived in an impressive apartment, where they hosted festive dinner and cocktail parties.

When Marilyn divorced and moved to Oakland with her six-year-old son Skip to live with one of her sisters, Ferris took the young boy out riding in his exotic, red MG TC. The boy couldn't get enough of the thrilling ride in the two-seater car.

It was still a good thing Ferris liked kids, since his mother was no better as a grandmother. She didn't even have any toys or treats for the grandkids when they came over.

Ferris got along with all his siblings but seemed to have the closest relationship with Marilyn. When her son Skip began drawing cars and hotrods in 7th and 8th grade, Ferris wanted to encourage him to push his artistic skills to another level. He purchased a watercolor kit and gave it to the young man. "Look at all the art prints your aunt and uncle have on their walls," he said. "You can copy these famous paintings and learn."

Ferris felt gratified to see Skip take up the challenge and move from cartoons to what he considered more serious art.

By the early 1960's, Ferris and Robert had split up and Ferris's new partner was Rod Rodgers. Rod seemed to really love Ferris, hovering next to him constantly at gatherings, but some of the family began to wonder if the man might be a bit too controlling. He always had his hand on Ferris's shoulder or arm or neck, almost as if he were afraid he might get away.

But Ferris and Rod seemed happy enough. Ferris still encouraged Skip to pursue his artistic dreams, paying his freshman-year tuition to San Jose State for an art degree, even paying to repair the engine in Skip's van.

The last big family gathering Ferris attended was his mother's birthday party in 1968. Shortly after, "the rift" occurred. It was all quite confusing. Ferris worked as a checker in a local grocery while he and his partner rented and lived on an acre of land to raise rabbits for food. The problem was that the land's owners were the ex-in-laws of Ferris's sister Marilyn.

Marilyn's ex-father-in-law was young, in his late fifties, but suffered from early-onset dementia and needed that rent money since he could no longer work himself.

Ferris had always been generous with his money, but soon he and Rod were borrowing money from more than one relative. And then they stopped paying rent on the land, without explanation, while moving to a property right beside it. When they refused to come up with six months of back rent, Skip's paternal grandparents took them to small claims court.

In return, Ferris sent an itemized bill for all the financial assistance he'd previously offered Skip.

The act was so out of character for Ferris that the family felt sure his partner was behind it. But they never found out because shortly after, in 1970, both Ferris and his partner disappeared. As 1971 passed into 1972 and then into 1973, the family could hardly believe Ferris still refused to contact them. They could only assume he was too embarrassed by his partner's behavior and by his own willingness to put up with it.

Then Ferris's mother died and Marilyn felt horror on Ferris's behalf. "Our mother's dead and Ferris doesn't even know!"

The years continued to pass. Long after Ferris was killed at the UpStairs Lounge, they waited for him to call. They didn't know he'd even moved to New Orleans, that he lived on Royal Street, that he received extensive 3rd and 4th degree burns over 80% of his body. They didn't know he'd been identified by an anonymous caller who described an antique spoon ring he was wearing.

They didn't know he'd been killed while out celebrating his 50th birthday.

And because they didn't know, there was no one to claim his body. Ferris LeBlanc was buried along with three other victims of the fire in an indigent graveyard, his burial site unmarked.

It wasn't as if his siblings didn't search for him, however. Over the years, Marilyn and her sisters contacted California's DMV but found no record. Marilyn knew that Ferris had worked for years as a hairdresser, so she asked her current stylist to contact the Board of Cosmetology, but there was no information there, either.

Then, sometime in the 1980's, the family had a breakthrough. Robert, Ferris's former partner, left a note on the door of one of the sisters. "Call quick!" The sister followed up, sure Robert had news about her brother. Robert explained that one of his clients swore she saw Ferris walking down Broadway in Oakland. The family tried searching once more but again found nothing.

As the years continued to pass without contact, the family never grew angry at Ferris for abandoning them. They simply worried more. Had something happened? Had Ferris succumbed to AIDS? Was his partner not allowing him to call?

So 1990 came. And 2000. And 2010. And there was still no word.

But maybe soon he'd call. Maybe soon he'd knock on someone's door.

Soon. Maybe soon.

Photos

Buddy Rasmussen at the UpStairs on Mardi Gras (courtesy of Napoleon and Stanley)

Buddy Rasmussen at the UpStairs (courtesy of Napoleon and Stanley)

Stanley Plaisance (left) with Gene Davis (courtesy of Napoleon and Stanley)

Stanley and Napoleon at the UpStairs Lounge

Theater at the UpStairs Lounge (courtesy of Napoleon and Stanley)

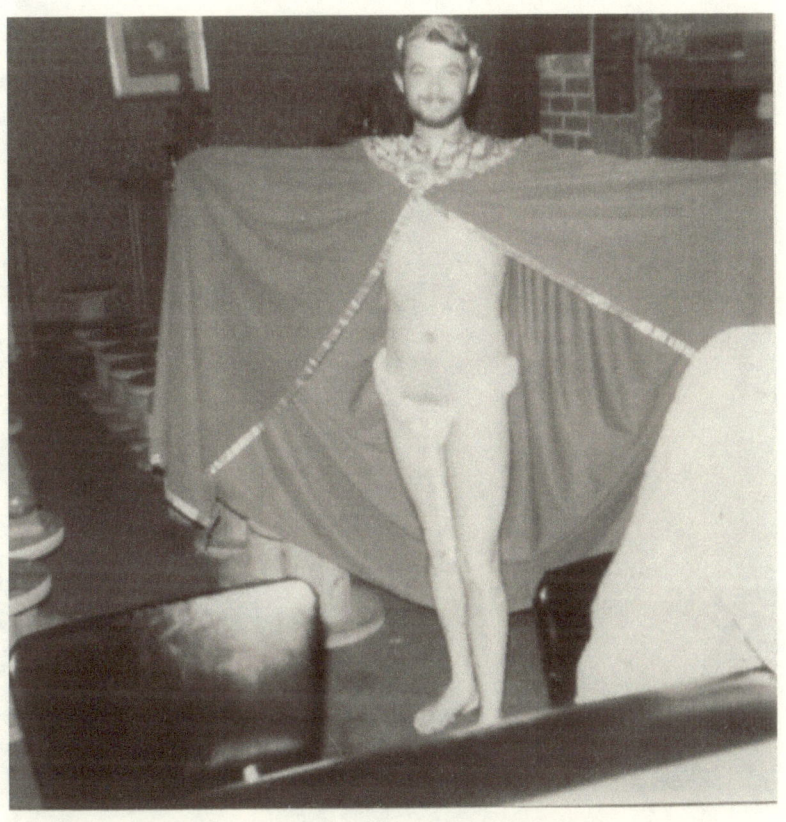

Bill Bailey in the UpStairs Lounge theater
(courtesy of Napoleon and Stanley)

Michael Scarborough (foreground, left) at the UpStairs. Bettye McAnear is behind him. Reggie Adams is covering his face in the center. Luther Boggs is on the lower right with glasses. (courtesy of Napoleon and Stanley)

Michael Scarborough, Ginny Lynch, and Reginald Adams at the UpStairs Lounge (courtesy of Napoleon and Stanley)

Buddy Rasmussen at the UpStairs, with Burt Reynolds and Mark Spitz posters (courtesy of Napoleon and Stanley)

Adam and Buddy at the UpStairs (courtesy of
Napoleon and Stanley)

Duane "Mitch" Mitchell at the UpStairs on Mardi Gras

Duane "Mitch" Mitchell and Horace Broussard

Rodger Dale Nunez in Abbeville High School

Phil Esteve, owner of the UpStairs Lounge

Skip Getchell (courtesy of Peggy Stewart)

Bill Larson at the MCC

Perry Waters

Adam Roland Fontenot (courtesy of Rose Clark)

George "Bud" Matyi (courtesy of Rod Wagener)

Ricky Everett in the UpStairs Lounge theater
(courtesy of Ricky Everett)

"Egad, What a Cad!" at the Upstairs Lounge, Michael West (center) with Ricky Everett (right)

Reggie Adams

Ken Harrington (left) and Frank Landry
(courtesy of Roseland Revaldo)

Leon Richard Maples the afternoon of the fire
(courtesy of Larry Raybourne)

Robert Keith Lumpkin (courtesy of David Crumley)

Ferris LeBlanc on left, with Robert Guillaume, at the Purple Onion (courtesy of Skip Bailey)

Robert and Ferris (courtesy of Skip Bailey)

Corner of Chartres and Iberville, with Jimani Bar under the former UpStairs Lounge (courtesy of Lori Bailey)

Marilyn LeBlanc Downey kneeling beside memorial plaque (courtesy of Lori Bailey)

Skip Bailey and Marilyn LeBlanc Downey searching for Ferris LeBlanc's grave (courtesy of Lori Bailey)

Rev. Paul Breton waving handkerchief during second line procession for the 50th Anniversary Memorial. Photo by Johnny Townsend.

Robert Fieseler, Clayton Delery, and Johnny Townsend speaking at the 50th Anniversary Memorial events. Photo by Amy Williams (courtesy of The Historic New Orleans Collection)

Hunter Burke, Max Vernon, Monica Ordoñez, and Brad Dalton at the 50th Anniversary Memorial events. Photo by Amy Williams (courtesy of The Historic New Orleans Collection)

The View UpStairs by Max Vernon. Photo by Kurt Sneddon.

Max Vernon's *The View UpStairs*. Photo by
Kurt Sneddon.

Mélange Dance Company. Dancers portraying John and Jane Golding. Photo by Samuel Birdsong.

Mélange Dance Company. The UpStairs
Lounge. Photo by Mike Yoder.

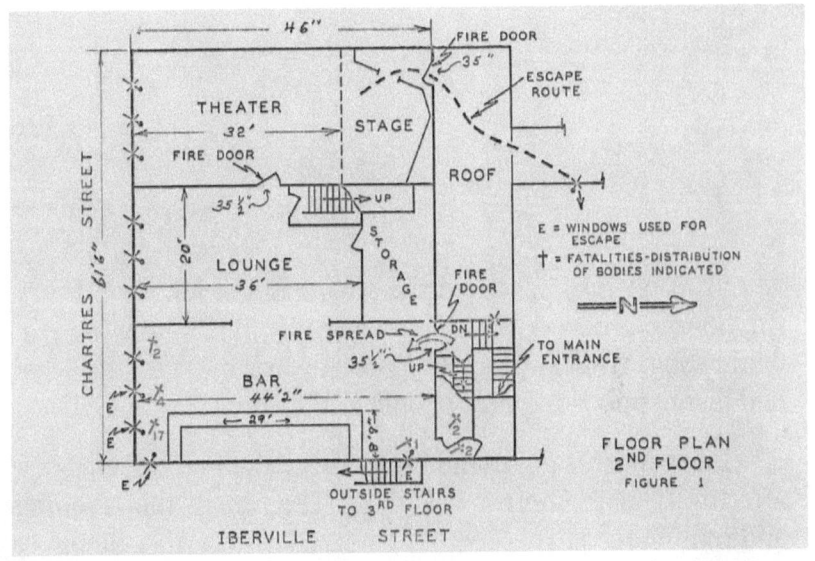

Floor plan of the UpStairs Lounge, showing the three rooms, the escape route, and location of the fatalities. (Source: "The Upstairs Lounge Fire" by A. Ellwood Willey in *The National Fire Protection Association Journal*. 1974)

Grieving

"I'm on fire!" shouted the singer in the jukebox. Larry Raybourne groaned, wishing people would stop playing that damn song, "Burning Love." Sure, it was a hit, but after what had just happened, didn't people realize how it sounded?

Larry and his girlfriend both missed the fire, arriving just after most of the horror was over. The rest of that evening and on until dawn, people gathered down the block at Wanda's to grieve together.

When Rusty Quinton came in, crying and cursing, everyone turned to look at one of the fortunate survivors. "Oh, fuck!" Rusty moaned. "Oh, shit! All those bodies! Oh, fuck!"

A rather butch-looking woman turned to him and said, "Please. Watch your language." Some thought the woman was an insensitive idiot, while others felt she was trying to defuse some of the tension.

But the tension and grief endured all evening and throughout the coming weeks. A couple of days after the fire, Larry was able to go up into the bar with a friend. After poking around a few minutes, his friend picked up what at first looked to Larry like a big piece of charcoal briquette for a barbecue. When his friend opened the charred, black thing, they realized it was a wallet which had been almost totally burned. Only the very middle was unharmed, and Larry looked down at a photo of his friend Glenn Green.

Larry also learned that his friend, Leon Maples, had been killed. Here, however, is where there is some discrepancy. Larry insists that Leon was killed when he jumped out a window and landed on the back of his head, breaking his neck. The autopsy, though, states that Leon received 3rd and 4th degree burns over 90% of his body. His face was destroyed, there was a loss of some fingers, and he was charred to the bone on his lower left leg. Enough of a few fingertips survived to identify him through fingerprints.

It would be easy to discount Larry's claim and accept the apparently more reliable coroner's report. However, there were several witnesses who claimed seeing someone killed by leaping into the street, and yet not one of the autopsies shows this to be the case. Someone who was already on fire could have jumped and only his burns reported, or the person who appeared dead from the fall might only have been unconscious, but more than one witness seemed convinced that someone was killed by his fall to the ground.

Perhaps Leon did die this way and another body was accidentally labeled as his. Certainly, the body finally identified as Leon was terribly mutilated, so it's difficult to know who's correct. If Leon didn't die from a fall, why would Larry continue to insist this was the case?

Perhaps it's simply easier to believe his friend died a relatively quick and painless death, that Larry couldn't face the idea of Leon being burned beyond recognition. Whatever the case, someone was likely at least injured in a fall, and someone, Leon or not, was seriously burned over 90% of his body.

Another discrepancy appears in Reginald Adams' coroner's report. Not only was Reggie black, but photos show he was relatively dark. The first page of his autopsy labels his color as N, but the second page states, "The body is that of a somewhat slender white male...There are only a few portions of the skin of the anterior legs remaining and being recognizable as white skin... and only a small portion of the skin of the left fifth finger is intact."

But if the coroner thought the body was white, why did he mark N on the preceding page? Did the pages of a couple of the reports get jumbled? Even if that were the case, no other report on the fire victims mentions a black body. Whatever the reason for the discrepancy, the fact that the report goes out of its way to point out the "white" skin of the legs, while the reports on several of the other victims make no such claims, is disconcerting.

Other difficult points include a witness who claimed that an unidentified man injured in the fire died a year later at Charity hospital without ever having regained consciousness. Perhaps this could be the man people saw injured in the fall. There seems, however, to be no report or article to confirm the existence of this victim. According to another person, a homeless man crouched underneath the stairs was also killed, but again there's no official mention of a body found at the base of the stairway, and this is probably a false rumor.

Some of these issues might be attributable to the development of mythologies that frequently grow out of mass tragedy. "I heard that..." "A friend of a friend told me..."

The New Orleans fire department has a diagram showing where twenty-nine bodies were found in the bar, but the National Fire Protection Association has a similar diagram showing the position of only twenty-eight bodies, saying that a twenty-ninth victim died on the way to the hospital and three more died later, still making thirty-two. William M. Roth, Jr., one of the state investigators, wrote in 1982 that thirty-three had died in the fire, so he may have included an injured survivor who died a year or more after the fire, but that person's identity, if his tally is accurate, remains unknown.

Despite the uncertainties, the one thing known with surety is that at least thirty-two people were killed, and grief hung in the air for weeks. Larry watched as people came for months to place flowers at the entrance to the bar, sometimes being met with taunts of "Faggots!" from people driving by.

Not long after the fire, a friend of Larry's handed him a photograph of Leon. "I took it Sunday afternoon," the man told him. "I knew he was leaving town, so I said, 'Hey, let me get a picture of you before you go.' I know you liked him. Here, take it."

It helped a little.

When the Post Office bar opened later, Larry went to support Phil Esteve's new venture. He watched as the survivors gathered in a circle, holding hands at the end of each beer bust and singing the song they'd sung at the UpStairs: "United we stand, divided we fall—And if our

backs should ever be against the wall, we'll be together—
Together—you and I."

Larry thought singing those lyrics was perhaps a bit
maudlin, but they'd done it before, even without the added
significance it now carried, so he tried to accept the ritual as
part of their grieving process and listened to them sing and
hug each other, hoping that one day all their pain would
finally go away.

Michael Scarborough and Glenn Green

Bill Goodrum was part owner of Gertrude's at 125 Chartres, along with his two friends, Bob Rosenman and Clayton Gould, from 1970 to 1975. Bill was working at the bar one Sunday evening, planning as usual to head over to the UpStairs for a while after he got off from work. About a half hour before his shift was over, two young men ran into the bar.

"The UpStairs is on fire!" they shouted.

Bill lost several acquaintances but no close friends in the fire, but being a witness to the scene was something he could not quickly erase from his mind, especially since he continued to work just half a block away from the scene for the next two years.

He was just getting to where he didn't think of it so much anymore when an old acquaintance of his walked into the bar.

"Oh, my God." Bill dropped a glass, which shattered on the floor, as he looked at his friend, Michael Scarborough. Michael had formerly been an attractive, blond-haired man. His hair, what was left of it, was now white, and one of his ears had been half burned off.

"I thought you died," Bill gasped.

"I did," Michael replied.

Michael Wayne Scarborough was born on January 8, 1946. His parents, Mr. and Mrs. Loy W. Scarborough, still lived in West Monroe, Louisiana, in the northeastern part of the state. Michael worked at Bethlehem Steel on the Westbank, and he and Glenn Green became lovers during the summer of 1972.

Glenn Richard Green was a shipping clerk, a little short, with a relatively slight build and brown hair. He'd been born on November 1, 1940 to Forrest Charles and Beatrice D. Jeaniott Green, who lived in Wall Lake, Michigan, and was a Navy veteran.

The two men lived together on Bourbon Street for a while but then moved to 446 Pacific Avenue in Algiers, on the Westbank. While living in the Quarter, they often had dinner with friends Bill and Clarence, Mitch and Horace, and Rusty. Sometimes, they'd all go bike riding together in Audubon Park. Even when they moved to the Westbank, they still got together often with their friends. Algiers was, after all, right by the bridge, and it also had a ferry, so they weren't going to let a little water keep them apart.

Michael lost several friends in the fire, but most importantly, he lost his lover. Glenn received 2nd and 3rd degree burns on his hands and head, having the hair burned from his scalp. His fingers were destroyed and his facial features distorted. His red shirt and red socks survived. Glenn died not of burns but of smoke and carbon monoxide inhalation. He was identified through the dental charts of his dentist, Dr. Perry Waters.

Michael's hands were seriously burned, some fingers exposed to the bone. Six fingers and both thumbs were amputated either at the first or second joint, depending on the severity of his injuries.

Michael was naturally quite despondent for a good while after the fire, but he did have police come to his hospital room in Baton Rouge so he could tell them his suspicions that it was Rodger Nunez who'd set the fire. He kept waiting to hear that Rodger had been arrested, but that news never came.

It was nine months after the fire before Michael moved back to New Orleans, after living briefly in West Monroe at 322 Stuart Street for further recuperation. Though he tried to adapt to his new life, it wasn't easy. When Phil Esteve opened his new bar, the Post Office, Michael began visiting. It wasn't the UpStairs, but at least there was something familiar about it, and any little anchor at all was better than just drifting about. If only they'd convict Nunez, maybe he could get enough anger out of his system to move on with his life.

Then on Monday, November 18, 1974, while Michael was casually chatting with Phil at the Post Office, Ralph Forest came in crying, saying his best friend had just killed himself.

"Who was it?" Phil asked, trying to show some concern. "What happened?"

"Rodger Nunez."

Before the man could continue, Michael burst out laughing. Phil, too shocked to say anything at first, finally became angry and almost threw Michael out for being so callous, until Michael explained who Nunez was. Michael would rather that Nunez spent the next fifty years in prison.

He didn't believe in an afterlife during which the guy might suffer and would have preferred making sure the arsonist suffered here and now for killing all those people. But at least some form of justice, Michael felt, was served by Nunez's suicide.

Michael learned to accept his disabilities, and when friends Napoleon and Stanley returned from North Carolina, staying with him a few days before finding their own place, he could play cards with them, dealing them swiftly and accurately, even with only partial fingers. Within a couple of years, he became roommates with Richard, another man who'd been at the UpStairs but who had left shortly before the fire. In 1977, they moved to Baton Rouge, and a year later, they moved to a small town in Arkansas to enjoy "the quiet, country life." The town was also only sixty miles from where Michael was raised.

Michael had not seen the last of fire, however. Several years after settling in Arkansas, his and Richard's home caught fire, and the two men lost most of their possessions, including irreplaceables such as photographs. Michael had lost irreplaceables before, though, and was happy that neither he nor his roommate was injured, knowing that health and life far outweighed mementos of any kind.

Almost eighteen years after the fire, Michael and his roommate seemed to be doing well, Michael laughing easily and wanting to avoid talking a lot about the fire not so much for the painful memories it invoked, but to spare his grown son and other family members possible embarrassment, wanting to respect their privacy. Michael himself seemed to have adjusted to meet the changes his injuries made in his life, and though it had been a few years since he and his roommate had traveled to New Orleans, he said they were saving and planning a trip, and he hoped to drop in and say hi to his old friend, Phil Esteve.

David Gary

David Stuart Gary still listed his parents' home at 1601 Piper Place in Greensboro, North Carolina, as his permanent address, but he'd lived in New Orleans long enough to work regularly as a piano player, specializing in ragtime, at the Levee Bar, for a barbershop quartet, and at the Marriott hotel just across the street from the UpStairs. He'd only been playing at the UpStairs, where he worked simply for tips, for a few months. David had just moved to a new apartment on Bourbon Street a week before the fire.

Born on July 8, 1950, to Elwyn Ray Jr. and Becky Byrum Gary, David had two brothers, Douglas Ray and Stuart Ray, both living in Greensboro, as were their parents. Twenty-two-year-old David Gary received 2nd, 3rd, and 4th degree burns over 80% of his body and was found near the piano he'd been playing. His scalp was charred, with the cranial bones exposed. His boots protected his feet, but only portions of the lower parts of his pants remained attached to his body. He was identified by dental charts.

Rodger Nunez and Miss Fury

On the day after the fire, Miss Fury, 6'2", with long, frizzy, blazing red hair, went Uptown with her husband to pick up a food voucher. Miss Fury, a drag queen, was still reeling from the events of the evening before when several of her friends and acquaintances, Luther Boggs, the Warren boys, Perry Waters, and others, had died or were mortally injured. When she reached the front of the line today to get her voucher, the woman at the counter glared at her and said, "You should have been in that bar yesterday."

Three days later, as she was drinking with a friend at the Society Page, a woman came into the bar with a picture. "My son hasn't called in four days," she explained. "His pick-up truck is parked on Chartres. Do you know if my son is alive?" She showed her the picture, and, not even knowing the answer to the question, Miss Fury burst into tears.

When people announced the memorial service later, they'd walk past Miss Fury and tell others of the meeting but not her. "Hey, us drag queens are people, too," she said. She went to the service.

Over the years, Miss Fury noticed that on the anniversary of the fire, Bobby Hernandez, who often worked offshore, would return to the UpStairs to place a bouquet of flowers at the entrance, kneeling down to offer a short prayer. It seemed that everyone else had forgotten what happened, so she was glad to see somebody cared.

In the late '60's and early '70's, Miss Fury worked as a hustler on Bourbon Street and sometimes waited tables. When Wanda Long, "an ex-whore from Texas," opened a bar at 604 Iberville, Miss Fury became a regular. Many of the bar's customers were drag queens, but when Phil Esteve took over, he discouraged drag queens from coming to the new bar.

Miss Fury was afraid to go back to the UpStairs, feeling she'd be unwelcome, and once, when she was walking with Luther Boggs, and Luther wanted to go up, Miss Fury said, "Oh, they won't let me up there." Luther took her and led her up the stairs. Miss Fury never did go regularly, but enough to see there was a strong camaraderie among many of the customers. They seemed so proud of their plays and trying to keep the bar looking nice.

In the Spring of 1973, Miss Fury was arrested and sent to Parish Prison. She wasn't in for long, just time enough to meet a man named Rodger Dale Nunez. Rodger was born on February 22, 1947, to Rose Choate and Mansel Joseph Nunez, Sr., and grew up in Abbeville, Louisiana. He was 5'7" and weighed 140 pounds, with a stocky build but not appearing overweight. Rodger's thick hair was dark brown, his eyes brown, too. He often wore plaid pants with plaid shirts. Other than a burn scar on his right elbow, however, there were no distinguishing features. He did have a history of epilepsy, so he took Dilantin regularly.

Rodger said he'd briefly been in the Navy, and he worked on oil rigs for a while. On May 29, 1970, he was arrested for driving while intoxicated and fined. On August 27 of that year, he was admitted as a patient at Central Louisiana State Hospital in Pineville with a diagnosis of "Conversion Hysteria." Rodger also went to a psychiatric clinic on February 5, 1973, shortly before his arrest.

Rodger, it seemed, a maintenance man at the Marriott hotel, had stolen a Texaco credit card from Lloyd J. Zirkenbach back in December of 1972 and used it twice, once on December 4, buying gas, oil, and accessories to the value of $184.57, and then ten days later, charging $22.25 more on the card. He was arrested once in the Second District on December 14, and his mug shot is on file at the New Orleans Police Department as #164505/121472. At this arrest, he claimed his occupation was that of nurse.

Rodger was again arrested on April 4, 1973, on the Algiers Ferry Landing. After insisting on reducing the $184.57 charge to $99.00, he confessed and gave a written statement. He was sentenced to six months in Parish Prison, which was commuted to time served and a one-year probation beginning on April 10.

When charged with the $22.25 theft, Rodger stated that his address was 624 Oliver Street. When charged with the larger theft, he listed his address as 111 Oliver Street. By August 7, he had not reported to his probation officer, who also discovered that Rodger could not be found at either address, and that one of the addresses didn't even exist. A warrant was issued for Rodger's arrest, but he wasn't located on this charge until March of 1974, almost sixteen months after the theft, and more than eight months after the fire.

At that time, Charles Adams, the district supervisor, could see that Rodger had recently undergone brain surgery, and he wrote to Judge Frank Shea on April 11 that the "subject was under the mistaken impression that he had not been on probation." Since the year of probation had technically passed by this time, and since Rodger had paid back the money he'd stolen, the probation was declared complete and that was the end of that.

But this wasn't the only thing going on in Rodger's life. He and Miss Fury became friends, and he told her he lived with his sister on the Westbank. Rodger often went to Gene's Hideaway or to Wanda's but occasionally did visit the UpStairs. All three were near the Marriott hotel.

Rodger worked briefly for Eugene "Gene" Davis at Davis' bar, Gene's Hideaway, at 608 Iberville, almost next door to the UpStairs. Gene, forty-nine, had opened the Hideaway on June 19, 1972. It wasn't a gay bar, but Gene considered turning it into one and having Rodger work for him again. Ultimately, he decided to keep it mixed.

Gene liked Rodger, and they talked often when Rodger came in. Rodger was also friends with fifty-two-year-old Dorothy Jean "Dottie" Rikard and Jacqueline "Jackie" Bullard, bartenders at the Hideaway. He was also friends with twenty-five-year-old Kay Keath and forty-year-old Angie, both of whom he met at the Midship next door, and with Foxey, who worked at the Society Page on St. Louis.

Rodger met Cynthia Ann "Cee Cee" Savant and her boyfriend, Michael "Snake" Medford at Gene's Hideaway and became friends with them, too. Michael's record included a burglary arrest in February of 1968, an arrest for using stolen checks in August of 1970, arrest for public drunkenness in Arkansas and Mississippi in 1970 and 1971, a DWI in March of 1971, the theft of two cases of beer in February of 1972, and possession of stolen property the following month.

When Rodger no longer had a place to stay, he asked Cee Cee if he could stay and sleep on her couch. Cee Cee, twenty-one, who'd run away from home in Lake Charles eight years earlier and come to New Orleans, could understand needing a place to stay. She told him yes, and so in the middle of June in 1973, Rodger moved into her place at 608 ½ Iberville, just above Gene's Hideaway. He kept some of his clothes down in the bar.

Another of Rodger's friends there was nineteen-year-old Mark Allen Guidry. Allen's parents lived in Houma, but Allen liked the French Quarter and lived at the Savoy hotel in the 100 block of Royal Street, a block over from the UpStairs. He worked sometimes in construction but was presently earning his living as a hustler, turning tricks for $15 or $30. And when he had a few dollars in his pocket, he was always willing to buy drinks for his friends.

Rodger had friends, and Rodger had johns, but he didn't often have someone he was really interested in. For a few days in the middle of June, though, Rodger spent some time with James Calvin "Jamie" Larson, an eighteen-year-old drag queen who lived in the 1400 block of Terpsichore. But after only a week or so they broke up. Jamie, born on June 25, 1954, had been arrested in October of 1972 for possession of marijuana and in early June of 1973 for the sale of obscene books.

On June 24, 1973, Rodger went to the UpStairs Lounge and began to cause trouble. He was kicked out of the bar. An hour or so later, the bar burned.

What Rodger did immediately after the fire is almost impossible to determine because of contradictory reports. He and most of his friends each gave two or three different versions. Steve, a "Mexican guy," said he knew who started the fire but wouldn't tell his friends. Michael Medford, though, identified Allen Guidry as the guy named Steve.

Gene Davis said that Rodger ran up to him, breathless, just as the fire trucks were coming up, saying he'd just made it out of the bar. At 4:00 the next morning, he told the same story to Jackie Bullard. No one from the UpStairs remembered him being inside during the fire.

Rodger was standing on the corner of Iberville and Royal a few minutes after the fire when Buddy Rasmussen saw him, grabbed him by the collar, and said, "Where have you been?"

"At Wanda's."

Buddy started dragging him toward a police officer.

"Why are you holding me?" Rodger asked.

"I'm going to have you arrested for questioning." He brought Rodger to an officer, but the officer sent them on, so Buddy reluctantly had to release him.

A few moments later, Courtney Craighead went up to Buddy and pointed to Rodger. "I know," Buddy said. "The police weren't interested."

Courtney couldn't quite believe that, so he walked over to the officer himself. "You think you know police business better than I do?" the officer sneered. "Get back across the street. You're in the way."

When Allen Guidry talked later of the fire, he said he saw fire trucks driving up as he came out of Wanda's. This apparently didn't interest him, as he walked in the opposite direction to Royal Castle to buy a hamburger. Someone ran into the little restaurant, told everyone about the fire, and so Allen left. He didn't go to see the fire, though. He went back to Wanda's for another drink. He also said he didn't see Rodger after the fight at the UpStairs until sometime the following day. At another time, however, he said he saw the confrontation between Buddy and Rodger after the fire.

When investigators asked Allen if he'd bought the can of Ronsonol, he answered with the question, "What is Ronsonol?"

"It's lighter fluid."

"No."

"You know what a Ronsonol can looks like?"

"Yes. It's yellow and blue. Small."

So much for not knowing anything about Ronsonol. But the cashier on duty at the Walgreens drug store on the corner of Iberville and Royal couldn't identify either Allen or Rodger from photographs.

On the following morning of June 25, Cee Cee noticed that Rodger's jaw was swollen. He told her he had a toothache and she said later she thought it must have been an abscess. But she asked him at the time what the fight the night before had been about. He replied, "Forget about it. I don't want to talk about it."

A few days later, Cee Cee heard Rodger screaming in his sleep, waking himself up. He was shouting, "I didn't do it! I didn't do it!" When Cee Cee went to see what was wrong, he said, "Cee Cee, help me. I didn't start it. Tell them I didn't start the fire."

On July 2, eight days after the fire, Allen Guidry finally admitted that the guy he'd told police was named Jerry or Johnny and who lived somewhere in the 2700 block of Esplanade and who was then one of a few vaguely defined suspects, was actually Rodger Nunez, and Allen took the police to Cee Cee's apartment on Iberville, where police found Rodger sleeping on the couch.

His jaw was swollen, and police, who knew he'd been struck a week earlier by Michael Scarborough, asked him when his jaw had been hurt. Rodger said that three men had taken his wallet the night before. No, he did not have any trouble at the UpStairs, but he did admit to being there.

Rodger was taken in for questioning, but while he was waiting, he suffered a seizure, so the police took him to Charity Hospital. While in the admitting room there, he had a second *grand mal* seizure. Doctors noticed something besides the epilepsy, however. They noticed that Rodger's jaw was fractured. He remained in the hospital five days with his jaw wired and was released on July 7. He was told to return on the 13th for a checkup on the jaw, but he never came back.

Rodger moved back to Abbeville shortly after the fire, moving in with his mother and stepfather, Sale, in a trailer park at 305 South St. Valerie Street. His mother had been living there for four years. Rodger began working as a deckhand at D & B Boat Rental Company in New Iberia in July and continued to work there for at least two months.

One day while working, however, he was on board a boat when a cable broke and he was thrown against the side of the vessel. The blow knocked him out but didn't appear to seriously hurt him. He walked away with just a couple of bruises. Within a few days, though, he noticed he was having seizures more often.

His mother and stepfather moved to Dallas in early September without giving Rodger their new address, and Rodger left the trailer and moved to 113 South Lamar. His father had moved to Grand Chenier, Louisiana, sometime earlier.

After the questioning of several witnesses led investigators to believe more strongly that Rodger was an important suspect, he was asked to come to New Orleans and was questioned on September 18, 1973, by Edward S. Hyde and John M. Fischer. At that time, Rodger said he'd been living in Abbeville for four months, but he was clearly living in New Orleans at least until July 7. He also said he'd been working with the boat rental for two months but then later said he was injured in the cable accident 2 ½ months prior to the questioning, which would mean two weeks before he was even on a boat.

Rodger also seemed confused on a few other points. He couldn't remember if he was at the UpStairs the evening of the fire. He couldn't remember being with Allen Guidry. He couldn't remember just when his jaw was broken, though he was sure it wasn't in the fight with Michael Scarborough.

Rodger couldn't remember having owned a 1966 Plymouth Fury, which was registered in his name and which he later transferred to his mother. He couldn't remember having been to Morgan City or having been stopped by police there, though the police had the car's description, license, and registration. Perhaps most important, he said he couldn't remember whether he was at the fire scene while firefighters were putting out the fire. He couldn't remember if he saw the fire or not.

Despite the claims of several people who did see Rodger at the scene and heard his threat in the bar, and despite the many inconsistencies in Rodger's story, there wasn't enough evidence to hold him, so he was released.

Rodger told police he would willingly take a polygraph test, but doctors wouldn't allow it because of his epilepsy and medication. Investigators were able to give him a psychological stress evaluation, however. Each of several times he was administered the test, whenever he was asked what he knew of the fire, and he insisted he knew nothing, the test showed a great deal of stress.

Of course, what person knowing he was suspected of killing thirty-two people wouldn't feel stressed when asked about it?

In one version of the test, Rodger was asked each question twice and told to answer yes one time and no the next. First, he was asked what his name was and if he smoked, to establish his stress pattern. Then when he was asked if he set the fire, the test only showed stress when he said he didn't. Likewise, when he was asked, "Regarding the fire do you intend to answer these questions truthfully?" there was no stress when he said no, but there was stress when he said yes. Finally, Rodger's attorney, Albert Boudreaux, advised him not to answer any more questions, that his answers might incriminate him.

How much Rodger's friends knew or were involved themselves, either as accomplices or accessories after the fact, is unclear. When investigators came one time to question Allen, Dottie Rikard told him, "Keep your big mouth shut."

When Cee Cee was asked, "Did he [Rodger] tell you that he had anything to do with setting the fire?" she replied, "No. Not that I can honestly remember, he didn't." She didn't remember if he'd told her he killed thirty-two people or not.

Gene Davis reacted strongly when taking the Dektor PSE-I stress evaluation. "Now did you see Rodger come out of the place?" he was asked.

"No." The comment following his answer, written by the test evaluator, is, "Stress indicated, he is lying here."

"Do you know of your own knowledge if Rodger Nunez set the fire?"

"No, I do not." The evaluator adds, "Stress indicated, he is lying."

"If you knew who set the fire, would you tell us?"

"I sure would." This is followed by the comment, "Stress indicating that he is lying. Lots of nervous tension."

When Allen Guidry also took the stress tests, he showed stress when denying he knew who set the fire. Allen in one stress test said that Rodger had a Ronsonol lighter fluid can. Then in the same test he said Rodger did not have the lighter fluid. Only when he said Rodger did not have the can did the test show stress.

By Christmas of 1973, Rodger was back in New Orleans, and he and Miss Fury got together at Wanda's on the 25th and had a few drinks. Suddenly, Rodger began crying, saying he'd been the one who set the fire at the UpStairs Lounge. He was so mad after being kicked out that he walked to the nearby Walgreens and bought a seven-ounce can of lighter fluid. He said he squirted it over the bottom steps and then tossed a match inside. He'd only meant to cause a little fire and some smoke, he said, weeping. He'd only meant to scare everybody. He didn't realize the whole place would go up in flames.

Rodger told Miss Fury he'd been interrogated by the authorities, and that he'd even confessed, but that they said they had no evidence. They knew that the fire originated on the left side of the second and third steps, and that it did not originate in any of the three electric meters in the stairwell, as all three were still intact, and all the lines were tight.

But New Orleans didn't have an arson team, so to prove *he* did it was something else. Some in the gay community felt they didn't try very hard. According to Rodger (well, according to what Miss Fury *said* Rodger said), one of the authorities had told him, "You can burn down every faggot bar in town for all we care." But as often as Rodger clearly lied, we can only put so much weight into his accusation. And we only have Miss Fury's word that he made the accusation or the confession in the first place.

During the first week of January 1974, Rodger met thirty-five-year-old Ralph Spencer Forest. In March, they became roommates at the Imperial Hotel, a halfway house at 609 St. Charles. Ralph was a cook there. Shortly after Mardi Gras, as the two were talking, Ralph mentioned the fire, noting that he'd moved to New Orleans just before it occurred. Rodger laughed and said he'd started it. Ralph laughed, too, thinking it was a joke, and he soon forgot about it.

A couple of months later, though, while the two men were drinking at Wanda's, Rodger told him again that he'd started the fire. He seemed serious, but he was so drunk that Ralph couldn't be sure. Ralph asked him the next day when Rodger was sober, and Rodger denied it. But another day while in a bar drinking, Rodger confessed again.

He also said he'd used Ronsonol lighter fluid he'd bought at Walgreens on the corner of Royal and Iberville. The details were beginning to convince Ralph, but he didn't know what to do about it. He liked Rodger and didn't want to see him get in trouble, and Ralph really didn't have any proof.

Rodger also confessed to several smaller crimes, such as passing bad checks at the Holiday Inn, Winn-Dixie, and some businesses in Abbeville, so it sounded like he was honestly trying to list the things he'd done, but Ralph just couldn't be sure. When Ralph took a stress test and told police what

Rodger had told him, it appeared that Ralph, since he showed no signs of stress, was not making up the allegations for any personal reason.

While at the halfway house, Rodger went to a nun a few times to talk of his problems. Sister Mary Stephen Ledet of the Sisters of Christian Charity said that Rodger spoke of the fire and of being suspected but that he never confessed to her he set the fire. He seemed so sweet that she never even felt she had to ask if he set it. His biggest problem, as far as she could see, seemed to be his difficulty in dealing with being gay. He simply couldn't accept himself. She was also upset to see that he was too nice and let people use him for the $146 in disability money he received every month.

Early 1974 saw another development in Rodger's life. He stayed with Ginger Bruno, a woman he knew from Wanda's, and babysat for her. While at her home, he met Ginger's neighbor, forty-nine-year old Elaine Wharton Bassett. Twenty-seven-year-old Rodger and Elaine were married on May 17, 1974, in the Algiers Court House, and they lived at Elaine's home at 9200 Hayne Boulevard.

But Rodger didn't stay in the house. He slept in the trailer behind the house, and he and Elaine never did sleep together. After they were married, Rodger told her he was homosexual and impotent. And though Rodger continued to receive his disability from Social Security, Elaine learned he had forged several checks on her checking account.

Sexuality and theft were not the only problems, however. In March, just before the marriage, Rodger was operated on for a brain tumor at the U.S. Public Health Hospital at 300 State Street. He also received psychiatric treatment there under Drs. J. R. Smith and Alvin Rouchelle. In addition, he was treated at Southeast Louisiana State Hospital in Mandeville, a hospital for mental illnesses.

It seems likely Rodger did confess to starting the fire, but does that mean he actually set it? Did the tumor in the right frontal area of his brain already exist on June 24, and did it affect his judgment to some extent? Or did the tumor affect his judgment later and make him believe he'd caused the fire simply because he'd been accused several times? Could Rodger have confessed as a means of feeling important or getting attention? Was he trying in some bizarre manner to look for sympathy? Was his confession a form of self-destructive behavior?

If he was, in fact, telling the truth, could he really have expected the "innocent" little scare he said was all he'd planned? By several accounts, he was drunk, so his reasoning would have been impaired, with or without the influence of a brain tumor, but would it have been flawed to that extent?

And what about the epilepsy? It may have played absolutely no part, but what if his epilepsy was caused by a blow to the head in his youth? Some studies indicate a correlation between head injuries and violent outbreaks later in life. Perhaps the records of his doctors and psychiatrists, unavailable to the investigators, would have cleared up some of these questions.

The investigation suggests that Rodger did commit the crime, and that his friends learned of it afterward but covered up for him. Phil Esteve suggests another possibility. A bartender from Wanda's told him that he saw Rodger come into the bar and talk to Gene Davis, and that then the two of them went into Davis' office for about half an hour. Rodger then left the bar and headed in the direction of the drugstore. Minutes later, the UpStairs was on fire. However, since Gene Davis was murdered years later and since the bartender who reported this meeting has since died of a heart attack, Davis' alleged involvement must remain apocryphal. Rodger himself apparently never implicated Davis in the fire.

On Thursday evening, November 14, 1974, around 8:30, after Rodger had been drinking, Elaine saw him drink the contents of containers later determined to hold phenobarbital, chlordazepoxide, and diphenhylhydantoin. Then he left for the trailer behind the house. Around 10:30 the next morning, Elaine tried to wake him but couldn't. She called an ambulance.

According to chemist Angela Comstock and toxicologists Rubye Ory and Monroe Samuels, Rodger died on November 15 around 12:30 p.m., of an overdose of prescription medication. Rodger had a blood alcohol level of 0.14%. There was a Dilantin level of 0.3 mg% and a phenobarb level of 2.2 mg%. He tested positive for barbiturates with an Rf value comparable to phenobarbital. The death was classified as a suicide.

At the time of his death, Rodger's weight had gone up from 140 to 160 pounds. He'd had another operation on his brain just sixty days prior to his death. It's possible that the suicide was in response to despair over his brain tumor, that it was due to remorse over the fire, or that it came as a combination of the grief he felt over both situations. He could have killed himself purely over self-loathing for being gay.

And, of course, it may have been due instead to circumstances about which we know nothing at all.

During the autopsy, assistant coroner Ralph Lupin described the tumor as "a 2x2x3 cm thick walled, fibrous cystic nodule densely adherent to the dura in the right frontal area. The cerebral gyri are widened and the sulci narrowed. There is uncal grooving and tonsilar coning at the base of the brain." Also, "the dural nodule is composed of dense fibrous tissue with few nuclei and the polarizing pattern of mature collagen. Suture material with surrounding foreign body giant cells is scattered throughout the sections. The central cystic area is surrounded by relatively acellular myxomatous tissue."

Although Rodger was the primary suspect, he wasn't the only one. At least two other people also confessed to starting the fire. The first of these was David Ronald DuBose. When David had been kicked out of the UpStairs for pestering customers and redeeming beer mugs, James Smith watched him leave. Jim, thirty, thought that eighteen-year-old David was kind of cute, so he followed him out and invited him over to his apartment at 1508 Erato Street Uptown. There they had dinner and then Jim performed oral sex on David, paying him ten dollars.

Around 9:15, David asked Jim to drive him to the Golden Slipper Lounge in the 100 block of St. Charles, and David arrived there at about 9:30, joining his roommate, Francis "Pepper" Barker, a musician and waiter, who was thirty-nine.

Floyd Michael Villarreal, eighteen, who lived at 722 ½ Kerlerec, was walking down Iberville when he saw someone run out of the stairwell of the UpStairs just seconds before the fire started. He was too far away to make a positive identification, but while he was watching the fire, he overheard someone describing a man wearing a blue and red striped shirt with the words "Ponchartrain Beach," the name of an amusement park on the lakefront, over the left breast. The man had come running out just before the fire. Floyd recognized the description of David and told police. The man Floyd overheard could have been deliberately lying, or perhaps he only meant he knew David had been kicked out, not that he'd seen him leave seconds before the fire. But the police thought they'd check it out anyway.

At 10:30, the police came into the Golden Slipper, looking for David. They found Pepper on the phone to Jim Smith, asking him to be their alibi. The police took David in for questioning, and he confessed to Captain Anthony Polito. He told the captain that he'd brought the can of gasoline and Jim Smith had set the fire. Then David changed his mind, saying he didn't set the fire. When he took a polygraph test, the results suggested that he was not the arsonist.

Another man, thirty-two-year-old Raymond Wallender, named Ken in one account, apparently only confessed to police in Sacramento in hopes of going to prison in Louisiana rather than in California, where he was wanted on a charge of grand theft and larceny. After being extradited to New Orleans, Wallender was charged on November 16, 1973. He then said he'd "made up the story" because he was afraid if he went to prison in California that "someone would kill [him]" there. It didn't take long for the police to discover that Wallender wasn't even in Louisiana at the time of the fire. Arson charges were eventually dropped against him.

Other suspects included thirty-six-year-old Daniel Patrick Kimball, who'd been arrested in February of 1972 for simple arson and who lived at 1720 Fairway in Kenner (right where a plane crash in 1982 would kill 154 people). Michael Garry Butler, a twenty-one-year-old busboy from Spartanburg, South Carolina, who was arrested in January of 1971 and who served in Angola state prison in Louisiana from September 1972 until April 1973, was still another suspect. Jerome Wayne Griffith, a twenty-two-year-old carpenter, and Kirk John Kirkland, a twenty-three-year-old bricklayer, were suspects even without an arson record. But none of these proved worth investigating at length.

William White, eighteen, and Gary Williams, nineteen, both of Pineville, told police that they needed to be looking for two men. William and Gary had started up the stairs to the bar shortly before the fire but stopped when they saw two men arguing at the top of the stairs. They decided to try someplace else and left, but they'd only gone about half a block down the street when they looked back and saw the bar in flames.

Could these have been two friends who were leaving the bar because of an argument they'd just started inside? Were they two men who, despite their argument, went on into the bar and were soon killed? No one remembered anyone entering or leaving just before the fire, but that isn't a point many people would have any reason to notice before the fire started. Could the two men arguing have been on their way to the bar and because of their disagreement have turned around and left, just moments before the arsonist arrived?

Could William and Gary have stopped "half a block" down the street at Wanda's and lost track of time? The argument could then be totally unrelated to the fire, or they may have witnessed Buddy or Hugh throwing out David or Rodger from the bar earlier that evening.

Or the men from Pineville may in fact have seen two men arguing about where to set the fire. In any case, the two men were never identified either as victims or as suspects.

Yet another theory about the arsonist was that a hustler had gone to the bar with a john, but the man decided not to pay him or go with him after all, and they started to argue, after which the hustler was thrown out. Seeking revenge, he started the fire. No names are mentioned in connection with this theory, and apparently the fact that no one was ever prosecuted led people to continually think of other possibilities as to who or what caused the fire. One woman was convinced the cause was that all the men at the bar were using flammable amyl nitrate, or poppers.

For years, many gays across the country, unaware of any of these suspects, believed the bar had been torched by some right-wing homophobe, and though it seems unlikely in this case, the belief still shaped their lives, adding another layer of oppression that might have been avoided if the police could at least have tried to prosecute Rodger. But arson is a notoriously difficult crime to prosecute successfully even in the best of situations.

Rodger Nunez seems the most plausible suspect, but plausibility is not fact. The reality might be too bizarre to be plausible but still true. In 1980, though, Frank J. Locascio, Jr., chief of the arson division, set up a few years after the fire, wrote to the Department of Public Safety that "The investigators were completely satisfied that he [Nunez] was the person who set the fire. No charges were ever accepted by the D.A., N.O., LA."

However, because of the homicides involved, making this even fifty years later one of the largest mass murders in U.S. history, the case is still officially open. It's unlikely, though, given the passage of so many years and the loss of records after Hurricane Katrina, that any further investigation will be conducted or any stronger conclusion determined for Rodger's guilt.

Bud Matyi

Born on September 2, 1945, in Perthamboy, New Jersey, an industrial suburb of New York, George Steven Matyi was only a child when he moved along with his family to southern California, to the Pasadena/Glendora area. His parents, Betty Jane Julian and George Matyi, were divorced soon thereafter, and Betty kept her two boys, George and Kenny. George hated his name, preferring to be called Bud. But Bud and Kenny were not long without a father. Betty remarried an Italian-American named Conenna, and the family was again "traditional" and complete.

Bud worked often in his stepfather's carpentry shop, remembering always the discipline he learned both there and at home from having an Italian stepfather. Opportunities for friction were ample, with Conenna's strength being carpentry and Bud's early interests developing in music, but though the family may have thought Bud a little odd, they could clearly see his remarkable talents. Perhaps music wasn't as stable a career as they would have liked him to pursue, but he was good at it, and since they loved him, they accepted that music was what he was going to do.

The same understanding was evident when he told his folks he was gay. Certainly, it wasn't what they wanted to hear, but Bud was their son and they loved him and that was that.

Bud became sexually active with men at seventeen, but this wasn't the time he really "came out." He felt enormous confusion over his sexual identity, and since he wanted children, not only because he was "very Catholic" but also because he liked kids, he decided to marry.

Mary was Hispanic, from Mexico, and they were only married a short while. They broke up when Bud started going out again with men. Mary felt that Bud leaving her for a man was the lowest thing he could do. And for him to leave her with an infant son, Shawn, was even worse. What was she supposed to do now as a single mother raising a baby? Bud was nothing more than an irresponsible and repulsive human being.

Bud did keep in touch with her over the following years, however, and did take an interest in his son. He could hardly deny the fact that Shawn looked a great deal like him, and he felt he owed something to the child. Just what he owed he wasn't sure. First, Bud had to take care of himself and get his own career going, and besides, was a gay father really what the kid needed?

But Bud couldn't quite give up the idea of children or marriage and thought he'd try again. He met and married Pamela, but Pamela's parents didn't like Bud. For one thing, Pamela was too young to marry anyone, and certainly too young to be pregnant by a would-be musician who couldn't support his family. Bud and Pamela were so poor they sometimes literally ate out of the trash, and even when Bud did have a paying gig, Pamela resented him being out so late.

Sometimes, she'd show up where he was singing and plop their infant daughter, Tina, in his lap and say, "Here.

You deal with it." Bud and Pamela fought a lot the short time they were together. Once, Bud even threw a vase which struck her in the head, giving her a cut requiring stitches. Well before Todd was born, the marriage was essentially over, and a divorce followed quickly.

Bud was the parent who received custody of the children, but he couldn't face the responsibility and so let Pamela keep them. She, too, could only think of Bud as despicable for leaving her for men, and leaving her with two young children. At least, this was Bud's impression. It was partly out of a hope to pacify his wives that he let them keep the children, hoping they'd see that as a privilege and not just as a burden, that type of double standard even more prevalent at the time.

After the divorce, Bud traveled across the United States, listening to various performers, trying to gain some experience, and thinking about what to do with his life. Passing through New Orleans, he found he liked the city and decided to stay. Once there, his love for the city grew daily.

And his music career took off. He totally enjoyed not only composing songs but also playing the piano and singing. It was while playing at The Grog on Rampart that he first met Rod Wagener. They became acquaintances and then casual friends. They enjoyed hanging out at the same places, and they both held similar political beliefs, both liberal Democrats. Bud had been a strong supporter of Kennedy and Johnson, and he absolutely despised Nixon.

Despite enjoying each other's company, their relationship seemed destined to remain casual, until late one night, or rather, early one morning. It was about 7:00 a.m., and Rod had recently been released from the hospital after the removal of his gall bladder. He was still wearing bandages and a loose jumpsuit, and the previous days of pain had left him looking far from his best. But Rod ran into Bud leaving Lafitte's that morning after a long night out and said, "I need you. Please come home with me. I need you very much."

Bud did go home with him, and the next day, he moved into Rod's apartment at 511 Esplanade. When Rod came home from work, he found a piano in his apartment. "What's going on?" Rod asked.

"You do like me very much," said Bud. "You love me, don't you?"

"Yeah."

"Well, I'm moving in."

"You really go around believing what drunks tell you?"

"Yes."

They laughed, and the partnership was accepted. The two considered December 27 their anniversary, and they both wore wedding rings to let others know they did indeed consider themselves a couple. Rod liked Bud because of Bud's "great personality." He also admired Bud's music, and it didn't hurt that Bud was great at sex, able to teach the older Rod a few new tricks.

Bud, on the other hand, liked Rod's stability, liked the way Rod made him (let him?) feel important, since feeling important was something Bud needed to feel. Rod was also good at getting rid of guests who stayed too long, something

Bud could never manage to accomplish, and having a "heavy" around could be useful at times. And of course, Rod was pretty good in bed, too.

Rod was meanwhile prospering in his career, doing an afternoon talk show each weekday afternoon for WDSU, the NBC affiliate. Bud's career was continuing to blossom as well. They were both making lots of money and moved to an exclusive condominium, $300 a month in the early '70's, at Regency Park, near the Lakefront airport. Because of Bud's music connections and Rod's broadcasting connections, they knew most of the musicians in the area, including Ronnie Cole and others. They became friends and acquaintances of many who were then or were later to become stars.

Bud liked to be domestic. It was he who did the cooking, usually serving meals with a formal dinner setting. He took pride in his meals, and once when Rod commented, "These potatoes are awful," Bud stood up, reached across the table, and dumped the potatoes in Rod's lap. Rod never criticized the potatoes again.

Bud liked to keep their place clean, too. If someone put out a cigarette in an ash tray, Bud would dump out the cigarette, clean the ash tray, and set it back down. He kept the carpets in the house clean and fluffy, and it was he who decorated the place, mostly with French Provincial furniture. He often spent $1000 a month or more on furniture or other items for their condo.

He decorated their trailer in Slidell, on Mickal Street, and he decorated the apartment they kept in Montreal, Quebec. Bud spent a lot of time in Slidell at the trailer, driving up from New Orleans in his 1966 Camaro convertible. He enjoyed all the pine trees, the peacefulness of the area. It gave him time to think, and after over four years with Rod, he had to make some serious decisions about his kids. He knew he shouldn't have put them off for so long. Sure, he called them, and of course he sent them bikes and toys and lots of other presents, but he knew he needed to take a more active role in their lives.

He'd liked being free, of course, and it was true he needed a lot of time to get his career going, but could there really be much of an excuse not to raise his own kids? Especially when the courts had given him custody of two of them?

He was afraid of Pamela, though. She could cause a big stink if she wanted to and maybe hurt his career. Who would want to support an artist who'd "run out on his wife and kids"? He knew now, though, that his relationship with Rod was stable and permanent, and that he'd already achieved a level of success with his music that many musicians never achieved. The new song he'd just composed, "The Kingdom of Love," was as good as anything he'd yet written, and he was sure he could have some commercial success with it.

Rod was quite willing to take in Tina and Todd, and Shawn, too, for that matter. Bud and Rod began looking for a governess, what we'd call a nanny today, since they knew they'd both be too busy with work to be there every minute for the kids, and they knew they couldn't fully change their characters; they'd still lead fairly independent lives. But they could make some changes, and so Bud began making phone calls to California to see what his chances might be in gaining custody of Shawn.

Meanwhile, things continued much as always for Bud and Rod. There were tiny arguments occasionally when one would ask the other, "What are your plans now?" or "What are you going to do next in your career?" But most of their arguments were over the lack of time they were able to spend together, with Rod working weekdays and Bud working mostly weekends. They always seemed to get over their arguments quickly, however, and get on with better things. Bud enjoyed sitting at his Kawai grand piano, polished so that he could see his face in it, sitting beneath his elaborate crystal chandelier. It was awfully nice to be comfortable, and it was fun, too.

They both enjoyed weekend trips to Las Vegas, Lake Tahoe, Chicago, and San Francisco. They had fun together, but it was more than just fun. Despite the differences in their careers, they each had a deep appreciation for what the other was doing. And though at times they both felt they didn't see enough of each other, there were other times when even just a few moments seemed to make everything worthwhile.

One weekend, for instance, they decided to take off for Florida. They knew of a particularly secluded beach where they could be alone without any disturbances, even from friends. In warmer weather, they might take off their clothes and stroll down the beach naked, but it was winter, and it was more the seclusion they were looking for now.

They arrived around 3:00 a.m. and trudged into their room. It was freezing cold outside and none too warm even inside. Rod sure looked like he could use some warming up, and Bud figured he knew a way to do it. He got out a bottle of Baby Magic skin lotion, warmed it up, and then rubbed it gently and slowly into Rod's skin. Rod looked up at him and realized again what an incredible feeling it was to be in love. "Why me?" he thought. "What does this guy see in me?"

And of course, there were always good times in Montreal. In May and June of 1973, Bud and Rod were able to spend four weeks together in their Canadian apartment. Their place was near the university, the Offertoire de San Josef, on top of a mountain. It was beautiful there and gave them time to be alone together as well as be with friends they'd made in the area. There was enough time to reflect on how fortunate they were to have one another, how rare it was that they both received love and acceptance from their parents, and to reflect yet again on what their responsibilities would be as father and "stepfather" to Bud's children.

While in Montreal, Bud received a phone call from New Orleans. Could he play at a fundraiser for the Metropolitan Community Church? Maybe. When was it? The 24th of June. Would he be back in town by then? Yes. So would he do it? Sure.

The 23rd was Rod's birthday, so they'd planned to be back for that, anyway. Bud arranged a surprise party and did manage to surprise his husband. They both had a wonderful time at the party, but the next day they were arguing.

Rod couldn't believe Bud wanted to go to the UpStairs. Didn't they have drag shows there sometimes? Rod and Bud were both "straight appearing," and Rod felt little connection to many of the French Quarter gays who were "obvious." When Rod learned that the fundraiser was for the MCC, to support a church that wanted to hold religious services "for drag queens," he looked at Bud sternly.

How could Bud want to raise money to help drag queens? Weren't they part of that fringe element of gay society that gave gays a bad name in the first place? If there were any aspect of the gay community they could do without, it was certainly drag queens. "Why do you want to associate with those people?" Rod demanded.

"They can't even go to church," Bud replied. "No one will let them in. It's not right." Someone had to stand up for those who were inarticulate or otherwise unable to stand up for themselves. MCC did that and so merited his service. And Bud felt he had a responsibility himself to stand up for the rights of all gays, even those who weren't deemed "acceptable." After all, how acceptable were he and Rod to most of society? He may not have been the world's greatest activist, but if he could use his talent to help in some small way, he was damn well going to do it.

The argument continued. Bud wanted Rod to come, but Rod insisted he had nothing in common with those "queers." Neither would back down, but they at least stopped trying to force the other over to his side.

"I'm going to the UpStairs now," Bud said finally.

"All right," Rod replied. "Then we'll go back to Montreal."

Rod knew they couldn't spend too much more time up there, but Bud had just signed a contract in St. Louis for his personal management, and he'd just been to Memphis, where he'd signed a contract that would take him all over the southeast to perform, so Rod wanted just a little more private time with his husband before all the chaos started.

As Bud walked toward the door, Rod watched the religious medal dangling from Bud's neck. It had a dove on it, and a priest in Montreal had told him that the design on the medal was the symbol for marriage. Rod was still upset from arguing, but he knew that would pass just as had all their other arguments. And really, when he thought about it, wasn't the way Bud was willing to stand up for his beliefs one of the things he genuinely liked about the man anyway?

Rod remembered Bud's lyric from his latest song, which spoke of how service brought love. "Before you receive it, you have to give it," and Rod, though still grumpy, realized Bud was probably right after all, though Rod couldn't let Bud know that yet.

He almost smiled despite himself, nodding as Bud walked out the door.

Napoleon and Stanley

Lyn was working on an oil field derrick and living with his fourth wife in Hattiesburg, Mississippi, when he first earned his nickname of Napoleon. His wife was attending beauty school and one day told him she wanted to color his hair. Lyn grabbed a beer and sat back as she worked, first turning his hair white and then honey blond, and then adding a perm which swept his hair forward.

Walking into the Red Maple bar later, a guy named Dale saw him and squealed, "Ooh! You look like Napoleon!" The name stuck with him the rest of the time he worked in the oil field. Then, six months after moving to New Orleans in 1967, he went to Wanda's bar one day, and Dale came in. "Napoleon!" he shouted. Lyn didn't like going by his real name, Kerry Lyn, which said quickly and in a gay bar too often sounded like Carolyn, so he shrugged and let Napoleon remain his name.

Born in Laurel, Mississippi in 1942, Napoleon was only ten hours old when he left his native city, moving with his family to Washington, D.C. A few years later, though, he was back in the South, living on a farm just outside McComb, Mississippi. At age eight, he was guiding a plow horse and plowing three or four acres a day. He had his first official job at eleven, working as a carhop at a burger restaurant for thirty-five cents an hour.

But he still worked on the farm, too. They had a few milk cows, a few beef cattle, and a few pigs, but their crops brought the big workload. Napoleon tried to talk his way out of helping if he could, but with a brother on the farm, and cousins on neighboring farms, he had time enough to relax and play when he needed to. The boys would go swimming together or ride their bikes twelve miles into town to see a movie for ten cents. They brought their hatchets to the woods and chopped down trees to build a log cabin for camping. They had fun enough.

When Napoleon was six, he was introduced to a new kind of fun. His fourteen-year-old male babysitter molested him. "Don't tell anyone," the older boy warned. Napoleon didn't, but he didn't feel traumatized by the incident, either. He'd enjoyed it.

There was a little more "fooling around" during Napoleon's early teenage years, but he didn't really come out until after he joined the Navy. At five, he'd seen an older cousin in a sailor uniform and thought the man looked wonderful, so he'd planned for years to join. At sixteen, after finishing ninth grade, Napoleon dropped out of Amite High School, took his GED, and joined the service, saying he was seventeen.

He was stationed on the ship Missouri, in San Diego, then in Washington State, and again in San Diego. The city was large enough that Napoleon felt he could look for men and not be caught. When he began his last six-month cruise in March of 1961, he told his superiors that his term of service would be over in one month, before the cruise would be finished. They expected him to reenlist, but a month later, he was discharged on Treasure Island near San Francisco. Of the 300 or so men leaving at that time, Napoleon saw that about twenty or thirty of them were being kicked out for homosexuality. They were all "obviously" gay, though, and he wondered how they'd ever been able to enlist in the first place.

Despite his own homosexuality, however, Napoleon had already been married twice by this time. He married his first wife at sixteen shortly after he joined the Navy. He met a twenty-one-year-old from Washington State and went to Tijuana with her. She was old enough to buy beer, he thought, so why not get married? With that firm foundation and two dollars for the license, they were wed.

The next morning, they realized their mistake, so for five dollars more they bought their divorce, but they still liked each other and continued to live together for the following two years.

Napoleon's second marriage lasted a bit longer, two months and eight days. His wife was a young Hispanic woman from Texas. He had two more marriages after that, and with the four wives, Napoleon fathered three daughters and kept in touch with his ex-wives and children over the following years.

In New Orleans, he quickly found the gay community and began going to the bars. In 1967 or 1968, he went to the Stand In on Burgundy and Conti, to the back room. The main bar was in front, but in back was a room for their private dancing club. For two dollars, a man could go in back and dance with other men.

One evening around 10:00, Bunny Day was working the front bar, and when she saw two young, cute, well-dressed men come into the bar, she invited them to the back. They went to go dance, but when the first song was over, they very politely held out their badges and arrested everyone. The charge was "obscenity for dancing with a member of the same sex in an intimate embrace."

Joe, who owned the old Pete Herman place where they were dancing, went to jail to bail everyone out, and within four hours, almost everyone was back dancing at the bar. Their names would all be in the paper the next day, but as Napoleon was the name in the paper and he was only known by his real name at work, there wasn't a problem for him.

Napoleon soon heard about a new bar called the UpStairs which would be opening on Halloween of 1970. Phyllis Teve would be running it. "What kind of name is Teve?" Napoleon wondered and so ended up at the bar to take a look at the owner, finally realizing the name he'd overheard was Phil Esteve.

Napoleon's main job at this time was hustling, $5 for oral sex and $20 for anal sex, and he went to Phil Esteve and asked, "Is it okay if I pick up guys at Wanda's and then come spend my money here?"

"Sure," Phil told him. "That's great. Just don't hustle anyone in my bar."

"Okay."

Napoleon had a reasonably good reputation as a sex worker. Someone once asked a bartender if he knew a good hustler, and the bartender pointed to Napoleon. "He isn't the youngest, but he's honest and won't rob you." So the guy, about twenty-five, went up to Napoleon, twenty-nine at the time.

"How much will it cost for you to spend the night with me?"

"The whole night?"

"Yes."

"Dinner, breakfast, and $50."

So they went to dinner and then to the man's hotel room, where the man handed Napoleon a briefcase. Inside were handcuffs and a cat o' nine tails. Napoleon quickly looked back at the guy. He was small enough to handle if things got messy.

"I want you to tie me up and beat me."

"Look, man, I'm not into this shit."

The man tried to persuade him without success. Then he picked a new strategy and grew angry. "You mean I spent $20 on you for dinner and you won't beat me?" He punched Napoleon in the face. Napoleon punched back and then grabbed the handcuffs, fastening him to the bed but next to the phone. Then he walked over to the man's wallet.

There was $600 inside. Napoleon took $50 and left.

The next day, the man came back into the bar where he'd met Napoleon and demanded to know where he was. "I need him again," he said. "He was great." But Napoleon had had enough of that and declined.

Incidents like this made Napoleon consider leaving hustling, but it was easy money. When he met Glenn Green, though, he took a breather, hustling a little less. During the last few months of 1971, they were roommates. Napoleon took care of the house while Glenn paid the bills. They weren't lovers but friends.

Glenn Green, who Napoleon liked to call "Gangrene," was outgoing yet private, rarely revealing anything deeply personal. He was loving and friendly, but Napoleon could never tell if anything was going on beneath the surface. There was that one week, of course, when a sixteen-year-old boy stayed with them. The boy absolutely loved oral sex, doing Napoleon first one night and then Glenn, then Napoleon, and then Glenn again. Finally, Napoleon told him to stop. "I've got to get some sleep," he protested. "Besides, I've got to have something left for work tomorrow." Even easygoing Glenn seemed glad when the boy left a few days later.

After a few months, in January of 1972, Napoleon, still on friendly terms with Glenn, moved out.

Napoleon went to lots of bars but became a regular at the UpStairs. Sometimes, he'd get so drunk he'd crawl underneath the piano out of harm's way and go to sleep. He became friends with Buddy Rasmussen, Tad Turner, Debbie Dyke, Ricky Everett, and Uncle Al. Uncle Al was apparently heterosexual but liked the gang at the bar enough to bring big bunches of bananas he grew in his back yard and divvy them out to his friends.

Napoleon also came to know Rusty Quinton, Michael Scarborough, and Bob and Bettye McAnear. He would never take part in Bettye's plays, but he did enjoy watching them.

They were fun even after seeing them a dozen times. Phil became angry with him one night, though, during a performance. Buddy had put out popcorn for people to throw at the villain, but Napoleon felt mischievous and picked out the kernels at the bottom of the bowl instead, flinging them toward Tad Turner on stage. Tad finally tired of the little rock-like projectiles and turned to him during the play. "Get out!" he ordered, and Phil told Napoleon to calm down or leave. Napoleon calmed down.

In June of 1972, after dancing aboard ship at a gay function, Napoleon stopped by Gertrude's for Carmen Miranda night. There at the bar was Howard, an old friend he hadn't seen in some time. Pleased to see him, Napoleon went up behind him and began scratching his back.

The man turned around and wasn't Howard. Embarrassed, Napoleon walked away, but when he turned back to look at the guy, the man didn't seem upset. He was kind of cute, in fact, and he seemed alone. Napoleon walked back and this time officially met Stanley.

Stanley Plaisance, born and raised in Westwego, on the Westbank of the Mississippi, had almost always known he was gay. It seemed so natural to him that he had a regular lover by his senior year in high school. But just as he graduated in 1968, his lover was killed in a car accident.

An introvert anyway, this added emotional burden kept Stanley from going out for quite a while. He spent most of his time at work, as a cashier and then assistant head cashier, at B & C Supermarket on Airline highway from 7:00 a.m. to 7:00 p.m., but eventually he started going to the Quarter bars, which was how he met Napoleon.

He really liked Napoleon, but there was a problem. Stanley was down to earth and not morally offended by Napoleon's hustling, but it still did present some difficulties. The largest was that it seemed to keep Napoleon from becoming attached to any one person. When the two started dating, all of Napoleon's friends got together to make a pool, each picking a different date as to how long the relationship would last. The winner would take the money from the pool.

But the furthest date was three weeks away, and four weeks later, the two were still together. And four weeks after that. And four weeks after *that*. It was getting serious, and Napoleon found himself picking up fewer and fewer johns. He even decided to try finding a job as a welder. And did.

Stanley had been to the UpStairs a couple of times before meeting Napoleon, but now they both went together regularly, and Stanley quickly became friends with many of the others. He always sat with Adam if he could. Poor Adam couldn't hold his alcohol very well, getting drunk after just three beers, but he was still good company.

It was Stanley, rather, who got into real trouble with alcohol one evening. Buddy and Adam had invited Napoleon and Stanley over for dinner, but Napoleon had to work, so Stanley went alone. And Mike Wolf came, too. There was red wine with dinner, and Stanley became too drunk to think clearly. Mike began making advances and was about to succeed in making a conquest, but Adam wouldn't have it.

"He's Napoleon's lover and he's drunk," Adam said pointedly. "Leave him alone." Mike didn't convince easily, so Adam took Stanley to another room, made him lie down, and closed the door against any unwanted guests. Stanley's honor was preserved for the evening.

Stanley was grateful and liked Adam even more after that. He also liked Mitch, whose dog, Pooky, fathered his and Napoleon's puppies. Mitch and Horace lived almost right across the street from them on Polymnia, and Horace was okay, too, but he knew one way sure to make Stanley furious and used it far too frequently.

One evening after Napoleon and Stanley walked into the UpStairs, Stanley overheard Horace say, "God! Who cut Napoleon's hair? It looks like fucking shit!"

Stanley went over to him and said, "If Napoleon ever comes to you to have his hair cut, that's the day I'll shave Napoleon's head bald." Horace always seemed to criticize other people's hair, and it never failed to get Stanley pissed. If they talked of something else, though, things were okay between them.

Bill Bailey and Clarence McCloskey were two others Stanley liked/didn't like. They were nice enough guys overall, but every once in a while they'd try to cause trouble. Bill would go to Napoleon and say, "Did you hear what Stanley did?" and Clarence would go to Stanley and say, "Did you hear what Napoleon did?" They finally accepted that the other couple just liked to gossip, and after they stopped taking it seriously, things went more smoothly.

For the Fourth of July in 1972, the UpStairs crew decided to prepare months in advance by giving out a ticket with each drink purchased. Then on the day of the drawing, they'd call out several of the numbers and give out free drinks. Napoleon would ask those he knew didn't come often or people from out of town if they wanted to keep their tickets. They let him keep them, and with others helping by shouting periodically, "Napoleon's collecting tickets!" he'd sometimes go home with forty or fifty tickets a night.

As the holiday approached, he put all the tickets in numerical order and wrote out a list, and on the day of the drawing, he was ready with 2500 to 3000 possible winning numbers. The first number called wasn't his, and neither was the second number. But the third was, and the fourth, and he kept his friends in free drinks the rest of the afternoon. The Fourth was also the day of the tricycle race, and Napoleon won the $25 bar tab.

And he soon used it. So of course Napoleon and Stanley also knew bartender Wayne and his lover Lonnie. Wayne didn't particularly look Native American, despite his black hair, but when the couple left to raise pigs in Alaska on the two or three hundred acres he received for being one-quarter Indian, Napoleon could then see the features. Napoleon himself was 1/32 Cherokee but being predominantly Caucasian had no typical Native American features and wished he had. Heck, all three of his girls were even blondes.

Wayne's departure was a good opportunity for Napoleon, however. Clearly, Phil needed to hire another bartender. "Phil," Napoleon asked, "could I have the job?"

"Are you out of your fucking mind?" Phil asked in return. "You're the last son of a bitch I'd ever let work in here. You'd drink all my profits away."

But Phil saw the change in Napoleon since he'd been with Stanley and did hire him to work Fridays, Saturdays, and Sundays, and things seemed to work out fine. There was that one time, however. Napoleon knew Phil was planning to go to a Mardi Gras ball and offered to come in early, around 5:00, to give Phil time to go home and get ready. Phil agreed, but Napoleon stopped off at Wanda's on the way and was drunk by the time he showed up.

Phil was mad but already set on leaving, so he decided to chance it. "*No* booze!" he ordered, and Napoleon complied. As the hours passed, however, he began sobering up with a hangover. He felt absolutely awful by 1:00 when Phil returned.

"You look good," said Phil, impressed by the sobriety.

"I feel terrible."

"Okay, you can have one drink."

"Make it a double."

Napoleon and Stanley went to the bars together, certainly, as part of their dating and courtship, but they also went to the movies together, and as they became closer, they went hunting and fishing with Stanley's brothers on the Westbank. Stanley was still working six days a week, for $125 a week, at the supermarket in Kenner, so there wasn't a lot of free time, but enough for them to realize they were falling in love.

When they could manage it, they took off for the Gulf coast for a night at the beach, but whatever they did, they just enjoyed being together. And the shy Stanley found himself opening up more and more.

The couple also came to know "Marriott" Dave, the piano player. Buddy had a gallon bucket in which he saved pennies, and since everyone knew Dave always drank sangria, one day the group got together and filled the gallon goblet with several bottles of Dave's favorite drink and put it on the piano. He did drink a lot of it before finishing that evening.

They also knew Mother Cross, who started the beer bust ritual of singing, "United We Stand." And they of course knew the Warrens, "the rectum mother and her two asshole sons." There was just something irritating about that family. At one beer bust, they were even thrown out. Buddy liked to create some variety at the busts and sometimes arranged the tables to make an S shape or a U horseshoe shape. On the horseshoe evening, Inez stood up to claim a pitcher of beer she hadn't paid for. Then her two sons stood up to defend her claim. And then thirty others in the room stood up to testify against them. Buddy, tired of their attitude, handed them their deposit and told them to leave.

At another beer bust, Napoleon was faced with more serious trouble. A short guy, about five feet tall, came in, and when he wasn't served quickly enough became enraged, lifting up the bar on the Chartres end, ripping it from the floor and then storming out, yelling, "Fuck all of y'all."

Buddy called out to Napoleon, "Go after him."

"Are you crazy?" returned Napoleon. "I'm not messing with anyone who can do that."

But he did follow him, saw which bar he went to next, Gertrude's, and called the police, who picked him up there.

Meanwhile, the months wore on, and Napoleon and Stanley were still together. People finally began accepting it. Phil Esteve, though, did occasionally tell Stanley jokingly, "If you ever need to throw Napoleon in the doghouse, feel free to toss him under my piano."

After six months working in the bar, almost ten months after they first met, Napoleon thought they ought to try something different with their lives. At the end of March 1973, just after Mardi Gras, they thanked Phil for all the good times and moved to Durham, North Carolina, to work for Manpower, hanging sheetrock, hauling asphalt, taking care of animals for Burroughs Wellcome research, moving furniture, working as operators for the phone company, and whatever else they were assigned to do.

And as June came and their anniversary approached, they remembered fondly all the fun they'd had together with each other and with their friends at the UpStairs Lounge.

Then, on June 25 when they saw the headlines, they pulled out a batch of old photographs and started trying to find out who was still alive.

Donald Dunbar

Twenty-one-year-old Donald Walter Dunbar listed 212 Cedar Avenue, Tampa, Florida, as his last address. Born to Warren Sr. and Beatrice McKuen Dunbar on Valentine's Day in 1952, Donald was presently working as a carpet cleaner. He'd graduated from the Custer Job Corps Center in Battle Creek, Michigan, before moving to New Orleans. Donald received 2nd degree burns on his face and hands and died of carbon monoxide asphyxia.

Howard Johnson's, Rault Center, and UpStairs Fires

At about 7:50 p.m. on June 24, 1973, Mrs. Katherine Kirsch left her apartment to get her husband a milkshake and some cigarettes. Walking down the street at approximately 7:53, she heard another woman say, "Look, there's a fire over there." Katherine turned and saw the second and third steps of the UpStairs on fire. She walked immediately to the Midship bar a few feet away and announced in the doorway, "Someone call the fire department. There's a fire next door." No one seemed to believe her, and four men sauntered out to look for themselves. Katherine went in and made the call herself. When she went back outside, the fire already reached almost to the top of the stairwell.

The fire department received a call at 7:56. The fire station at 317 Decatur was the headquarters for the city and just two and a half blocks from the UpStairs. Decatur is only one street away from Chartres, and from the corner of Decatur and Iberville, the fire station is one and a half blocks further down the street, just past Bienville. Because of one-way streets, however, the actual route was four and a half blocks, but that's still an insignificant distance.

It took roughly two minutes for the crew at the station to respond and reach the scene. The bar was already fully involved when they arrived by 7:58 or 7:59, and so four more alarms were sent. Twenty-one pieces of equipment, including thirteen engine companies and four ladder companies, were at the scene, and 87 firefighters battled the fire, which was then fully extinguished by 8:14.

7:53 to 8:14. Twenty-one minutes. But the twenty-eight men and one woman who died inside the bar were already dead or severely burned by the time the first trucks arrived on the scene by 7:59, so the real destruction was done in the space of a few minutes. Even the time of 7:53 is only approximate. The first verified time is 7:56, when the call was received, and the fire was reported surely in its first seconds of existence since only two steps were on fire when first seen. When the call was finished, the fire door at the top of the stairs still had apparently not been opened yet. The fire simply could not have been reported any faster or responded to any more quickly.

But that stairwell, with a small, open window at the top, acted as a chimney, funneling all the heat and fumes right at the door, so when it was finally opened, the blast just flew into the bar.

Combustible wood paneling, carpeting, and fabric along the ceiling to cover pipes provided the fuel in the stairwell. A lighter fluid can was also found on the stairs.

The first step at the bottom of the stairs was concrete, but the others wooden. The fire started on the second step, at the bottom of the staircase. It was fully raging by the time Luther Boggs opened the door, and patrons certainly had not been listening to the buzzing for several minutes before finally responding, so it would seem likely that any short which might have caused the buzzing occurred after the fire was well on its way up the stairs. Though the classification made on the coroner's reports was "Accidental—Fire Fatality," the investigators finally concluded that the fire was indeed deliberately set.

Inside the bar, there was a rayon fiber-flocked wallpaper on plaster-and-wood-lath walls. There were glass fiber ceiling tiles which were suspended underneath a plaster-and-wire-lath ceiling. The floor was wood, and carpet was cemented to the floor. The carpet was 5/32 of an inch thick and made of polyvinyl chloride and cellulose fibers, felted together in four layers, the carpet having a flame index of 535, which put the carpet, the same as that in the stairwell, within the Class E flame spread classification. The cocktail bar was made of wood, as were the window frames. The barstools were padded, and there were plastic tablecloths on the tables.

There were two illuminated exit signs in the bar, one over the main exit, which was of course unusable during the fire, and the other over the second fire door which led from the second room into the third room of the bar. The four available windows in the first room were nine feet high and forty-two inches wide. Since the windowsills were only a few inches above the floor, the building's previous owners had at some time before the UpStairs opened installed three metal rods across the lower portion of each window except for the one leading to the fire escape.

The most persistent misinformation about the UpStairs Lounge was that there were burglar bars on the windows. There weren't. No one gets through burglar bars. No amount of squeezing will force a skull between them.

There were fourteen inches between the windowsill and the first rod, and ten inches between the next two rods. In addition, there were wooden shutters which closed over the lower portion of the windows, just enough obstacles to create a delay that considerably slowed down the exit of the customers. None of these devices completely blocked the windows. Ten inches is a tight squeeze but not impossible. Fourteen inches is even better.

But for those too large, it was still possible to go over the rods, since the window raised up well above the three-foot level where the rods ended. And the rods themselves could be easily knocked out, as Buddy Rasmussen demonstrated to a fire department official. Perhaps the panicked customers never considered the possibility and so didn't even try to remove the bars.

Even with the rods in place, though, people could get through the windows. The problem was simply that going over or through the rods took extra seconds, and in a flash fire, there were no seconds to spare. Even with the windows completely unobstructed, it's quite possible that many of the patrons at the Chartres end of the bar would still not have had time to escape.

We know that several at the other end of the bar died within feet of a totally unobstructed window. The combination of the obstructions in the windows, the flash fire, and the number of people trying to escape created a situation that was hopeless.

In all of New Orleans in 1973, there were 2,128 fires, including that at the UpStairs. 100 of these fires extended to adjoining buildings, and ten of those extended even beyond that. During that year, there were 473 injuries to firefighters, and a total of forty-nine people fatally burned in fires. To compare this number with the totals of fire fatalities from previous years shows the impact of the UpStairs fire.

1964—24 fire fatalities

1965—10

1966—20

1967—22

1968—28

1969—12

1970—20

1971—29

1972—17

1973—49

More people were killed at the UpStairs Lounge in one day than were killed in any entire year for at least the previous nine years. Of those forty-nine killed, forty-two were male and seven female. Forty-four were burned, four died of asphyxiation, and one died from injuries suffered in escaping. In the category called "trapped by rapid spread of fire" was the telling number—thirty-nine.

New Orleans has a history of major fires, with the French Quarter being almost totally obliterated more than once. In 1990, the Louisiana State Museum displayed an exhibit noting all the major fires in the city's history, but the UpStairs wasn't included, though as far as can be determined from historical records, more people died in that fire than in the fires which swept through the Quarter in earlier centuries. In 1998, however, the Louisiana State Museum provided an exhibit at the old U.S. Mint in remembrance of the 25th anniversary of the UpStairs tragedy.

The period just prior to the UpStairs fire was a particularly grim time for New Orleans. On November 29, 1972, an arsonist set a fire in a downtown high-rise, the Rault Center. Dozens of people cowered on the roof as helicopters battled updrafts while trying to rescue those trapped. Two men died of smoke inhalation.

The most terrifying episode, however, was captured on live television. Most of the city watched in horror as five women, trapped in a beauty parlor on the 16th floor, screamed for help from their window. Flames blocked their exit into the hall and up to the roof. As they stood at the window and begged for help, flames entered the room.

The women, in desperation, tried to lower one of their group to the floor below. The dangling woman kicked at the window but was unable to break it. She kicked again, and her shoe fell off. The other women, no longer able to hold her, watched as she slipped from their hands and fell to the concrete below. Then the other women, one by one, with their only alternative a fiery death, each followed the other woman out the window, bouncing against the side of the building until crashing to the pavement with the others.

One woman, Natalie Smith, miraculously survived.

Most of New Orleans became part of this fire as they watched it happen. There was an incredible sense of frustration and helplessness as people watched the trapped women die. For years, one could walk up to people in New Orleans and say, "Rault Center," and the almost immediate response was, "Oh, God, those women." Not, "Oh, yeah, I remember that," but, "Oh, God." For a long while that sense of horror made this a personal experience for many in the city, including undoubtedly many of the customers at the UpStairs.

Only a couple of months after the Rault Center fire, there was another major fire in New Orleans, this one at the Downtown Howard Johnson's (later a Holiday Inn). The fire itself might have killed no one, but several people did die, because the arsonist also became a sniper.

Mark Essex was disturbed by the prejudice and abuse he received in the military. After killing a couple in their hotel room, he set the fire, and when firefighters arrived, he began shooting at them, too, eventually going to the roof and shooting more people in the street below. After several hours, Essex himself was also finally killed. Fewer people remember this fire, but certain stories, such as the firefighter fleeing Essex by jumping into an elevator shaft, sliding down the cable and ripping the flesh from his fingers, remained vivid even years later.

Both the Rault Center and the Howard Johnson's fires occurred mere blocks from the corner of Iberville and Chartres. Then, only five months after the latest tragedy, the UpStairs burned, leaving the city with a new set of catastrophic, unwanted memories.

Suzanne Joslyn

Suzanne Joslyn was eight years old when she came down with chicken pox at her home in Hartford, Connecticut. She was furious at the little dots all over her body. How *dare* they come now? Not now, when the Barnum and Bailey Circus was in town! It was July 6, 1944. She'd been fine for the July 4th celebrations and knew she shouldn't complain too much. But this was the *circus*. She'd looked forward to it for so long. Maybe she'd sneak out of the house. No, that wouldn't be fair to the other kids who'd get sick. But then, kids were *supposed* to get chicken pox.

Suzanne sat in her room, looking glumly out the window as she fantasized about miraculously getting well in time to join the other neighborhood children she saw trotting off to the circus. Hours later, two of her neighborhood playmates would be among the 168 killed in the big top fire.

Narrowly escaping tragedy did nothing to dampen Suzanne's natural exuberance toward life, and she played as hard as ever over the following years. It was a couple of years later when the young girl first heard the word "homosexual" and asked her mother what it meant. "It's when someone loves someone of the same sex," her mother explained in a solemn tone.

"Oh," Suzanne replied easily. It sounded okay to her. She would joke years later with friends about what she'd say when she met her first Martian, purple and with six arms waving about. She'd say, "What kind of plants do you have over there?" She just didn't understand how people could be upset over the color of someone's skin or who they loved. People were people, as far as she was concerned.

She was so easygoing, in fact, that while she was living in Greenwich Village in New York, when she met an eighteen-year-old runaway named Phyllis, she took the young woman in instantly, knowing nothing of her background. Just how little she really did know became apparent when Phyllis received her first letter at Suzanne's address six months later. When Suzanne saw the envelope, she realized she was learning Phyllis's last name for the first time. That just hadn't seemed important enough to ask before.

Suzanne loved painting with oils, having decided at the age of five she wanted to be an artist. The problem was that she liked to paint things life-size, and throughout her life, no one wanted to buy her huge paintings. She didn't really care, though. Whenever she could afford the materials, she'd paint, and then she'd hang the paintings in her apartment. At least *someone* appreciated them.

According to Susan Finch, Suzanne studied art at San Francisco State College, at Yale, and at the Berlin Art Academy. In 1960, Suzanne married and soon gave birth to Annette Grefe, but after she divorced six years later, the German courts ruled that the American-born girl should live with her paternal grandmother in Germany.

Back in America, Suzanne lost contact when her ex-husband moved without leaving a forwarding address.

Suzanne would marry twice more, becoming first Suzanne Vogel and then Suzanne Fosberg, and bear another daughter, Mary Ellen Cohane. She'd think frequently about her lost daughter, hoping one day to see her again. Maybe in 1978, when the girl turned eighteen, she'd start looking for her mother.

In the meanwhile, Suzanne tried to live life to the fullest. She moved to New Orleans shortly after losing custody of her daughter and, according to Susan Finch, studied art at Newcomb College. She also took a job as housekeeper, saying, "You don't make a living as an artist unless you're Picasso." Suzanne began teaching art for the New Orleans Recreation Department in 1972, and she organized the Artists' Information Bureau.

Shortly after arriving in New Orleans in the mid-1960's, Suzanne also decided to try acting. While performing in *The Time of Our Lives* at the Gallery Circle Theatre, she met Tad Turner, with his turned up, waxed moustache. Tad was the stage manager, and he and Suzanne hit it off right away. Her role didn't begin until the second act, and since the place was an arena theater without a curtain, there was a blackout while the actors took their places. When the lights came up, she was supposed to lift a glass and drink. Often, actors used Coke or iced tea instead of alcohol, but when Tad asked Suzanne what she'd like to drink on stage, she mischievously replied, "Oh, anything ladylike."

Every night for the two weeks the show ran, Tad placed a different, elegant drink in a different glass on the table. In the dark, she had no idea what it was and didn't find out until she drank it in front of the audience. She expected real alcohol the last day of the performance, but the alcohol began five nights before closing and continued through the last show. The first time she drank the liquor on stage, she was so surprised she blew her lines. She was ready for him after that and simply looked forward to the different drinks. On closing night, Tad prepared a five-layer pousse café for her. Suzanne knew she wanted someone who could be so playful to be her friend.

She did become good friends with Tad and his longtime companion, Luther Boggs, having them over for dinner many times over the next several years. Tad also taught Suzanne directing and how to do lighting for the stage.

Suzanne did Greek plays, Shakespearian plays, and children's plays, performing at the Old Rep, in Audubon Park, at People Playhouse, at a library, at a youth center, or wherever. When Tad took her to the UpStairs Lounge, Suzanne remarked, "Oh, Tad, we should do *Lady Windemere's Fan* here in drag!" They laughed, but a month later, a stage was built in the third room of the bar and Bettye McAnear was directing their first nelly drama. Each play ran for a few months. Bettye directed a few and Suzanne directed a few as well.

When the nelly dramas were just starting, Buddy Rasmussen announced that anyone who wanted to be an understudy could sign up at the bar. Suzanne thought most of the players were pretty good, but there was an older man with a bit part who wasn't great, so Suzanne signed up. When the man was ill one evening, Suzanne borrowed her husband's suit, taped down her breasts, and stepped in. Speaking in her lowest voice and smoking a cigar, she tried to act as gruff and fearsome as possible. Tad, at least a foot taller, played the man's wife. To look a little more feminine, he put sequins in his moustache. "My dear," Tad's character complained during their scene, "we haven't had any fun in years."

"You forget," replied Suzanne's character. "We're married. We're not supposed to have fun."

Suzanne was working just around the corner from the bar, so she stopped in every day after work for Happy Hour, in addition to attending or participating in the plays. She also attended many of the beer busts, but she didn't feel compelled to make every single one. She loved the crowd at the UpStairs, finding them clever as they'd all joke back and forth, the whole gang getting involved in wordplays.

It was also a relief not to worry about men trying to pick her up. Oh, there was the one time a guy started coming on to her, thinking she was just in drag, but when Buddy said, "Careful, that's a real woman," the guy backed off quickly enough.

Suzanne liked Buddy's sense of humor. When one of the bartenders he'd hired would flirt with guys for a few days, then flirt with the female customers a few days, and then flirt with the guys again, Buddy finally told him, "Pick a team and stick with it." Just as there was plenty of confusion over the distinction between drag queens and trans women at the time, many gay men didn't believe bisexuality was real.

Suzanne didn't meet Buddy's lover, Adam, through Buddy, though. One day when she brought her husband, Ben Fosberg, to the bar, Ben recognized his old college roommate. Adam was mortified to have the man realize he was gay, but Suzanne felt glad to meet him. Adam, with his hair often falling over one eye, was a bit shy, but she could tell his eyes were expressive, and she looked forward to getting him to perform in some of her plays.

Ben didn't much like theatre or gay men and resented the amount of time Suzanne spent with both. She introduced him to photography and helped him set up a darkroom, hoping to keep him occupied with a hobby of his own. Before long, his theatre photographs were published in the *Times-Picayune.*

Suzanne was continually on the lookout for actors to perform in her plays, and she found many of them in gay bars. One time while looking to cast a small role for a psychiatrist, she noticed a middle-aged man who seemed just right. She walked over, complimented him on his beard and voice, and told him what she was looking for. The man laughed. "I *am* a psychiatrist," he said. He took the role and continued acting thereafter.

She met Bill Bradford at the UpStairs and had him work with her. And Courtney Craighead, who sometimes did her lighting, and Ralph Davis, who she asked to choreograph *The Tempest* for her while also playing the part of Ariel. Tad and Luther were both also cast in *The Tempest* as noblemen. Suzanne's idea was to have the nobles swish a lot, and figured a gay cast would already know how to do it.

Tad also played the lead when Suzanne directed *Salome.* Luther appeared as the king. Though offstage Luther had a wicked sense of humor and a droll delivery, on stage he seemed to have a wooden face and make stiff gestures. He wasn't a great actor, but he was reliable, so Suzanne tried to compensate a little for his lack of expression by costuming him with a big hat that had fringe dangling down, casting drifting shadows across his face. In the right light, it might look like he was acting.

Suzanne finally managed to get Adam to act in her plays. He insisted on small roles and only performing when there were others on stage to take over if he forgot his lines, but with his remarkable memory, he was rehearsing without the script long before the other cast members, and Suzanne began giving him larger roles. He was good not only in classic plays but also in children's plays, and he also was just a nice guy to have around, giving Suzanne a sweet, sincere compliment on the score she'd written for one of her children's plays.

But then one day while Adam was alone on stage, about to give the speech on tragedy in Anouilh's *Antigone,* he froze and forgot his lines, with no one to cover for him and no way to prompt him without the audience knowing. So the other cast members came on early and turned the monologue into a conversation. Adam felt terrible about letting everyone down, but the others hugged him and comforted him. "The audience never knew," they told him. "We covered for you. We're here together. It happens to every actor once—it's happened to all of us. Don't be sad—you'll go out tomorrow night and be brilliant." And he did go back out and perform again.

Adam and Luther were both in Suzanne's production of *Much Ado about Nothing* in 1973. She gave trial performances of her plays, children's plays as well as Shakespeare, at the UpStairs. Suzanne found that the fun-loving crowd there was also literate enough to get all the jokes, laughing in all the right places during the performance of a Shakespearian play, and giving the cast such positive feedback that it got them off to a good start.

During one performance, a man who was playing the leading lady brought his small dog to hold in an early scene. The dog was to be kept backstage during the second act, but it broke loose and wandered out on stage, looking for its master. With a quick swoop, Suzanne picked up the dog and held it out to the audience, saying, "Out, damn Spot!" The audience howled.

So life went on, usually fun, with Suzanne working as a bartender at Bonaparte's Retreat, where Luther also did some part-time work as a landscape gardener, partly paying his rent since the bar owner, Victoria, was also his landlady. Suzanne joked with him when they met there or elsewhere, but she did sometimes go out with a female friend, Nila Lytrell, not only hanging out with gay friends. Suzanne would tap dance on bars or grab someone to Apache dance with, do anything that sounded fun and crazy. And she and Nila both often went to the UpStairs. Suzanne fit in so well at the bar that she was even voted "honorary lady faggot of the year."

But Ben simply didn't like the same things Suzanne did, and they separated in December of 1972. With three failed marriages and having lost custody and even track of one daughter, it was impossible not to feel something was wrong with her. But was it wrong to enjoy life? That simple thing seemed to drive other people crazy. But how could she give up living? She wasn't sure there was really any point to life, but if there was, it had to be that we make the most of it while we were here.

Tad was a major support during her divorce, helping her get through it reasonably well. Tad was always a support not only to her but to all his friends, she noted, remembering also how he helped another friend of his who'd been arrested on Halloween for stepping out of a Bourbon Street bar in drag.

So life wasn't perfect for Suzanne or for her circle of friends, but for the most part, things were going okay. In June of 1973, Suzanne had a male lover, one who liked theatre a little more than Ben had, and who didn't seem as uncomfortable around gays as Ben had been.

In fact, on June 24th, Suzanne and her lover arranged to meet and head on to the UpStairs together for the evening. Since Luther, Tad, Adam, and Nila would be there, too, she was sure to have a good time. And maybe she'd find a new cast member for her next play as well. She smiled into her bathroom mirror and put on the finishing touches of her make-up.

Adam Fontenot

In the small Cajun community of Ville Platte, in southern Louisiana, sharecropper Dillard Fontenot and his wife Mary had their first child, Adam Roland Fontenot, on January 13, 1941. Neither Dillard nor Mary could read or write. Mary spoke only a little English, enough so she could "defend herself" or get by, and Dillard spoke only a few words of English in addition to his native Cajun French.

Dillard, an outgoing man, raised cotton and corn, plus enough vegetables for Mary, a quiet woman, to can for the winter. They had a couple of cows, so there was milk for the family. Their place had no well, but they did have a cistern, though sometimes they'd have to pour the water through a strainer to take the worms out.

Roland spent his first six years without books of any kind. He had routine childhood diseases such as measles and chicken pox, but when he was six, he had an appendectomy and a tonsillectomy. The illnesses, operations, and recovery kept him out of school for four months.

But Dillard finally brought Roland into town. The boy's teacher told Dillard she'd take him to class, but he should understand that Roland was so far behind there was no way she'd be able to pass him to the second grade. Dillard understood and accepted that. He just wanted his boy in school.

A month later, the teacher sent a note home with Roland, a note his parents had to ask him to read to them. "Please don't let Roland open a book at home. He's caught up and passed all the other children in the class."

Roland did like to read, now that he knew how, but that wasn't all he'd do. As a young child, he liked to play with the chickens, naming them such things as "Mr. Rooster" and "Mrs. Chicken." He played with his cousin Rose, who was five years older than he was, and he played with his younger sister, Patricia. When he was a little older, he played football with his cousins, but it was true that his most enjoyable pastime was reading. By junior high, he was reading the newspaper daily.

At Ville Platte High School, Roland excelled in every subject, so much so, in fact, that when Patricia came through a few years after him, all the teachers expected the same from her. Patricia was intelligent herself and a straight A student, but she was not the genius her brother seemed to be, and she was not always happy to follow in his footsteps.

In the 10th grade, Roland began working at KVPI as a disk jockey, playing soft music, which was his favorite. At school, he also learned to play the clarinet. He worked at the radio station throughout high school. Then, having earned a scholarship to college, he studied at a Louisiana university as well as Vanderbilt in Tennessee. He studied Spanish on his own and so was able to study as an exchange student in Mexico, where he was able to polish his Spanish even more.

Fascinated with languages, Roland eventually became fluent in seven, including his native Cajun French, English, Spanish, Italian, Portuguese, German, and Russian, getting

Master's degrees in a few of these. He was a speed reader with a photographic memory, and his mother called him "the bookworm" since he always seemed to have his head in a book.

Apparently, there was a gene for intelligence in the family. In addition to Roland's gifts and Patricia's straight A's, there was first cousin Jimmy Fontenot, who became a lawyer in Abbeville, and there was first cousin Sue Fontenot, a lawyer who became a judge in Acadian Parish.

However, something else seemed to run in the family, too. One of Roland's cousins was gay, another was suspected of being gay before he committed suicide, and another cousin was transgender. Roland himself eventually realized he was gay like a couple of his cousins, but it was not something that pleased him.

And there was yet one more family trait. Alcoholism. Many of his relatives had a problem with alcohol. When Roland started to go out, he wasn't aware of any genetic predisposition toward alcoholism and so had no real reason not to drink, and being a progressive disease, the alcoholism took a while to develop.

Roland intended to teach after finishing college, and he did teach at Vanderbilt briefly. He didn't like it as he'd hoped, however, finding that the students didn't respond well to him, often ridiculing him, perhaps because of his slight effeminacy, or perhaps because of his unpracticed teaching abilities.

He moved to New Orleans around 1965, moving in with his cousin Rose for a couple of months, sharing her trailer in

Mereaux, near Chalmette. She tried to get him a job at the nearby Tenneco Oil refinery, but he was told he was too educated. He eventually found a job and moved out, but he never seemed able to stay with a job too long, either because he felt stifled if the job wasn't challenging enough, or later because of his developing alcoholism.

Roland visited his parents often, feeling close to both. They didn't fully understand their son, either his homosexuality or his genius, but they were proud of him for his accomplishments. When he wasn't around, there'd be talk such as, "Hey, you know he's living with a known homosexual?" but when Roland was around, the conversation would be on less touchy subjects. When he'd visit them, they'd speak Cajun, and Roland would sit on the porch in the rocking chair, rocking for hours. His family made sure the chair was in good rocking order if they knew he was coming for a visit.

Dillard eventually changed jobs, working now cleaning huge storage tanks. Toxic gases collected in one of them, and when a cousin was trapped inside, Dillard went in to rescue him. Both men, along with a couple of other rescuers, died.

Roland was deeply affected by his father's death, which helped his alcoholism develop further. Roland wasn't continually drinking, of course, and regularly visited his mother for a few days or a week at a time as they both learned to adapt to life without Dillard. Mary was able in time to fall in love again and remarry.

Roland met Buddy Rasmussen in late 1969, while Roland was a ticket agent for Greyhound. Because of his photographic memory, Roland could remember not only all the information on a page in a book but the page number as well. When customers asked at the Greyhound station, "Are you sure about that price?" Roland would answer, "*Of course I'm sure.*" For Roland, having a photographic memory was as natural as seeing or hearing was for most people. It was difficult for him to understand why it took so long for other people to learn things, and he found he had little patience to wait for them.

Roland and Buddy soon became lovers, buying a home on St. Andrew near the St. Thomas projects. About a year after they married, Buddy began working at the UpStairs Lounge. Having a bartender for a husband wasn't the healthiest thing for Roland, whom Buddy and most of the others at the bar called by his first name, Adam. Though almost everyone felt that Adam was nice and sweet, the continual drinking began to get on Buddy's nerves. Still, Adam hadn't yet hit "rock bottom" and wasn't willing to take the steps necessary to start recovery.

Adam confided to Buddy that he'd never learned to accept his homosexuality. He never told his family he was gay, though he brought Buddy to Ville Platte a couple of times and everyone knew. Being gay was also one of the reasons teaching had been so difficult. He'd be in front of the class and think, "It isn't right for a queer to be up here teaching these students."

Adam worked for tour buses for a while, but that didn't work out, either. Finally, Buddy asked Wayne, another bartender at the UpStairs, to have his lover Lonnie, who worked at the Petroleum Club, find Adam a job there at the private club for oil people. So when Wayne and Lonnie moved to Alaska, Lonnie arranged for Adam to work at the club. In addition to being a secretary, Adam also made menus, earning little more than minimum wage. In early 1973, one of his cousins, Matt Clark, Rose's son, ran into him on Baronne Street and reported back to his mother that Roland was wearing a nice jacket for the Petroleum Club and apparently doing well.

Adam knew that Buddy was becoming good friends with Bill, a regular at the bar. Adam was jealous, but there was little he could do. He knew Buddy was upset with him over the drinking, but he just didn't seem able to stop. Adam would stay at the bar until closing time, leaving with Buddy for breakfast together, but several times Adam was so drunk he threw up. Still, he and Buddy never argued or fought. Until one time when Buddy invited Bill to join them for dinner. That was going just a little too far.

When Adam was sober, he looked quite respectable and behaved in a nice, quiet manner. But things were getting worse. While he and Buddy had been together now almost four years, and Buddy had promised never to leave him, their relationship was becoming more and more strained as Adam's alcoholism progressed. He knew Buddy was wondering how much longer he'd be able to keep his job, and he wondered himself. The job was so far beneath him considering his abilities, but he didn't know how to make things better.

When he'd think about these things, he'd grow depressed, and depression was best dealt with by drinking. He'd been working earlier the afternoon of the 24th on a play that would be performed soon at the bar as a benefit for disabled children, and he needed to relax from that, too. That Sunday afternoon, Adam began drinking even before the beer bust.

He was quite drunk well before the bust was over, always pleasant even when drunk, enjoying the company of those around him, while also happy Bill never came to the beer busts. He listened to the singing around the piano and watched a few couples dancing. And he kept on drinking. He had a drink in his hand when the fire burst into the bar just before 8:00 that evening.

Ken Harrington

Born in West Covina, Florida, on January 7, 1925, Kenneth Paul Harrington was raised in Ocean City, New Jersey. His mother, Ada Spence, died early, but Ken was close to his sister and absolutely loved his father, William. Working as an usher in the Paramount theatre in New York, Ken lived near enough to visit his family often, which they all enjoyed.

However, one day when Ken was twenty-seven or twenty-eight, he met a man visiting from New Orleans. Frank Landry, who was from Prairieville, Louisiana, was a hair stylist at Maison Blanche on Canal Street on the edge of the French Quarter. Ken and Frank hit it off immediately, and soon Ken moved to New Orleans to be with the man he loved.

Ken found a job as a lab technician at the U.S. Department of Agriculture in the Milk Division at 3400 S. Carrollton. He liked his job and his coworkers liked him. Frank was also well liked at the beauty parlor. In the 1950's, the salon at Maison Blanche was where many Uptown society members came to have their hair done. The gang working there were mostly young and single and good friends having a great time together. In addition to the stylists, there were six attendants, in the cloak room or sweeping up hair that had fallen to the floor. Everyone seemed to like each other, which made the work fun.

One day, though, one of the women started screaming and shaking as her hair dryer began electrocuting her. Everyone else stood petrified, but Frank grabbed a towel and yanked the hair dryer out of the wall socket. He didn't think twice. If someone needed help, he helped.

Frank was religious in the sense that his God was important to him. He didn't know many of the answers, but living a good life was important. It was important to Ken, too, and was part of what drew them to each other. And it was what drew their many friends to them as well.

One of Frank's friends and coworkers was Roseland Revaldo, who was raised in the French Quarter. She'd gone to beauty school with Frank back in 1943 or 1944 and had been close to him over the next eight years when Frank was single. But Frank's marriage to Ken didn't seem to change him much. He was still friendly and maintained all his friendships. Ken just seemed to slide right into those friendships. People didn't put up with Ken because they liked Frank. Both men were well-liked by the others, and Ken seemed to fit right into several pre-existing friendships.

Ken and Frank were one of the first households in their group to buy a television, and since Roseland's only other opportunity to watch was to stand in front of a store window, Ken and Frank invited her over regularly to spend an evening watching the Texaco program and Milton Berle. Yes, she had to put up with that terribly boring western, too, but she also had the chance to spend the evening with some good friends.

They also socialized together at parties. Someone in their group was always hosting a dinner party, and everyone would visit each other regularly. Ken and Frank moved around a bit, living in a beautiful place Uptown on Napoleon Avenue for a time, then in Gentilly, and out on Hermes St. in New Orleans East. While there, Frank's father in Prairieville died, and he had his mother move in with him and Ken.

She eventually joined the parties as well. Frank had regularly visited his parents, Angel and Joseph, in Prairieville, enjoying his mother's chicken jambalaya, and they'd always seemed to accept the fact that Frank was with Ken.

Since Frank was an only child, they couldn't help but regret not having grandchildren, but Frank was impossible not to love, and so was Ken. Ken, who loved his own family as well, thought it perfectly natural to have Frank's mother move in. He still visited his own family when he could, but it was never often enough.

The years passed, the 1950's running into the 1960's, and the years continuing to fly by. The times always seemed good. Ken and Frank were always smiling, always happy, always making others laugh, and life went on. They traveled when they could, went to the opera at every opportunity, worked hard while at work, and went out with Roseland and other friends to different lounges when various performers would come to town.

They enjoyed hearing Dwight Fiske sing innocent songs in a naughty way, they enjoyed listening to the pianist at the Hotel Astor, and they enjoyed staying home with their cats who tore up their curtains. They enjoyed growing vegetables in their back yard, trying anything new that looked like it might be worth tasting.

They exchanged gifts with various friends. Roseland would give them wool sweaters or wool scarves or gloves, and they in turn would give her perfume or a nice pin. "When you die, I want to buy all your sweaters back," she joked once, only giving them sweaters she really thought were beautiful.

Then one day in the late 1960's, as Ken and Frank were traveling out of state, Frank suddenly began feeling ill. He was still young, in his forties, so it probably wasn't serious, but they decided to see a doctor then and not wait. The doctor told them that Frank was indeed very ill, that his kidneys were failing, and he'd better get right home.

As Frank lay in the hospital back in New Orleans, Ken smiled and joked and tried to make Frank's last days as pleasant as possible. But all too soon, after only a few weeks, Frank was dead.

It was a devastating blow. Ken and Frank had been together seventeen or eighteen years by this time. They'd had a wonderful life together. They loved each other.

Ken had his friends to help him through this period, of course. Roseland was there for him, as were the others.

But life would never be the same.

Still, though he and Frank had never been much for going to the bars, preferring Saturday evenings at this or that friend's house, he did start going out again.

He lived at 611 Dauphine Street in the Quarter for a while, and at 700 N. Rampart above Alice Brady's bar. Alice liked him, as did another lesbian friend, Charlene Schneider, who would one day have a bar of her own. Ken met with them often at Brady's to talk and drink coffee together.

On June 24th, according to Charlene, Ken, now forty-eight, went to the UpStairs with a friend of his, a young, attractive man who played piano in the back room at Brady's. Ken was wearing white jeans, a black belt with a gold buckle, sandals, a gold ring with several white stones on the ring finger of his left hand, a gold ring on his right ring finger, and a black and white checkered flannel shirt.

Roseland was at work only a few blocks from the UpStairs when she received the call the next day. "Ken was killed in the fire!" She stood there completely shocked, in disbelief. They'd been so close that she couldn't believe there wasn't some kind of psychic connection. How could he have been in trouble and she not sense it? Could it be true? Could her friend of over twenty years be dead? Just a few years after Frank had died, too?

Ken's body was indeed found in the bar. He received 2nd and 3rd degree burns over 35% of his body and died of carbon monoxide inhalation. Though the skin of his fingers was peeling away, it was intact enough for identification. However, after friends called Ken's sister, she came from New Jersey to personally identify the body. Though his face was blackened, it was still identifiable, and his sister was able to give a positive I.D. Then she brought his body back home with her.

Roseland, alone in her apartment, would take out a photo of Ken and Frank once in a while and remember. It was all she could do for them now. But she would do at least that much for them. She would remember them, and miss them, for the rest of her life.

June 24th

Buddy and Adam arrived at the UpStairs at noon on Sunday, June 24th. The bar wouldn't open for two hours yet, but Buddy had to total up the previous day's receipts, make a deposit at the bank, and clean up the bar. At 2:00, Buddy unlocked the gate downstairs and poured Adam a Bloody Mary.

They were alone at first, and Adam looked around as he sipped his drink and let Buddy work. There was a bulletin board on the left as one came into the bar, up above the jukebox. People put up announcements, fliers, business cards, whatever. Behind the bar, there were pictures of winners of the Mardi Gras and Halloween contests. Over the piano were oil paintings for sale.

Adam looked back at his drink, wishing they made bar stools with rockers.

Around 3:30, Lindy Laurell "Rusty" Quinton came into the bar. He lived next door to Buddy and Adam at 921 St. Andrew Street. Born on March 21, 1948, red-haired Rusty was twenty-five and worked full-time as a welder at Vic's Ornamental Iron Works at 1539 North Claiborne Avenue. He had lived in Houston for five years before coming to New Orleans, and his mother, Mrs. T. J. Quinton, still lived there on Bancroft Street. She worked for the phone company and had done so for as long as Rusty could remember, for twenty years anyway.

Rusty liked Buddy, and he liked the group at the UpStairs, so he'd asked if he could work part-time there, just to serve the beer bust two hours each week. Phil had hired him three weeks previously for $2 an hour. Rusty didn't need the few extra dollars, but he enjoyed the bar on Sunday evenings and liked having an additional reason for being there. Though he didn't need to be at work until just before 5:00, Rusty liked to get there early to chat with Buddy and Adam.

Richard Robert Cross was one of the next customers to arrive. Born on February 9, 1944, "Mother" Cross was twenty-nine. He was six feet tall and slim, weighing 145 pounds. "Mother" had brown hair and wore a brace on one leg. He'd been living in New Orleans for four or five years, having relocated from Miami Beach, though he was born in Chicago, where his father, Lloyd L. Cross, still lived. Ricky's mother, Anna, was dead. His father, on South Shore Drive, worked as a foreman in a steel mill. Ricky worked in retail.

"Mother" arrived at the UpStairs around 4:30 or 4:45 with his lover, Dean Morris. Dean, who was thirty-seven, had been in the service for several years. He'd lived in Ft. Worth, Texas, and had been in New Orleans about a year. He and Ricky lived at 1115 Burgundy, so the walk to the bar took them almost completely across the Quarter.

A few doors down the street from the UpStairs, at Gene's Hideaway, Rodger Nunez and Allen Guidry were talking, drinking, or shooting pool off and on all afternoon. When Allen left for a while, Rodger started talking with an "old man." The man, who was drinking heavily, bought Rodger a couple of drinks, and Rodger hoped to soon encourage the man to pay for sex.

Then Allen came back and joined the two. Somehow, Allen seemed to take over the situation, and before Rodger knew it, Allen and the old man had gone off for a quick trick. Rodger sat at the bar fuming, and when the two came back later, Rodger was still mad. He tried to get the old man to go with him to the UpStairs, but Gene Davis wouldn't let the old man leave.

"You're too drunk," Gene told him. "You'll fall down those stairs and break your neck." To keep him there, Gene refused to cash another of the man's checks unless he'd stay. But it wasn't a total loss for Rodger. The man did give him a $20 bill.

Back at the UpStairs, Buddy grabbed his hand mic and announced, "Here's J.C.!" as J.C. Carrier stepped into the bar.

J.C. came to the bar one or two times every week, always trying to make it for the beer bust. He liked going to the UpStairs because of its casual atmosphere. There wasn't nearly the sexual tension here that existed in some bars. Oh, sure, there was a little groping beneath the tables at times, but nothing major.

J.C. had first met Buddy one Mardi Gras at the UpStairs. They'd talked and quickly become friends, a friendship they continued both in and out of the bar. Looking about him now, J.C. could see Adam at the end of the bar, drinking heavily. J.C.'s friend, Sid Espinache, was there with his lover, Joe

Adams, who was a comptroller. Sid was fifty and Joe, whose full name was Joseph Henry Adams, Jr. was fifty-one, born on August 26, 1921. They both always dressed nicely, in dress slacks and starched shirts. They sure looked good together. Kip was also there, and so were Mitch and Horace, and Fred and Earl. And there were the Warrens, Inez and two of her sons.

And there was Luther Boggs, who was dressed nicely, as usual. Also as usual, he was smiling and joking, his large Adam's apple bobbing away and his deep voice carrying easily to his friends. Often, after the beer bust, J.C. would go home with Luther over at the Avenue Plaza on the upper floor, or Luther would go home with J.C. They'd talk for a while and fall asleep together, but there was never any sex between them. They just enjoyed each other's company, and who else did J.C. know who had a goldfish pond in his apartment?

J.C. was raised in a small town in Texas, but he moved to the city after high school, taking a part-time job and enrolling in business college. There was a naval base near the city, and the sailors passing by nearly drove him crazy, though it took him a while to figure out why.

It wasn't until he moved to New Orleans in 1962 that he first learned about gays. He was living in Kenner, just outside New Orleans, and went downtown with an uncle. As they walked past a particular bar, his uncle said, "Don't go in there. You'll get in trouble." J.C. wasn't quite sure what his uncle meant, but he found out shortly thereafter when he went to the Quarter by himself one Sunday, playing the tourist and walking around. It was a hot day, so J.C. popped into the bar to get a beer.

The bar was Lafitte's. As J.C. sipped his cool beer, he saw one man approach another, saying, "Oh, Mary! It's been so long since I've seen you!" and then the two men hugged. This must be one of *those* bars, J.C. realized.

Still, J.C. felt too awkward to come back. He continued with his job managing an estate but kept putting off dealing with his homosexuality. J.C. worked hard to maintain a straight appearance so that people wouldn't suspect him.

One man saw past the shield, however. J.C. had to redo the bedroom of a woman at the estate, so he hired an interior decorator. One freezing, cold day, the man arrived, and after the man had finished his work for the day, J.C. decided to do something nice before sending the guy back out into the freezing weather.

"Would you like to stop by my place for a few minutes?" J.C. asked. "I'll fix you a drink."

The man went home with him and had a drink. J.C. had hurt his knee recently and was wearing an ace bandage. He slipped into some shorts so he could work on the bandage, but then the decorator offered to rub his knee for him. J.C. was still too naive to suspect anything, but after the man rubbed his knee for a while, the man began to rub higher and higher on his leg.

He stayed the night. This was the first gay person J.C. had ever really met, and through him, J.C. was able to meet other gay men, so soon a new world was opened to him.

Tonight, as J.C. sat at the bar, he noticed a cute guy sitting nearby. J.C. had never picked anyone up, and he'd never gone off with any stranger, either. He did like to go to the bars, however, and he thought one day he might go home with someone. Maybe this was the day.

Jean Gosnell arrived at the beer bust a little later than usual. She'd had an appointment at her office Sunday afternoon, but she'd told Luther she'd meet him at the UpStairs when she was finished. Her client dropped her off at 6:00, and she joined Luther upstairs near the jukebox. They sat at the curve of the bar near the bathroom. Jean drank a tequila, but then remembering that Buddy made good Margaritas, she had those for her next two drinks. She wasn't there for the beer bust but for the company.

Frank Thomas Gaalema, a self-employed display freelancer, arrived at about 5:45. He was twenty-nine, born on November 5, 1943, and lived at 3028 St. Joseph Street. From Indianapolis, he'd been in New Orleans seven years. King of the Apollo krewe, he hoped to run into his friend Skip Getchell tonight.

Edwin J. Engeron had come into town this evening from Baton Rouge. He joined his friend Richard Travis, and then they went on to the UpStairs. They stayed a while but left by about 7:25. Nineteen-year-old Robert Thomas Price arrived around 6:00. When asked by someone he was first meeting what he did for a living, he would often reply, "Just about any kind of work I can find." He lived a block away from the UpStairs, at the Savoy hotel on Royal Street.

Kenneth Charles Kirkwood, thirty years old, who lived at 2501 Metairie Lawn, Apartment G-107, went to the

UpStairs once or twice a week, driving in from Metairie. He arrived around 6:15 on the 24th and talked with his friends, Mitch, Horace, Bill Larson, and Ricky Everett, for a while. A few minutes before the beer bust ended, Kenneth left and headed for Lafitte's.

Some of the others who came that evening were Adolph Medina, who lived at 1037 Esplanade and worked for a wig shop on Carondelet; Jessie Baker, twenty-eight, of 4031 Rye Street, Apartment E, a beautician with long blond hair; Philip Byrd, who lived at 915 Dauphine; Francis Dufrene. who lived at 307 VFW Boulevard in Harahan; Roger Dale Dunn, who lived at 2434 General Collins Street in Algiers; Jim Peterson, thirty-one, who lived at 1421 Polymnia Street; and Frank Dean, thirty-four, who had served in the military fourteen years and lived at 1373 Magazine, at the MCC building.

Michael Scarborough and Glenn Green arrived at the UpStairs around 4:45. Michael particularly enjoyed the beer bust because the only alcohol he ever drank was beer. He was sitting with Glenn, talking to him and their friends, Sid and Joe, Dean, Ricky, Frank, and others, when he inadvertently became the catalyst that set off the unstable Rodger Nunez.

Rodger had come over to the bar with Allen, but after Allen left, Rodger locked himself in a bathroom stall for a long while and kept peeking through a hole at the guys using the urinal. Michael apparently said something to him because when Rodger finally came out of the bathroom shortly before the beer bust ended (witnesses give widely varying times for this fight, from an hour and a half before the fire down to five or even just three minutes), perhaps 6:45 or 6:50, he went over to Michael and Glenn's table and started smart mouthing them.

Michael stood up and almost unconsciously curled his fingers into a fist. Before he knew it, he'd struck the stranger on the jaw and knocked him to the floor.

Lying there, raised on one elbow and rubbing his jaw, Rodger looked directly into Michael's eyes. "I'm going to burn you all out!" he said coldly.

Buddy came over with Hugh Cooley then, and Hugh picked Rodger up by his belt and stood him up on the landing just outside the door. Rodger still wanted to smart-mouth, so Hugh dragged him all the way down the stairs and put him out on the sidewalk.

"Freak," Michael muttered.

"Come on, let's forget about it," Glenn told him.

"Well, Sid," said Michael, trying to smile. "You're a trouble consultant at Sears. How come you couldn't take care of that?" They laughed, and then the friends began talking again as they had before they'd been interrupted.

J.C. used the fight as a reason to motion to the man he'd been cruising. They both stood and moved into the second room, passing under the archway covered with decorations for the upcoming Fourth of July. J.C. usually stayed in the main bar, but he'd said hi to his friends, and there was no more need for distractions. Besides, there were only three tables in the front room but several in the second, so it was easier to find a place to sit. The two men sat next to each other and finally began talking.

Nothing too serious at first. J.C. told the guy where he was from, and the other guy in turn told him of his hometown, Morgan City, an oil town along the Louisiana coast. As they continued chatting, J.C. also thought about how he usually had a sure ride home each Sunday with his friend, David Jones, if he didn't go home with Luther. Tonight, though, David could only drop J.C. off at the bar because he had to go on to a meeting of his carnival club. The two usually arrived long before the bust and stayed long after, but now maybe J.C. could go home with this young man.

A group around the piano held hands as the beer bust ended a few moments later and sang, "United We Stand." Michael went to get a last refill on the beer, and he, Glenn, Joe, and Sid decided to go on to Burgundy House when they finished this last mug. They were in no hurry, though, talking and joking with others as they slowly sipped their beer.

"Hey, Buddy," said Rusty shortly after the beer bust ended. "There's a guy over there who keeps bothering the customers." Rusty pointed out David DuBose, an eighteen-year-old with blond hair hanging down below his ears. David operated some of the kiddie rides at Ponchartrain Beach.

Rusty had seen David deliberately fill his sixteen-ounce beer mug to the brim a couple of times during the beer bust and then purposely spill some on the carpet. He punched some of the customers, pretending to be playful, and he kicked some of them, too. David came up to Rusty once during the beer bust and said, "Man, I'm stoned." But Rusty was too busy during the bust to do anything about the guy.

When the bust was over, David went about, looking for untended beer mugs, and cashing each one in for fifty cents.

After Rusty pointed him out, Buddy went up to him. "I think you should leave now," Buddy said calmly but firmly.

"I want my deposit back."

"You're turning in other people's mugs. I think you should leave."

"Who are you? The FBI? Here's a mug. Now give me my deposit."

Buddy's patience was wearing, and clearly there was no nice way to deal with this guy. He pointed to the door and said in his sternest voice, "Get out of here and don't ever come back."

David made an ugly face, but he did turn around and leave, taking an empty beer mug with him. When he reached the street entrance, he threw it on the ground, shattering it at the bottom of the stairs.

"Hugh," Buddy said, "could you go sweep that up before someone gets hurt?"

Hugh, who'd arrived at 4:30, wasn't officially on duty yet, but that didn't matter. Hugh was there and willing, and so the glass was soon swept away.

J.C. watched as David sulked out of the bar. Things were sure wild tonight, he thought. This was usually such a quiet place. The Jimani bar down below was celebrating its one-year anniversary, too, so their place was packed. But there was enough noise here to drown them out quite well. It was just that somehow there seemed to be a little extra something in the air. Maybe it was just his excitement at the possibility of finally going home with someone. Or maybe, he wondered, maybe it was that extra something this evening which was giving him the nerve to pursue this guy in the first place. J.C. pretended to point to someone on the other side of the room, just to have an excuse to "accidentally" touch the young man's arm. Yes, there was definitely an extra something in the air this evening.

Downstairs in the Jimani bar, Denise "Denny" Le Boeuf was sitting with her friend, Stan Sherman. Denny had been working on a doctorate in Philosophy in New York and had taught philosophy at Hunter College, but she moved to New Orleans earlier in 1973, deciding she wanted to play for a few years.

Her sister was then dating Jack Curry, who along with Jim owned the "Jim and I" bar on the corner of Chartres and Iberville, so Denny naturally began frequenting the Jimani and making friends. She tended bar at the Chart Room on the corner of Chartres and Conti a few blocks away. She also had gay friends and sometimes went out with them. Musically trained, she could sometimes forget names but always remembered voices. She sat now among her friends, chatting and joking.

Outside on Iberville, Eddie Gillis was on leave with a pass from the Public Health Hospital on State Street. He'd recently had a bone operation on his left hand, but it had healed enough now that his doctor was willing to let him out of the hospital temporarily. Eddie headed for the 600 block of Iberville, hoping to run into some of his seamen friends. After talking with them for a while, he thought he'd pop in to the UpStairs for a few minutes. He was kind of low on money and wanted to see if he could borrow a couple of dollars from one of his friends there. So around 7:45, he climbed the steps and entered the bar.

In the front room, Reggie Adams went up to Buddy for another drink. He was having a particularly good time this evening, and so on the spur of the moment made a suggestion. "Hey, Buddy," he said, "how about Regina and I take you and Adam out to dinner tonight? You get off in a few minutes, don't you?"

Buddy glanced down the bar toward Adam, who was drunk but still looked reasonably in control. "Sure," Buddy replied. "Sounds great."

Reggie turned to Regina. "Sweetheart, I only brought enough money for drinks. Could you go back to the apartment and pick up my wallet?"

They kissed briefly and Regina headed for the door.

Just before she reached it, Jean stopped her. "Regina," she said, "could you bring back that hat you borrowed? I want to wear it this week."

Regina told her she'd grab the hat and then left to walk the short distance through the Quarter to her apartment.

Stewart Butler made his rounds as he prepared to leave, stopping for a moment by Horace and Mitch. "I need a haircut this week," he told Horace, and they set up a tentative time.

Everyone continued talking and drinking for the next several minutes. Fred and Earl put a couple of dimes in the jukebox and danced to some songs. The group around the piano decided to try one more round of "United We Stand," singing it for probably the fifth time that evening. "And if our backs should ever be against the wall," the group sang out, "we'll be together."

J.C. and his friend leaned over the table to hear each other over the sound of the others. Since the guy from Morgan City had never been here before, J.C. told him some of the history of the bar, mentioning the plays they put on. J.C. had read lines during a rehearsal once, he said, but he couldn't bring himself to really participate because it seemed too much like a drag show, and J.C. didn't want to be effeminate in any way. At least the cardboard and plastic whisky displays made the place feel a little more butch now.

In the main room, Buddy pulled Hugh aside in between serving drinks. "Time to go count out your bank," he said. "You'll be taking over in a few minutes." Hugh started for the storeroom where the safe was kept, but then the buzzer started ringing, and it kept ringing. Buddy looked at Hugh and rolled his eyes helplessly.

Frank Gaalema was near the door and thought about yelling downstairs to whoever it was to cut it out. Instead, he picked up his beer and started to move toward the second room to get away from the sound.

Buddy looked at his watch. Five more minutes and his shift would be over. Couldn't that pest at the buzzer wait five more minutes? Oh, well, that was why he was manager, because he knew how to handle these things. He tried to keep his irritation down. Just a few more minutes and he'd be going out to dinner. If he could deal with this last little problem, it would be time to go.

In the second room, J.C. finally worked up the nerve to put his hand under the table. He smiled at his new friend and patted him on the knee. The young man smiled back, and J.C. let his hand remain on the guy's knee. The guy in turn took his foot and put it under J.C.'s pants cuff, touching his leg and giving J.C. a little wink. It was almost sunset. They might take a stroll through the Quarter and then perhaps one of them would suggest something more.

Yes, J.C. thought, this might be the night. This might very well be the night.

Hell on the Second Floor

"Fire!" someone screamed. People turned to look, and suddenly everyone began shouting and running about in confusion. The oxygen inside the bar was now available to fuel the fire, making it practically explode into the room in a tremendous roar. The floor in the hallway was already warped from the heat, keeping the automatic closer on the door from functioning. The noisy blast and heat of a hundred furnaces filled the room. The sound of falling stools, glasses dropping to the floor, and Luther's agonized screams added to the terrified commotion.

There was no time to think, only to act. Buddy reached immediately across the bar to the two men in front of him. "Come with me!" he ordered loudly. He moved quickly to the next customers. "Come with me!" he commanded in a no-nonsense voice.

Fire jumped instantly into the space between the door and far end of the bar. The acoustical tiles of the ceiling began to ignite, along with the Burt Reynolds and Mark Spitz posters above the jukebox. Buddy knew the only way out was through that third room theater. They had to get there fast.

He moved down the bar, stopping for a brief second at every patron. "Come with me!" he demanded. "Come with me!"

Many of the customers didn't even hear him, too shocked or panicked or drunk or too far away to focus on his words. Many ignored him and headed instantly for the windows. For some, this may have been the only choice even at that stage of the fire.

One man was in the bathroom, near the entrance to the bar, just past the jukebox. A friend of his, unable to follow Buddy without first alerting his friend, burst into the bathroom. "Someone's started a fire!" he yelled. They looked out the bathroom door and saw the ceiling in flames.

The man who'd been in the bathroom ran toward a window a few feet away, between the bathroom and the end of the bar, the window facing Iberville which led to the fire escape. He began kicking out the panes as the fire scorched his back. After someone else finished breaking the window, he leaped to the street below, his clothes on fire. Gerald Todd Tyler, a patron of the Midship bar next door, ran out and threw a pitcher of water on the injured man as the man turned to look back up at the bar.

His friend never made it to the window.

Eddie Gillis had only been inside the bar ten minutes and was on his way to leave when the fire began. He ran for the window by the fire escape, where someone was struggling with it. Eddie pushed him away, picked up a chair, and broke the window. People were so frantic by the time the window was open that he was punched several times as people fought to get out.

His clothes on fire, Eddie ran up the fire escape, but people in the street below yelled at him to jump, so he ran back to the landing, jumped over the railing, hung from the escape by his hands, and dropped to the street. Gerald Tyler ran out of the Midship again and poured a pitcher of water on him, too.

When the window was finally open, Luther pushed Jean out ahead of him. He was in too much pain to aim well, however, and shoved her face against part of the window, breaking two of Jean's teeth. She spit them out and continued through the window. She and Luther both made it onto the fire escape. There, however, Luther began crying. "Jean, help me! Help me! I'm on fire!"

Jean looked in horror at her friend, who seemed almost totally ablaze. She tried to beat out the flames on his legs with her hands, but he finally could stand it no longer and climbed over the railing, walked a moment along the ledge, and then jumped to the street, bouncing on the pavement next to a car. Gerald Tyler came out of the Midship yet again with another pitcher of water and poured it on him.

Each of the four or five customers who escaped through the fire escape exit was already burned when they reached it, the fire having flown into the bar so rapidly. They had barely made it onto the fire escape when flames shot out of the window after them.

There was no ladder on the fire escape leading down. The steps only led up to the third floor. As the flames reached out through the window, the men jumped down into the street. Some of them, too injured to move, lay where they fell. One customer ripped off his flaming clothes, standing naked in the street until someone brought him a blanket. Then he wandered off in a daze.

Jean Gosnell couldn't bear to jump so far down. Each story in these old buildings was tall, almost like a story and a half. When the flames came through the window, she ran up the fire escape toward the third floor, hoping rescue would come before she was forced to jump from even higher. As she cowered on the top landing, someone threw a shirt up to her to wrap around her head against the heat.

The man who escaped from the bathroom kept looking toward the burning window in vain. No one else appeared. One body was later found sitting beside the toilet and another was found beneath the wash basin, both bodies largely unburned. Two bodies were found in the entrance to the bathroom, one on top of the other. One body was found right beside the window which opened onto the fire escape, crouched against the bar.

Robert Price was standing near the jukebox, heading back to his table to pick up his drink, when Luther opened the door. Suddenly, Buddy grabbed his arm and told him to follow him. Robert hadn't even realized there was a fire until then. He followed Buddy.

Buddy went from the end of the bar near the fire escape down toward the other end of the bar where Adam sat drinking. "Come with me, Adam!" he said. Then he moved on. Jimmy Demoll, Jr. blanched when he turned and saw the fire. He needed no urging to follow Buddy.

Buddy stopped at the group by the piano. Bud sat staring confusedly. "Come with me!" Buddy ordered. He stopped at the two tables in the front room, the customers staring in horror at the fire screaming toward them in the few seconds it had taken Buddy to reach them. The end of the bar and the first stools were already burning, the ceiling in the first half of the bar a sheet of flame. The 4th of July decorations ignited, sending bits of burning material drifting through the air. Thick clouds of smoke began filling the room.

Just as Buddy passed under the arch into the second room, the lights went out. It wasn't dark, what with the last of the daylight still coming through the windows, but the change was noticeable, yet another indication of impending doom, enough to send a few more people into a panic. The first of the windows on the Chartres side of the bar were open now, creating a draft which pulled the flames even more quickly through the bar. There was more shouting, more screams, the sound of chairs and stools falling, bottles popping, the sound of people tripping and falling into each other.

Ricky Everett was sitting in the second room, on the same side of the bar as the entrance, near the wall dividing the two rooms, so he couldn't directly see the door from where he sat. When he heard someone yell, "Fire!" as the door opened, he noticed an orange glow. Somebody must have set a trash can on fire, he thought. But why was everybody screaming?

A second later, Buddy grabbed Ricky, who was still sitting. "Come with me!" Buddy ordered.

Ricky stood, not believing this could really be serious. He turned to look into the front room and saw the carpet lift several inches off the floor as flames shot underneath it. He and his friend, Ronnie Rosenthal, quickly followed Buddy. Jamie Larson followed, too, as did Jim Peterson, Frank Dean, and Theo Ancelet.

Uncle Al had arrived at the UpStairs around 6:00 that evening, joining some friends and grabbing a pitcher of beer. He'd watched as Rodger was ejected from the bar and thought briefly to himself, "He'll cause trouble." When he saw the fire burst through the door, his first thought was, "Oh, my God! He did it!" Uncle Al heard Buddy telling people to follow him, but he saw the window by the fire escape and thought it was close enough to try.

He watched a few people in front of him trying to open the shutters, and after five or ten seconds, he realized he was going to be trapped. The door was almost closed, but fire had gotten in already and was burning the walls near the entrance, and he could feel the heat building up. He backed up, but as he ran past the door toward the arch, the door opened and a blast of heat scorched his head. He quickly joined Buddy's group.

Buddy stopped at each table in the second room, commanding everyone he touched to come with him. He touched J.C.'s arm as J.C. stood confused in the middle of the room. "Come with me!" Buddy demanded. J.C. and his new friend followed. Buddy grabbed Peter, a bank clerk and notary. He grabbed Harry and then Courtney Craighead. "Come with me!" he ordered yet again.

Then he reached the fire door which led to the third room. He pulled it open and ushered everyone through. Only twenty or twenty-five people passed through the doorway.

Frank Gaalema was near the entrance when the fire started and thought he'd try for the window, too. But it seemed to take forever for those people to get the window open, and the fire was spreading fast. He finally got down near the floor and crawled backwards away from the door.

Frank watched as the man who'd yelled "Fire!" earlier and the friend he'd been dancing with near the jukebox. Fred and Earl, both looked at each other and then made a mad rush for the door. They burst through it with such force that the door was lodged open. Then they tried to run down the burning stairs.

Frank, still crawling, saw Inez Warren and her two sons in the middle of the bar and tried to get them to come with him to join Buddy leading people to the third room. They wouldn't come, so Frank grabbed Jessie Baker and another guy.

Buddy led his group across the stage and behind the scenery to a door which opened out onto the roof. He moved a spool table and some costumes out of the way and then opened the door. Buddy then directed everyone to cross over the roof, go through a window into another building, walk through an apartment, and climb down a stairway which led to an entrance at 606 ½ Iberville.

When Dean Morris saw the explosion of fire into the bar, his first thought was that someone had thrown a Molotov cocktail in through the doorway. He stood just staring for several seconds but then heard someone shouting about a back door, and when he saw people lining up, he followed.

As Dean was about to climb through the window into the apartment in the next building, he suddenly realized Ricky Cross wasn't with him. "Buddy!" he wailed. "Where's Ricky? He was here a minute ago!"

Buddy ran back into the theatre and found Mother Cross in front of an open door.

"What are you doing?" Buddy demanded.

"My lover's still in there!"

"No, he's not. He's out on the roof."

"Thank God!" But then he turned back toward the open door and fell to his hands and knees, as if he were going to head back into the bar anyway.

Buddy picked him back up. "You can't go in there. You'll die."

"But maybe I could crawl underneath the smoke, grab someone by the legs, and drag him back."

Buddy knew too well the stories of people killed when returning for others. "Look," he said. "We'll hold the door open and call out. If anyone's able to come, they will."

Buddy and Ricky stuck their heads through the doorway and began calling. No one was in the second room. What with the lights out, the thickening smoke, and the customers pressing against the windows in the front room, the light was too dim for Buddy to see anyone. They were all past his line of sight anyway, past the arch toward the Chartres end of the bar.

They called again and again. No one came. No one could hear them from that distance, with the roaring flames just behind them and three dozen voices screaming together in terror in the front room.

Smoke began pouring into the third room. "Look," Buddy said. "This is a fire door. I have to close it. Are you convinced there's no one left who can get to this door?"

Mother Cross nodded reluctantly, and Buddy closed the door. Then the two joined the others on the roof. Buddy pushed Ricky into Dean's arms and forced them to leave together.

When Ricky Everett walked out onto the roof, he looked about for Ronnie, but he couldn't see him, and Ronnie wasn't one of the last few to come out of the door onto the roof. "Oh, my God!" Ricky shouted. He was so sure Ronnie had followed him out.

At almost the same moment, Mitch, standing near him, exclaimed, "Horace is still in there!"

Ricky and Mitch went back inside and up to the fire door. Buddy, ushering the last several people off the roof, was too busy to notice them. Mitch pushed the door open and the two ran back into the bar. Ricky stopped after only a few feet and stood there in a daze. Flames were everywhere. The front room was a mass of flames, and the second room had started to burn as well.

After staring for another moment, he stumbled back out of the room and crossed over the roof to leave with the last of the others. Walking down the steps leading to Iberville, he found Ronnie, who had somehow gotten ahead of him in line and wasn't still inside after all.

But three dozen other people were. A nineteen-year-old man was talking with friends when he heard a noise and turned to see the fire sweep into the room. God, the fire was coming in through the *door*! Fast! He ran instantly to the window. God, he thought. God! There were *bars* on the windows!

He was slim, though. He pushed his way forward, the first to squeeze through the bars. He hung onto the bars, lowering himself as far as possible toward the street, and then dropped to the ground. "I was the first to get to the window, and thank God…thank God I was able to get out," he said. "But the others…they…"

Many panicked. Since many of those trapped were regulars, they would have known of the third room and probably the roof exit as well, having seen the room many times as they put on the plays. The others who weren't regulars could have seen the other fire door if they'd just looked into that second room. Maybe they would have thought it only led to a storage room, despite the Exit sign above the door, but there would surely have been the possibility at least of more windows to choose from.

Then again, all the windows in the second room were covered with plywood. Even if there were other windows in that third room, who was to say they weren't boarded up as well? And who wants to run fifteen feet *toward* a raging fire to peek through an archway in the first place? Especially when there are windows right in front of them, and losing one's place in line was a death sentence. By the time it became obvious not everyone was going to be able to get through the windows, it was probably too late to head for the second room. After three hours of drinking, even a regularly clear-headed person could get confused when there were only seconds to make a life-or-death decision.

Bud Matyi didn't react as the others did when he saw the flames pouring into the bar. He could see there were too many people in front of the windows. He tried for a moment to push the others forward and get through himself, but he soon realized he'd never make it out that way. Looking back into the bar, though, he could see the flames leaping and jumping, surging towards him. There was nowhere to go.

But heat rose, didn't it? Certainly, the ceiling was already almost completely ablaze. Perhaps if he lay on the floor, he could escape the heat long enough for the firemen to get there. And that piano should help. It was thick enough to offer a shield from the flames at least for a few minutes, and maybe that was all he'd need.

He looked one last time at the screaming, frantic mob clawing at the windows and then crawled underneath the piano, huddling against the wall. He felt someone beside him and turned to see Inez Warren crawling next to him. As she lay on the floor, he lay on top of her, offering her a little more shielding.

Meanwhile, Denny Le Boeuf was downstairs in the Jimani bar with her friend, Stan Sherman. Just before 8:00, as she and Stan sat with friends at the far end of the Jimani away from the entrance, the lights flickered, and the jukebox cut off and on and off again. With the music off, Denny suddenly heard an odd sound, almost like thunder. It sounded like people were running upstairs above her. She heard the pounding feet and looked in puzzlement at Stan. What an odd dance they must be doing up there.

Stan noticed a very thin layer of smoke creeping along the ceiling above them. Having been in a terrible fire a few years earlier, he knew exactly what was happening. He grabbed Denny and told her they were leaving. He also shouted to the bartender, Billy Hoolihan, to get everybody out.

Despite being in the back of the bar, Stan and Denny were among the first to reach the exit. As Denny crossed the threshold, suddenly glass littered the street in front of her, and a man came sailing down from above, landing headfirst in the street, lying on his back, his feet toward Canal and his head downriver. Denny stood stunned, still not realizing what was happening. Why had this middle-aged, bald man jumped into the street?

As Stan pushed her out the door, Denny saw that the man's leg looked broken. And he wasn't bald after all. Part of his scalp was peeled back. A huge, dark cloud of smoke billowed out above her, and more debris and bodies came crashing down. Stan led Denny across the street, urging her not to look, but she had to make sure her friends made it out of the Jimani.

Then she heard the screams, not of the men inside, but of the men below, calling for their friends and lovers. She could *tell* they were calling for their lovers, just by the quality of the sound in their voices.

"Don't look," said Stan. "You don't want to see this."

As Stan led her away, the wails of the men calling out names followed her down the street.

Upstairs, Rusty Quinton had been standing beside the piano with Reggie Tubbs, Dave Gary, Mitch, Horace, and other friends, when he heard a boom and saw flames leaping through the doorway. He didn't know about the back exit and ran instantly to the Chartres window in the left corner of the room, the one next to the piano blocked by plywood and an air conditioner.

As he raised the window, another man crawled through ahead of him, and with smoke already in his face, he swung out by hanging on a sign from the Jimani bar below. Then he grabbed a pipe and slid to the ground, spraining his left ankle. He remained on the sidewalk below a few moments, helping break the fall of Roger Dunn, who leaped next. But the following two people were afraid to jump. As they hesitated, the fire stretched further and further into the room, scorching people with its intense heat even before the flames reached them.

"Jump! Jump!" shouted two girls from across the street. Passersby, tourists, guests from the nearby Marriott hotel, and patrons of the bars below filled the street, watching in horror as the terrified men in the UpStairs tore away at the plywood and bars blocking the windows.

Inside the bar, someone fell against Adolph Medina's leg, and he fell to the floor. When he scrambled back up, he realized he was missing a shoe. That was a new shoe, too. He had the bizarre thought that maybe he should look for it, but then he saw the flames again. He noticed Adam sitting frozen at the bar, and when he saw all the people trying to get out, he thought about hiding under the piano like those others were doing, but instead Adolph fought to reach the window. Bob was right behind him and helped him through the bars. It sure helped to be a slim 110 pounds. Out on the ledge, he hesitated a moment and then jumped.

A few of the men behind him had already collapsed or died from breathing the superheated air, but there were still many struggling forward. Now, though, the actual flames were beginning to reach the men, who fought to stay in control despite the pain long enough to escape. Burning ceiling tiles dropped down on top of them, starting this man's shirt on fire, melting that man's hair.

Michael Scarborough, his head, back, and hands burning, broke out through the corner Chartres window after Francis Dufrene and swung down a pipe to the street below, Rusty helping break his fall. Oh, God, he thought, lying in the street, looking back up at the window. Glenn had been right behind him. Where was he now? Moaning in agony, he tried to call out for his lover, who never made it to the window.

Another man jumped, seriously injuring himself when he hit the pavement. Then another man jumped, his clothes burning as he leaped from the building. Yet another man, his clothes also ablaze, was seen running down the street in terror. Someone grabbed him and beat out the flames with his hands.

The air was filled with screams. Screams of those watching the scene in horror. Screams of the injured lying in the street amidst pools of blood and patches of skin torn from their bodies. And screams of those still clawing desperately at the bars on the windows.

One man hung from a window, terrified of the flames behind him but also of the street so far below. "Let me jump! Let me jump!" he screamed, apparently trying to convince himself, or perhaps asking for the crowd below either to get out of his way or help break his fall. He did jump, but the two men screaming behind him never made it to the window.

When Adolph picked himself up from the sidewalk, he realized he was scorched on his back and shoulders, and the bars had already been so hot they'd burned him as he crawled through, but someone had broken his fall, and he was more or less okay. He looked back up for Bob, who'd been right behind him, but now Bob was on fire. Adolph watched him die there in the window.

Bill Larson made it to a window blocked by an air conditioning unit. He ripped it partially out of the window and began to struggle through the gap below the bars at the bottom. The window slid shut on him, and he couldn't get it to stay up. Its heavy weight kept pinning him down, and he couldn't get out.

He pulled himself back inside, letting the window shut all the way, and then he punched a hole in one of the panes and began crawling through. It was a snug fit, but those flames were getting closer. He got one arm out, then a shoulder, and then he squeezed his head through, tearing his skin on the glass as he pushed himself forward. But the flames were already licking at his heels. He had to get out fast, but he was almost stuck. "Oh, God, no!" he screamed.

A muntin, the thin piece of wood dividing two panes of glass, kept him from fitting through the hole he'd made in the window. He punched out the next pane and tried to struggle forward, but then his green shirt, covered with soot, began to burn. Bill reached out, crying for help. Then he screamed. Fire surged over him, covering his face. His hair disappeared into ash.

Rusty watched him burn. He also watched three people in the corner window burn to death when the window he'd come through slid shut again, and a man too agonized and frantic to lift it simply thrust his foot through and tried to back out. But the flames caught up to him and the others waiting behind him.

Only fourteen people, several seriously burned, had been able to escape through the windows, including the group that had tumbled onto the fire escape. In the two windows on the corner of the building where Iberville and Chartres met, seventeen people burned to death as they piled against each other in their attempt to escape. From the street below, people could see not only Bill Larson's body hanging partially through the window but also the foot and leg of another burned man thrust between the bars in one of the other windows.

When Ricky Cross ran out onto Iberville, the first thing he saw was Fred and Earl coming out of the UpStairs entrance. They were both covered in flames. People helped stamp the fire out on their clothing, and then Ricky took off his T-shirt and wrapped Fred's burned hands.

When Frank Gaalema saw the two men, he and others tried to keep them apart so neither would see how badly injured the other was, but Fred kept calling out for Earl, and Earl kept calling for Fred, up until the ambulances arrived.

When Buddy reached the street after coming through the adjacent building, he ran into Bill Duncan, who'd heard the screams from his apartment across the street and rushed out, searching desperately for Buddy. "Thank God," he said, hugging him.

Buddy turned to look back up at the bar. "Shit!" He could see Adam inside, still sitting on his bar stool, waving his arms and screaming amidst the flames, already fatally burned. A firefighter turned on a hose, and a thick stream of water knocked Adam off his stool and onto the floor. Now another hose was turned on, and another, and another, but for twenty-eight people upstairs in the bar, it was already too late.

The Dead

Joseph Henry Adams

Reginald Adams Jr.

Guy O. Andersen (sometimes written as Anderson)

Joe William Bailey

Luther Thomas Boggs

Louis Horace Broussard

Herbert Coolcy (sometimes written as Hubert)

Donald Walter Dunbar

Adam Roland Fontenot

Larry Norman Frost (was listed as unidentified white male until 2018)

David Stuart Gary

Horace Getchell

John Thomas Golding Sr.

Gerald Hoyt Gordon

Glenn Richard Green

James Walls Hambrick

Kenneth Paul Harrington

William R. Larson

Ferris LeBlanc

Robert Keith Lumpkin

Leon Richard Maples

George Stephen Matyi (sometimes written as Steven)

Clarence Joseph McCloskey Jr.

Duane George Mitchell

Larry Stratton

Willie Inez Warren

Eddie Hosea Warren

James Curtis Warren

Perry Lane Waters Jr.

Douglas Maxwell Williams

Unidentified white male

Unidentified white male

The Survivors

Marcy Marcell just couldn't take her eyes off that Bette Davis movie. Finally, at 7:55, she looked at her watch. "Oh, my god! I'm gonna be late!" But as she reached to turn off the television a few moments later, a news flash came on.

Marcy rushed down to the bar and saw the dead bodies. Her lover Terry heard about the fire and ran all the way over from the Pussycat Theater, afraid Marcy had been killed. They went to Charity hospital and watched as the injured were brought in. But they couldn't find all their friends. Eventually, Marcy learned that seventeen of her friends and acquaintances had been killed. For weeks, everyone went around trying to find out who was alive and who was dead. Most of Marcy's friends thought she was dead since they knew she was always at the bar on Sunday evening.

Marcy's brother-in-law, Clarence McCloskey, and his lover, Bill Bailey, both died at the UpStairs. Clarence received 3rd and 4th degree burns over 75% of his body. His face and legs were destroyed, but his brown shoes remained intact. He was identified by his brother Bernard through a key chain which had Clarence's name on it. The identification was confirmed by fingerprints taken by the New Orleans Police Department.

Bill received 3rd degree burns on his face and lower extremities, and 2nd degree burns on his face, arm, and trunk.

Hair was burned from his scalp, and his face was charred, but he'd died of carbon monoxide inhalation. He was identified through fingerprints.

Marcy was numb for weeks, in shock. About the only good thing was that the tragedy brought her and Terry back together. But then just as the initial shock of the fire was beginning to wear off, Terry was killed on August 16 in an auto accident.

Marcy spent the next year as little more than a zombie, having lost seventeen friends, a job, and a lover all within a couple of months. She moved in with Regina Adams, who was also in shock. Regina's lover, Reggie Adams, had been caught in the fire while waiting for Regina to pick up his wallet at their apartment. Reggie was near the piano with friends when Regina left him, next to Adam.

Regina arrived back at the bar just as the first fire engine was pulling up. She watched as an air conditioner blew out of a window from the heat. She looked at the burned, moaning people who'd barely escaped, but she didn't see Reggie among them.

For a week, Regina laid out Reggie's clothes, hoping Reggie would come home, hoping he was hurt and not dead, hoping he'd just lost his memory from shock. Regina fixed two plates for breakfast and kept hoping to find Reggie at home when she returned from work. "He'll be there," she kept telling herself. "He'll be there." But Reggie never came.

Regina's mother called Reggie's mother in Dallas, and Mrs. Adams came to New Orleans for a week. When Reggie's body was finally identified through dental charts, his mother took his remains back to Dallas, and Regina finally accepted that Reggie was dead. Reggie had received 3rd and 4th degree charring over 95% of his body, with only a few portions of his anterior legs still showing patches of skin. It was an image Regina could never erase from her mind.

Marcy and Regina spent the next several months trying to comfort each other. Once, in one of her zombie states, Marcy fell asleep with a lit cigarette and set herself on fire. Regina, fortunately, put out the flames before Marcy was badly hurt.

Though they only lived together a short time, Marcy and Regina remained friends throughout the next two decades. Regina began living full-time as a woman and in 1980 had her name legally changed to Regina Adams before moving to the Gulf Coast of Mississippi.

Marcy was deeply depressed and often suicidal for a year after the fire, but she eventually began to recover. She helped open the Cabaret, a show bar, in 1974, and over the years became one of the Quarter's best known drag queens, dancing and working in almost every gay bar. She worked part-time at the Municipal Court for a few years, quitting when she decided in 1976 to begin living as a woman. Feeling transgender rather than gay, but used to the gay world, Marcy began from that time on dressing exclusively as a woman, though she never underwent surgery. She said in 1990 that she never regretted her decision to live as a woman.

Marcy died in 2011 of pulmonary fibrosis.

Phil Esteve rushed over to the bar that evening but couldn't go inside until the following day. Then, he says, he watched as investigators tore names off of checks and took money from the cash register which they never turned over to him.

A few months after the fire, Phil knew he'd either go crazy or have to move on, so he decided to get over it. He eventually opened the Post Office, a bar on the ground floor of a French Quarter building, and still later another bar. In 1982, he opened the Apple Barrel, a restaurant/bar in the Faubourg Marigny, decorating the wall behind the bar with foreign paper currency from around the world which friends donated for the purpose. Fifteen years later, the Apple Barrel, serving a mixed crowd, was still operating successfully. Phil, however, grew increasingly tired of any mention of the UpStairs, wishing people would just let the story die and be finished.

Phil died in 2007.

Napoleon and Stanley were devastated, naturally, when they learned of the fire, knowing twenty of those injured or killed. Some even thought they were among the victims, since they were usually there every Sunday before they moved. After they returned to New Orleans in March of 1974, an old acquaintance turned pale upon seeing them in a bar. "You're dead," the man said shakily.

"No, we had just moved away. Now we're back."

But the man was unconvinced and soon hurried out of the bar.

They also ran into Bob and Bettye McAnear at the Post Office, back in town to visit Phil at his new bar. The tricycle had been in the storeroom and was unburned, so Phil kept up the tradition of the tricycle race for a few more years. Napoleon and Stanley ran into friends Michael Scarborough, Dale Dunn, and Fred Scharohway, all burned in the fire.

It hurt to see their injured friends, but it hurt, too, to learn from a neighbor what had happened with Mitch's family after the fire. His family had told his two sons they could either have Mitch and Horace's bikes or the men's dog, but not both. The kids, intimidated by the responsibility, chose the bikes, and the neighbor took in Pooky.

Napoleon and Stanley still had one of Pooky's litters, and over the years also had some of that litter's puppies. They kept in touch with their friends and led a quieter life now, Napoleon welding full time, and the couple living in a mobile home on the Westbank. In 1992, they celebrated their 20th anniversary together, still looking fondly back at their photo album of UpStairs friends.

Michael Scarborough died in El Dorado, Arkansas, in 2006.

Bettye and Bob McAnear moved to San Antonio a few years after the fire and eventually divorced. She remarried and continued her life of music and theater. Bettye died in 2014 at the age of eighty-one. After the divorce, Bob moved to rural Texas. In 2023, at the age of ninety-two, he was still helping out at a rural grocery, sitting on his porch watching the goats and donkey on the neighboring property, and carrying his gun wherever he went, always prepared for trouble.

The man from Morgan City did take J.C. Carrier home the night of the fire, but they were both so traumatized that of course nothing happened. J.C. remained deeply affected for years. He gave up drinking completely, though the fire was only one of the reasons for that. He also refused to ever step inside another bar.

Well, he made an exception once. When Phil Esteve opened the Post Office, he thought he'd go to show his support. The bar was on the ground floor and had plenty of big doors leading out onto the sidewalk along both walls which were facing the street. J.C. sat near one of the doors, but he shook so badly he never went back to that bar or any other. He was able to socialize through his involvement with a carnival krewe and other means, but bars were no longer a part of his life.

Bill Farrell was still playing the piano at the Burgundy House when he learned about the fire, and his worst fears seemed confirmed when Skip didn't come home that night. Bill wasn't up to identifying Skip's body, so their friend Mike Moreau went to the morgue and recognized the jewelry Skip had been wearing.

Horace "Skip" Getchell received 3rd and 4th degree burns over 90% of his body, with the loss of almost all skin and fat down to the muscle tissue. His fingers were lost, and his identity was confirmed through the dental charts of Dr. Perry Waters.

Bill also wasn't up to dealing with the members of Skip's family who came down to collect his belongings. They began packing many of Bill's things, too. "No, that's mine," Bill tried to explain, but they countered with, "No, he described this in a letter. I know it's his." Bill, too overcome to fight, let them take what they wanted.

Bill never did fully recover from the shock of Skip's death. Even though there'd been problems, they'd still loved each other.

But Bill did try to move on with his life, continuing to play the piano and go to parties with friends. The following year, he shocked everyone by appearing in drag for the first time, as a southern belle with a hoop skirt. He'd decided life was too short to worry so much about appearances and thought he'd let loose just a little. Life, it turned out, was indeed short for him, too.

Bill Farrell died of a heart attack in 1975.

Bob Babb never did get Wayne Barras to give in and go to the UpStairs that Sunday as they did almost every other Sunday. Wayne was just too tired with the routine. "Oh, Bob, I'm just gonna take a week off," he said. "Then when I go back, I'll be a celebrity." They both stayed home the night of the 24th.

David Crumley found love again after losing Bobby Lumpkin in the fire. He was partnered with Henry Kubicki for many years. David died in 2014.

Stewart Butler and Alfred Doolittle left the UpStairs around 7:30 and headed over to Wanda's. They were sitting there drinking when they heard sirens and turned to see fire engines rushing down the street. They ran toward the UpStairs but watched the scene from a distance. Ten people Stewart knew died in the fire. The hardest thing for him was going to work the next day and pretending nothing had happened, because he wasn't out at work yet.

At the memorial service, Stewart watched people going out the side entrance so they wouldn't be seen on TV. Stewart also walked out the side entrance. He had a hard time going to the wakes, not because he was afraid to be seen, but because the families of the dead often refused to notify any of the gay friends.

But Stewart eventually put the tragedy behind him and moved on. He was arrested for selling marijuana a few years later and gave up that sidelight, though he continued to smoke it, arrested once even in his eighties. His promiscuity gradually decreased until the early 1980's, when it then decreased dramatically after AIDS.

He and Alfred remained together the rest of their lives. Alfred continued to take medication, and Stewart worked over the years with gay youth on drugs, some who were emotionally disturbed or runaways or who'd been kicked out of their homes. He was a co-chair of the New Orleans chapter of the Louisiana Gay Political Action Caucus (LAGPAC) for years and became quite vocal on the issue of gay rights. And looking back on the fire at the UpStairs, he said, "It was a tragedy that, as far as I can see, no good came out of."

Alfred Doolittle died in 2008. Stewart Butler died in 2020.

Jane Golding finished toweling her hair dry and put the dryer cap on her head. It was 10:00, a little late for John to be out, but it wasn't as if she gave him a curfew. She had switched on the TV and turned it loud enough for her to hear even with the hairdryer on.

"A fire swept through the UpStairs Lounge tonight at 604 Iberville..."

Jane threw off the hairdryer and rushed to the television. He was there. She knew it. Oh, God, did he get out? Oh, God, look at those pictures!

Jane stayed up by herself all night. Their oldest daughter was twenty-four and had been married for six years, with two young children. Their nineteen-year-old daughter had recently moved out of the house. Only their eleven-year-old son was home, and he was sleeping. There was no need to bother the kids until she knew more.

She called the hospitals and the morgue, but they had no information on John. He was dead then. If he wasn't hurt and he wasn't home, he was one of the unidentified dead. The next day, Jane called the dentist to send some X-rays, but John had been arrested before on a gay-related charge, and the FBI had fingerprints on file through which he was identified.

The body was so badly burned that Jane could never quite convince herself she was burying her husband and not some other man. Over the next few months, Jane almost lost her mind with grief, but she pulled herself together, found a job, and began paying off her house notes and raising her last child alone. John had never been able to afford insurance, so there was no help from that, and the insurance at 604 Iberville only paid $300 apiece for Jane and her three children. Her daughters refused to accept the money, telling Jane to use it on the house or for their brother.

Jane didn't really want to capitalize on her husband's death even to that small degree, but at the same time, she felt overwhelmed by her new financial responsibilities. Even though it would have cost more money, though, she kept wishing John could have just been burned but lived. Even if he'd been disabled the rest of his life, she would have gladly taken care of him, just to still have him with her. She *liked* him.

She loved him.

As the years went by, Jane, who never remarried, watched her children mature and enjoyed watching her grandchildren grow. They were all good kids, smart kids, kids she could be proud of, that John would have been proud of, too.

Then, as the 1980's passed, and Jane watched the spread of AIDS, she could feel at least a tiny bit grateful John had been spared that miserable death. But she would grow furious when she'd hear people say, "Well, it's just gays. They deserve to die. AIDS is a good punishment." It was the same thing people had said about her husband. "It was just a bunch of faggots. Who cares?"

I do, she thought. I do.

Jane died in 2011 at the age of 86.

One of the initial results of the fire on Ricky Everett was that he came out to his family and coworkers. His mother, who knew Ricky always went to the UpStairs, now knew that it was a gay bar. She was upset at first but eventually became accepting and supportive. Ricky's brother started telling people at work, "Hey, my brother was in there!" until a coworker pulled him aside and whispered who the clientele of the bar were. Ricky's brother then called and demanded to know what he'd been doing in a gay bar.

"I have friends there," Ricky replied.

"What kind of friends?"

"Good friends."

They never did openly discuss Ricky's orientation. He never discussed it with his father, either. Once, his father called and asked if Ricky was dating any nice girls yet. When Ricky said no, his father continued, "Well, some guys like women and some guys don't," but no more was ever said.

When Ricky consented to do a TV interview with reporter Rosemary James, the studio insisted on filming Ricky from the back, but his voice was so distinctive that the following day at work, several people asked, "How's TV life?" He didn't lose his job, though. The only friends he lost were a couple of other gay men who were terrified of being found out if they associated with him.

He did lose a lot of sleep for a while, however, waking up from terrible nightmares. He took Valium for several weeks but finally decided to face the nights on his own and learned to live with the memories. Over the years, he continued to work closely with various churches, even becoming an ordained minister, though he earned his living through other jobs, for a time as a cook on an offshore oil rig. He kept in touch with his friends who survived, Ronnie

Rosenthal and Courtney Craighead, a bond having formed that night that endured over the following decades.

Courtney Craighead died in 2005, final services held on June 24th.

When Rod Wagener heard about the fire, he knew instantly his lover of four and a half years was dead. He remembered the time two months earlier when Bud had been reading a Taylor Caldwell book and said suddenly, "You're gonna miss me so much you're gonna ache for me." Rod had been surprised. What a weird thing to say. Was Bud thinking of leaving him?

"What the hell are you talking about?" he'd asked. But Bud didn't seem to know, either.

Rod called the hospitals just to be sure, but there was no George Steven Matyi listed among the injured. Twenty-nine people were dead, and one of those bodies belonged to his husband.

Some bodies were identified fairly quickly, but there were still so many left. Rod had to know which one was Bud. He finally went down to try identifying him.

And he found him. Bud had received extensive 3rd and 4th degree burns over 95% of his body. His clothes were gone. His skin was gone. Even his fingers were almost gone. In some places, he'd been burned down to the muscle and even to the bone. His face had been charred extensively and was unrecognizable.

But the body had been found with a medal around its neck, a religious medal with the design of a dove on it, the symbol of marriage that Bud loved to wear.

Rod moved out to the Irish Bayou and isolated himself for the next two and a half years. The loss was almost greater than he could bear. For the rest of his life, he was never able to get over the hurt, dismay, and anger he felt over the callous way his husband's death was treated by the community. He was mortified so many churches failed to acknowledge anything had happened at all. How could people pretend that thirty-two other people had not just died? How could so many priests and ministers, people of God, refuse to help?

And yet there was something even worse, and that was when Rod saw how many families refused to claim their sons. As Stewart Butler had seen, those families who did would often arrange funerals to which none of the gay friends was invited.

Bud was cremated and buried in Oakdale Memorial in Glendora, California, after a beautiful service with his family, children, and ex-wives. Rod wasn't able to attend but did fly out a few months later to spend a week with Bud's family. Rod let them know he and Bud were both committed to seeing that the children had everything they needed. Pamela had married an airline pilot and so was reasonably well off, but Rod let his offer to help stand.

Other than his visit to the family, he stayed pretty much to himself over the next couple of years. But then he met Alan Robinson, who asked for Rod's help in organizing a Gertrude Stein Society in New Orleans. Rod was reluctant at first to get involved, but then he thought about Bud. Wasn't this organization just what Bud would have wanted, a group of literate and articulate gay men and women who could speak up and act for the gay community?

When Rod was on the local board of directors for the National Federation of Television and Radio Artists in 1976, he pushed for a local boycott of Anita Bryant. The boycott was the first time a group of Bryant's peers, since she was a member of NFTRA, spoke out against her. Rod received scathing reviews in Louisiana for his actions, but he hoped he'd done something that Bud would have liked.

Rod left broadcasting in 1985 and was then able to come more fully out of the closet. He spoke often to groups of college students, trying to eliminate what he saw as one of the worst obstacles to progress—guilt. "Guilt is a useless emotion," he told the students. It was unproductive and even destructive.

In 1985, Rod established The George Steven Matyi Private Trust, a lobbying group that fought to gain civil rights for gays and minorities in general, reporting regularly to the New Orleans City Council. Rod worked with Mayor Sidney Barthelemy during the mayor's administration from 1986-90. He also took a leading role in the fight against Mike Early, a city councilman serving the heavily gay neighborhoods of the city, who many felt made promises to the gay community so he could be elected and then refused to fulfill those promises.

Rod also worked with Governor Edwards. His point was always to make Bud's position clear, that being gay was normal for gays, and that those who were intelligent and articulate had a responsibility to lift up not only themselves but the rest of the gay community as well. The Trust, in the first few years of its existence, performed work estimated at $500,000 in lobbying for civil rights. That made Rod feel good.

But there was one thing no amount of success could accomplish, and that was, of course, bring Bud back. Rod never did find again a love like that which the two of them had shared. Perhaps he was afraid to let himself feel so deeply again. Maybe he isolated himself from others too much. Or perhaps it was simply that the man best suited to fit his personality no longer existed, and there was no one else even in the same category.

In 1990, Rod Wagener, ill from two terminal liver diseases, debated over whether to share any information about this very personal and private part of his life. "But no group can exist without a written history," he said. Then he looked at the George Steven Matyi Private Trust agenda for the 1990's, which mentioned specifically the need for a written history of gays in Louisiana. "At least this is a start," he said. "And I think Bud would want me to talk about him, even though he was a private person, too."

Then, looking wistfully at a photo of Bud, he added, "He was a beautiful person, in every way." He paused a moment and then concluded, "I loved him." And there was nothing more to say.

Rod Wagener died in 1991.

In 1998, as Todd Matyi was nearing his thirtieth birthday, he decided to go to New Orleans to try making a stronger connection to his father. His mother, Pamela, never liked to talk about Bud, though she did always keep the vase he'd thrown at her. She gave Todd Bud's old suede jacket with fringes. Todd remembered Rod Wagener coming to visit once when Todd was a child, taking him to Toys "R" Us and buying him a race car track, but in later years, they lost contact, and Todd now regretted losing that tie to his father. Todd's grandmother had a reel-to-reel tape of Bud singing, "To Reach the Unreachable Star," and she'd converted it to cassette for Todd and Tina. It was the only time Todd could remember ever hearing his father's beautiful voice. It brought tears to Todd's eyes every time he heard it.

Todd was straight and married, but he had no problem accepting his father's gayness, and now that he was reaching a milestone in his life, he felt a need to understand his father, his own flesh and blood, so he went to the French Quarter for the first time. He had a vague idea where the UpStairs had been but once he reached the neighborhood, he picked a bar, the Jimani, and went inside to ask if anyone there had heard of the UpStairs. A man there said his father had died in that fire, so they talked and shared what memories they could. Todd would always miss his father, but at least having that stronger connection with him was comforting.

For some reason, Tom Struve and Paul Doll were distracted or delayed and never did make it to the bar that evening. After the fire, they were rarely able to go to another bar, or even to another building of any kind, without checking for exits.

They stayed with WWNO until 1977, leaving the radio station to open Flamingos, a café and bar on St. Charles. They enjoyed the restaurant business but lost money and so were forced to close in 1987. They bounced back quickly, though, Tom taking a job as limousine chauffeur in 1989 and Paul working at Pat O'Brien's annex on Bourbon Street catering for private parties and special events.

Together for twenty-one years in 1991, Tom and Paul described their relationship as one where they were mother, father, and child to each other, always there for one another no matter how rotten the other had been, and always there for those good times that kept coming after all those years.

Suzanne Joslyn didn't make it to the bar that evening, either, but she lost several friends who did go. She was upset at the way so many in the city made light of the fire, and she never could understand how people could consider some lives unimportant. Suzanne, always full of life, couldn't help but recover from the disaster, and continued to live her own life to the fullest. In 1996, she was able to fulfill a thirty-year-old dream when her daughter, Annette Grefe, now a physician, looked her up and came to New Orleans to visit.

Suzanne Joslyn died in 1998 of emphysema.

Denny La Boeuf was also horrified at the callous reaction of the news media toward the fire. She felt the attitude was basically that at least the fire hadn't killed any important people. The reporting trivialized the tragedy, implying that what she witnessed wasn't significant. Living in New York, even in the Village for a while, during Stonewall and seeing the succeeding emphasis on gay rights, having been an anti-war activist and a civil rights activist, she felt a natural inclusion of gays in her circle of friends and in her ideals of equality.

She was extremely angry at the indifference shown toward the dead, feeling that even the subsequent fire code inspections in the bar where she worked and across the Quarter carried the implication, "At least the UpStairs happened first, so we can prevent anything bad happening to people who matter."

Denny had come to New Orleans to party, but her ideals and determination to fight injustice were strong, and witnessing the fire and its aftermath only reinforced her commitment. She returned to school, earning a law degree from Loyola, and began fighting the death penalty and fighting against injustice and inequality in all the many forms that it takes.

Upon learning that inmates had been brought to pick up the burned victims in the UpStairs because the task was considered too traumatic for professionals, she huffed in disgust. "And it's not traumatic for prisoners?"

Photographer Pat Burke felt satisfied that the *Daily Record* hit the streets a full two or three hours before the *Times-Picayune* the morning after the fire. Pat's photos became some of the tragedy's defining images for years. In the major flood of May 1995, however, he lost twenty-five years' worth of negatives, including all those of the UpStairs. But he would always remember the devastating scene he saw, even without pictures.

Mitch and Horace never did pick up Duane Jr. and Steve from the theater. When the Disney movie was over, Duane Jr. and Steve remained in the theater. Mitch had told them they might be a few minutes late and to just start watching the movie again. He and Horace would come inside to collect them as soon as they could.

The boys were surprised, though, when fifteen minutes into their second viewing, their dad still hadn't shown up. They were even more surprised when they watched the closing credits a second time. And still Mitch didn't come.

But there was nothing to do but sit and start watching the film a third time.

And a fourth. And a fifth. In those days, some movie theaters ran films all night, even if only a handful of viewers came to watch. Duane Jr. and Steve sat through *The World's Greatest Athlete* seven times. They knew something was wrong but didn't know what to do. Who could they call? They didn't know anyone in New Orleans besides their father.

In the morning, though, Genevieve "Ginny" Lynch, their father's landlady, and neighbor Roslyn Joffe arrived with the police. They knew that neither Mitch nor Horace was on the list of injured and suspected the worst but didn't have confirmation. The boys didn't learn the truth until after they'd already returned to Ft. Payne. Horace, it turned out, had extensive 4th degree burns over 90% of his body. He was identified through fingerprints. Mitch, who had run back into the bar for his lover, was found with extensive charring over 100% of his body. No one knew those details yet.

Jim Peterson, a friend of their father who'd left the UpStairs shortly before the fire, took the boys on streetcar rides, to a museum, and to the amusement park at Ponchartrain Beach to keep them distracted before finally sending them back to Alabama. They returned to their mom's house without ever hearing their father and his partner had been killed.

Back home, of course, they eventually learned at least that much, but their mother was tight-lipped over the specifics. As the years passed, any time Duane Jr. asked about his father, the only thing his mother would tell him was, "Your father was a drunk and he died in a bar!"

And that was all he knew.

In 2011, though, his daughter, who worked as a bartender, called to tell him she'd read a book about the UpStairs Lounge. Duane was then able to read about those last terrible minutes of his father's life, learned that Mitch had escaped but run back inside for Horace, and finally had another account of his father than the one his mother told him over and over.

"My dad was a hero," he realized. "My dad was a hero."

Hugh Cooley, the bartender about to come on duty, was found with 3rd and 4th degree burns over 90% of his body, with extensive charring of his face and fingers. He was identified two and a half weeks later, on July 10, through dental records.

Adolph Medina's family already knew he was gay and accepted him, but he didn't want them to hear about the fire on the news. His parents were at the wedding of a nephew, so Adolph called a friend and had him tell the parents he was okay as soon as they came home. As Adolph had expected, they weren't worried that others might hear he was at a gay bar. They were simply glad he was okay.

A few weeks after the fire, Adolph moved back to San Antonio, and he and Chuck continued seeing each other. Still, it was hard to get over the horror he'd witnessed. A year later, in 1974, his baby brother was murdered, and Adolph was finally just overcoming that when in 1975, Chuck committed suicide.

That was the hardest blow of all. Despite their problems, they'd truly loved each other and were in fact each other's "first love." Adolph was never able to forget that, but he was a survivor with experience, and he managed to go on. In 1999, still living in downtown San Antonio, he felt that despite the hard times, life for the most part was still pretty good.

Bill Rushton, a local gay journalist, wrote many of the earliest stories about the fire and ended up covering the event for *The Advocate*, at that time still in newspaper format. He felt so impacted by the UpStairs arson that he also took part in the Anita Bryant protest in 1977.

Working in the emergency room the night of the fire reaffirmed Paul Villien's desire to pursue Emergency Medicine, and he made it his career, working until Hurricane Katrina devastated so many medical facilities across the region.

While Paul and Brock enjoyed going to French Quarter bars once in a while, they found the local gay community too incestuous. "You know you've been in New Orleans too long," he said, quoting a familiar joke, "when your new lover has your old furniture."

As a result, he and Brock didn't spend a lot of time in the bars. Self-professed "boring people," Paul and Brock legally married in 2014 and lived across the street from Skip Getchell's former home on Crete Street.

When Brock developed cancer several years later and it became obvious by 2022 the end was near, he struggled to hang on until their 50th anniversary on August 25, dying a week later.

Fifty years with the man he loved. Paul couldn't help but wonder how many of those who died the night of the fire might have had similar stories by now, if only they'd had the chance.

Ferris LeBlanc's family only discovered the truth by accident. One of Ferris's nephews had taken upon himself the task of doing the family history for over twenty years, so the others assumed if there was information to be found on the internet, the man would have told them. He did find it but for some reason chose not to share the information. Maybe he thought to "protect" the older family members. So still more years passed before Marilyn and Skip and the rest of the family learned Ferris had died.

Marilyn and Skip finally learned the truth in 2015. Skip did his own internet search and was the one to break the news to his mother. "We found him, Mom, and it's horrible."

Forty-seven years with no contact. Forty-two years since Ferris's death. But knowing what happened allowed them at last to reconnect. The details were horrific, of course. This wasn't what they'd hoped to learn. Still, after such a long time, they'd already begun to realize there was never going to be a phone call, there was never going to be a knock on the door.

Just as painful was knowing Ferris's body lay in some unmarked grave. Recognizing how many other gay men had been abandoned by their families, how many families of the UpStairs dead had refused to claim their bodies, while they *would* have claimed Ferris if they had only known.

Also frustrating was the knowledge that authorities *knew* Ferris's identity. With minimum effort, they could have looked up his military records and easily found numerous family members. Perhaps they assumed that with a name like LeBlanc, he was local, and local family members would already know about the fire and come looking. It felt, though, like neglect, like dismissal.

No longer trusting "the family historian" to keep him informed, Skip threw himself into internet research. He learned that Ferris's partner, Rod Rodgers, had been murdered in an alley in Oakland not long after disappearing. That raised a whole series of additional questions. Had the men borrowed money from a loan shark? Was Ferris on the run not only from family embarrassment but from actual danger?

What if Rod had been abusive toward Ferris and Ferris had really been on the run from Rod the whole time and not the family? Robert had told them shortly after Ferris's disappearance that Ferris had asked to sleep on Robert's sofa for a few days. But then one morning, Ferris was gone.

The biggest mystery, though, was the location of Ferris's body.

Skip found that the name of the indigent cemetery was Resthaven, not Hoyt or Holt as sometimes reported. The first time he arrived in New Orleans to look for his uncle in 2015, the graveyard was locked, the grass unmown, the cemetery right next to a site where the City stored its portable toilets. An employee cursed at Skip when he asked to enter the grounds and he was turned away.

But writer Clayton Delery was in contact with a former student who was able to help Skip gain access. Activist Sheri Wright joined Marilyn and Skip at Resthaven, where she filmed a short documentary, "Finding Ferris."

Filmmaker Robert L. Camina worked with them as well at the remote field off Old Gentilly Road in New Orleans East. Surviving records showed that Ferris was buried in Panel Q, Lot 32, but many maps and other records had been lost during Hurricane Katrina. The family even tried tracking down the gravediggers who'd buried Ferris, hoping against hope they'd remember what section they were working that day. But they weren't able to definitively determine which grave was his, weren't able to place a headstone or plaque, weren't able to relocate the body and bring him to California to be cremated and given a proper military burial.

They also spent years trying to persuade City and state officials that it wasn't only Ferris who needed attention. Skip Bailey felt that with advances in DNA technology, the three unidentified victims of the UpStairs fire could finally be identified too. Especially critical to confirm the tentative identity of Larry Norman Frost.

Skip contacted Louisiana Representative Clay Higgins to ask for help, and a couple of weeks later, Jeff Landry, the Attorney General of Louisiana, sent the family a five-page letter detailing multiple requirements setting up almost impossible conditions the family would have to meet to be allowed to retrieve Ferris's body.

Fifty years after his death, the family is still looking for Ferris.

Buddy Rasmussen naturally was deeply affected by the fire and witnessing his lover's death right before his eyes rather than just finding out later that he'd died. The body of thirty-two-year-old Adam Roland Fontenot was found at the end of the bar near his stool, making him probably the only person in the bar who hadn't even attempted to escape, his fantastic mind too dulled by the alcohol to realize what was happening until it was too late. He received 3rd and 4th degree burns over 90% of his body, losing his fingers and facial characteristics. He was identified by the dental charts at Dr. Perry Waters' office.

Even though the relationship between Buddy and Adam had been troubled, Buddy did still love Adam and felt his loss, even if there were fleeting moments of guilty relief intermingled with that. Buddy also felt a deep sense of frustration that more people hadn't followed him out the back way. Most if not all those who died by the front windows could have made it to the third room, and their unnecessary deaths irritated him. He was angry at them for dying. And he missed them terribly, as several had been good friends. He never did read any of the newspaper accounts of the fire. He knew more than he wanted to know about the fire already.

Buddy spent the night of the fire in Bill Duncan's apartment and stayed with him the next several days. It was awkward in a way since Bill had been Adam's rival, but Bill was also Buddy's best friend, and he needed Bill's comfort.

The Catholic Church in Ville Platte refused to bury Adam because he'd died in a gay bar, but when he was finally buried, many people came to the funeral. Thirty-five of them were gay friends, one of them Harry, who'd escaped with Buddy.

After the funeral, Buddy and Bill spent a week in Mississippi to get away from New Orleans, and then they continued seeing each other for the next two months while living separately before moving in together in the house at 923 St. Andrew Street Uptown. Buddy worked on house renovations for the first few years after the fire while Bill finished pharmacy school. They lived on Buddy's $9,000 a year and still managed to save.

He worked for a while at Phil Esteve's Post Office, but when Phil was bitchy just one time too many, driving off four customers at one time, Buddy walked out in the middle of his shift. The next morning when he returned, Phil taunted, "So you're coming back?"

Buddy said, "I just forgot to drop off your fucking keys," and he tossed them on the bar and walked off. They eventually made up and were on friendly terms again, but Buddy never did work for him after that. In fact, he never worked in any bar again.

After doing renovations for a while, Buddy decided to work offshore as well, continuing the renovations when he was back home. He started on the oil rigs as a galley hand and then worked as a roustabout. He finally tired of that and tired of searching in vain for good help with the home repairs, so he gave up both jobs and began working at Avondale shipyards in 1978, where he worked until he retired in 1991.

Buddy and Bill bought a house at 3119 Palmyra in Mid-City in 1983. They'd thought about buying a house a year or so after the fire, using Jean Gosnell as their real estate agent, but they decided against buying at that time.

Around 1977, Buddy joined the Amon Ra carnival krewe, a gay krewe that formed in 1965 and had its first ball in 1966. For 1983, Buddy was chosen as queen and kept the news secret until the night of the ball. When he'd leave in the evenings, his neighbor, also in the krewe, would ask if he was going over to the krewe den to work. He'd say yes, but when the neighbor went later and didn't see him there, he figured Buddy was out fooling around on his lover. What he was really doing was going to a friend's house to work on his costume.

When the queen was announced at the ball, a man sewed up in a bag squirmed around like a worm. Someone said, "The queen is dead," and the worm was carried off. Then while the New Orleans Gay Men's Chorus sang the Hallelujah chorus—repeatedly, because Buddy wasn't finished with his make-up yet—the metamorphosis took place. Out came Buddy as a butterfly. As he stood on stage, cables lifted his unfolding wings out of a box. They continued to unfold and spread out further and further until they covered the entire stage opening at the St. Bernard Civic Center in Chalmette. Then Buddy marched around for a few minutes to the 1812 overture. Buddy, forever frugal, had spent $2000 and hours of work for a few minutes of fun and glory, but somehow it was worth it.

Buddy dropped out of Amon Ra in 1987 and devoted more time to renovating the house on Palmyra, which took five years altogether, since he paid as he went. When he finished, though, the house was beautiful, with lots of pantry space in the kitchen, bookshelves upstairs, a built-in entertainment center, four-post beds, a brick patio out back with well-tended plants, and various framed prints and stamps hanging throughout the house.

Buddy and Bill rarely if ever went to the bars, Buddy having never much liked bars as a customer. The fire was horrible but not the reason he didn't go, and he was able to eventually put the tragedy behind him. In 1981, Buddy and Bill bought twenty acres of forest property near Calico Rock, Arkansas. A few years later, they bought sixteen additional acres, of cleared land this time, and moved to their property in 1991 after retiring early.

Buddy looked forward to years of relaxing yard work. "Can you imagine how long it's going to take to landscape sixteen acres?" he asked, smiling. He and Bill were still happy there in 2023, still in love after fifty years, enjoying the country more than they expected, canning vegetables, volunteering with the Food Bank, and working on their home until it was perfect. Though age had taken a toll, they planned to continue enjoying their little paradise and each other for the rest of their lives.

Researchers and Artists

The story of the UpStairs Lounge is primarily the story of those who were there that dreadful night or who lost people who were. It's the story, too, however, of the bar itself, which had a character of its own. It's one of many stories from the New Orleans LGBTQ community, and of Metropolitan Community Church history. It's the story of religious and political oppression. Even the story of anyone impacted when they first learned of the fire decades after it was set.

A tangential part of the story involves the researchers and artists who attempt to share the main story with the world.

In the process of my own research, I gained both respect and distrust of historians. Theirs is a monumental task, sifting through personal recollections of relatives and friends, always subject to distortion. There's plenty of misinformation from "official" sources as well. Articles stating that a Molotov cocktail was thrown into the bar or that patrons were in the middle of an all-you-can-eat buffet, neither of which is true.

Several people told unverified and unrealistic accounts of what happened that night. For instance, one story was that Mitch and Horace were found dead in one another's arms, but there's nothing verifying that detail in any official report. Another story went even further, claiming the two men were so badly burned that all that remained of them was their bones.

Of course, it would have taken quite the blaze to reduce Mitch's huge body to mere bones in the space of fifteen minutes, and we have the coroner's reports explaining what did and didn't happen. In the aftermath of tragedy, survivors often create a mythology surrounding it. The fact that Mitch gave his life for Horace is touching enough. There's no need to invent additional and overly grisly details about the event. The stories describing the locations of bodies, particularly those underneath the piano, are so persistent that I've kept some in this edition, but those details need to be corroborated by another source before being taken as fact.

Other aspects of the mythology around the UpStairs Lounge include the long list of people who experienced dreams or premonitions. I suspect most of those premonitions exist more in hindsight than they did as recounted here, but I reported what people told me.

In the past fifteen years or so, more researchers and artists have completed a variety of works incorporating the UpStairs Lounge story: art exhibits, books, documentaries, articles, screenplays, even musicals. I'm not able to provide an exhaustive list of people and projects, as I hope the list keeps growing, but it's probably already clear to anyone interested in the subject that there are other works to consult to gain a better understanding of the tragedy. Since most of this research postdates mine, it's likely to contain information I wasn't able to find at the time I pursued mine.

All these efforts have helped turn the tragedy into more than just a senseless loss of life.

Skylar Fein created an art exhibit called "Remember the Upstairs Lounge" featuring photos of the victims and items from the bar. The 2008-2009 installation was showcased at the Contemporary Arts Center in New Orleans.

Vincent Taughber Meis wrote a novel, *The Mayor of Oak Street*, which includes the fire as the climax of the story.

Wayne Self wrote a musical called *Upstairs: A Musical Eulogy*. Wayne died in 2022.

Max Vernon's musical, *The View UpStairs*, premiered Off Broadway in the Lynn Redgrave Theater in New York City on February 28, 2017, with a running time of one hour and forty-five minutes. It has since had 30+ productions in cities around the world, including London, Sydney, and Tokyo, nominated for 28 awards for its various productions.

Max is a three-time Drama Desk nominee, an Out100 honoree, and received the Lucille Lortel Award for Best Musical as well as the Richard Rogers Award, Jonathan Larson Grant, Pew Arts and Culture Grant, the New York Stage and Film's Founders Award, New York Foundation of the Arts Fellowship, and the JFund Award from the Jerome Foundation.

Max is a Tony Award nominated composer, lyricist, playwright, and performer. They earned an MFA from NYU's Graduate Musical Theatre Writing Program and have performed at the Kennedy Center, Lincoln Center, and the

Metropolitan Museum of Art. Their other musicals include *KPOP*, *The Tattooed Lady*, and *Show and Tell*.

Royd Anderson has long felt a fascination for New Orleans tragedies, of which there are many. In addition to his short documentary on the UpStairs Lounge, he's made documentaries on the Rault Center fire, the Pan Am plane crash in Kenner, the Continental grain elevator explosion, and the Destrehan-Luling ferry disaster. He's also written a book about the various tragedies.

Sheri Wright contacted me about the same time as Robert L. Camina. They had different visions for their projects and chose to make separate documentaries. I think that's wise. There will never be one book or film that fully tells this multi-layered story filled with so many characters. Each historian, filmmaker, writer, and artist will bring their own unique perspective and talent to their projects. There's room for everyone.

Some of the people I've spoken to over the years demonstrated a sense of possession over the UpStairs story, unwilling to share sources or contacts with others. But most of these folks were generous with their time and knowledge. For most, our main goal is to make sure the story is told, that these people aren't forgotten, that young LGBTQ folks today have an opportunity to know their own history.

Sheri Wright lives in Kentucky. She's an activist for women's reproductive rights, for Native Americans, and for racial justice. She was a live streamer in Louisville during the Breonna Taylor protests against police brutality and received multiple death threats. She'd already become friends with

Skip and Lori Bailey (relatives of Ferris LeBlanc) by that point, and they sent her funds to purchase a bulletproof vest to wear at protests.

Sheri has said that one of the most profound aspects of her research into the UpStairs fire was the opportunity to expand her extended chosen family.

For her documentary, Sheri filmed interviews with survivors, with witnesses who hadn't been interviewed previously, with first responders, reporters, city officials, and family members of those who perished, about forty people in total. She then went down to Orlando after the Pulse nightclub shooting and did some additional filming there, feeling a kinship with those impacted by this other horrific tragedy.

Sheri has accumulated enough footage for a 90-minute documentary and has completed a first edit but then ran out of funding before she could complete a second edit. She can still be contacted through her "Tracking Fire" website and Facebook page.

Sheri is serious and dedicated but that doesn't stop her from having fun, too. As a songwriter and guitarist for the band Auntie Madder, she expresses through hard rock/punk/sludge/metal her commitment to continue the fight for human rights everywhere.

Clayton Delery's book, *The Up Stairs Lounge Arson*, was a finalist for a Lambda Literary Award in LGBT non-fiction and was named Book of the Year by the Louisiana Endowment for the Humanities, the first time an LGBT-themed book won that recognition.

Delery shared the following with me about his research: I was a frightened, lonely gay teenager in 1973 when I was watching television and saw the news coverage of a fire in a French Quarter bar that had killed dozens of people. As the news coverage progressed in the next week, I learned that the bar had been a gay bar, and I thought that meant that one day, somebody would kill me! The story stayed with me.

I first started thinking about writing a book about the fire in 2003, when I read an article in the *Times Picayune* about the placement of the memorial plaque in the sidewalk outside of Up Stairs Lounge. For various reasons—none of them good—I didn't actually start serious research until 2009. I expected the work to take about two years. Instead, it took five, because I had to sandwich the research and writing in between my teaching career and various family obligations, including taking care of my parents, who both died during this period. So the active work took place between 2009 and the publication of the book in 2014.

I was surprised to learn that the fire had been set by a gay man. I assumed it had been a hate crime, but that theory was one of the first I had to let go of. I was also surprised to learn about how doggedly the State Fire Marshal's office tried to close the case. They worked on it for years after the New Orleans Police Department had given up.

The single biggest surprise was learning how few people who had been living in New Orleans in the 1970s remembered the Up Stairs. In the early days of my research, when I told people what I was writing about, some had only a vague, hazy memory about the fire, and others didn't remember it at all. It was—and remains—the deadliest fire in the history of New Orleans, and it was in very real danger of being forgotten.

Among the most challenging aspects of the project was locating the various primary sources. It was easy to find newspaper and magazine articles (many of them riddled with inaccuracies). It was more difficult finding things like the witness statements and the extensive investigative reports left by the New Orleans Police Department and the State Fire Marshal.

Equally challenging was finding former patrons and people who actually survived the fire. If they lived through the fire in 1973, and then survived AIDS in the 80s and 90s, by the early 21st century they were falling victim to heart attacks, stroke, cancer, and all the things that start taking people away from us when they're in their fifties, sixties, and seventies. In the six years that lapsed between the time I first thought of writing a book and actually beginning the work, a number of people died whom I would have loved to have interviewed.

Toward the end of my research, I exchanged several emails with a man whose name I won't mention for reasons that will become clear. He had been in the fire, and he'd survived it, though he'd sustained some painful injuries. He'd heard about my research and had some thoughts he wanted to share.

As I said, he and I exchanged several emails. He answered a number of questions for me, but in his last email, he said he wouldn't be writing to me anymore, because our emails had awakened very painful memories for him, and he'd been having nightmares about the fire.

I had incorporated several details I learned from him in the book, but after he stopped writing to me, my publisher told me I'd need to get him to sign a release to use that material. I didn't want to risk reopening his wounds. Rather than contacting him for a release, I just quietly withdrew those details. By that time, my book was under contract, and it would be published with or without him. I decided that my ability to use those details was not worth the price of his pain.

Among the most rewarding aspects was building relationships with many of the people who shared my interest in the Up Stairs Lounge. So many filmmakers and artists and writers—including you!

Another was to see how much interest in the fire has grown over the years. In 1973, city leaders seemed anxious to sweep the story under the rug, and it was only on the front pages of the papers for a few days. Now, fifty years later, interest in its history is stronger than it's ever been. It's the subject of at least three books, four documentaries, three plays, and countless articles. I've also read several screenplays attempting to tell the story, though I don't think any has yet made it into production.

The most rewarding things, though, have been the times when I've been contacted by the friend or family member of one of the people who died in the fire. It has been gratifying to learn that my book helped them learn something about a loved one. Those experiences have also made me realize that the story of the fire isn't over.

When I was just beginning my work, I became aware that a manuscript of your book, *Let the Faggots Burn*, was on file at the Historic New Orleans Collection (HNOC). The staff of the HNOC let me read it but were wary about letting me take too many notes or quote too extensively unless I had your permission, because your book hadn't been published yet. I contacted you, and you readily gave the permission to me. You had every reason to regard me as a rival, but you said, "I just want the story to be told."

You set an important example for me. I could never pay you back, but I could pay things forward. So whenever anyone else researching the book has contacted me with a question, I've done my best to answer it, sharing whatever materials I had that would support the answer: newspaper articles, autopsy protocols, police reports, witness statements, etc. I've also been filmed for several of the documentaries. None of us own the story. The best thing we can do is act as its stewards and share what we know.

I've written two books about the LGBT+ History of New Orleans: *The Up Stairs Lounge Arson* and *Out for Queer Blood*. Both involve the murder of gay men. I'm proud of the work I've done, but writing those books has had a price. When I've spent a day reading police reports and witness statements and autopsy protocols, it's very difficult for me to come back to the present and have a conversation, say, about the latest television show, or the hot new restaurant. And that, in turn, has had a negative effect on some of my personal relationships, because I was living more fully in the past than in the present. Nonfiction writers understand that there's very often a steep emotional cost in telling a story. Other people don't always understand that.

In the 1980s, there was a popular bumper sticker (memes hadn't been invented yet) that said, *Whoever dies with the most toys wins.* It's supposed to be about the power of money, and I can see why some people think it's important to die with a lot of toys, but I also think the idea is dead wrong.

I think whoever tells the most compelling stories wins. Ultimately the stories we tell define us. You see this all over the news these days, with everyone from Governor Ron DeSantis of Florida down to local citizens attending school board meetings trying to stomp out stories they don't like. We need our stories. We need them to be honest, and we especially need them to be honest when the honesty involves pain. And so I have two words to say to anyone reading this who thinks they have an important story to tell:

Tell it.

Frank Perez helped co-found the LGBT+ Archives Project of Louisiana and is its current Executive Director. He's written numerous articles about the fire, considering his extensive research a kind of bank account of knowledge he can draw upon to assist other researchers and write additional articles. He's organized three memorial services, including the 50th anniversary memorial in 2023, a three-day event with twenty-six speakers and panelists.

He says the story of the UpStairs Lounge gave him a greater appreciation for local queer history and a sense of urgency to get that history out of the closet. The most challenging aspect of his research and efforts to locate Ferris LeBlanc's body has been the emotional toll it takes.

Frank feels the folks at the UpStairs Lounge could never have imagined how far we've come in fifty years, but he warns that unless we're vigilant, we could lose many of those achievements.

Robert Fieseler wrote *Tinderbox*, the only book on the fire so far that's been reviewed by the *New York Times*. Robert grew up in Chicago, earned a degree in Journalism from Columbia University, and spent five years researching the UpStairs Lounge fire. He now lives in the Bywater neighborhood of New Orleans and has spent an additional five years since the publication of his book doing still more research while pushing policy supporting LGBTQ rights.

He wrote the resolution, passed unanimously by the New Orleans City Council, by which City leaders officially apologized for the City's initial response in 1973. He helped arrange for the LGBT+ Archives Project of Louisiana to place a marker on Reginald Adams's formerly unmarked grave in a Catholic cemetery in Dallas. And he helped Bill Larson's family finally place a marker on his grave, a marker which acknowledged Larson's service during WWII, which in turn led the National WWII Museum to acknowledge his service. Robert also pushed the *New York Times* to publish an obituary for Larson decades after his death in its Overlooked series.

He's helped people who were largely invisible during their lifetimes and all but forgotten after their deaths to exist and have meaning today. The UpStairs isn't torture porn, he insists. It's not a grisly story to endure simply to feel "educated" on LGBTQ history. No cause is dead, he says, so long as there is someone willing to take up the torch and help set the story in a contemporary context.

Robert disagrees that gay political activity in New Orleans began with the Anita Bryant protests. Charlene Schneider and Paul Killgore, who were marshals at that parade through the French Quarter, had both taken steps toward activism when walking out the front door during the memorial service at St. Mark's rather than exit through a side entrance to avoid TV cameras. Charlene, who'd been a friend of Ken Harrington, spoke about the UpStairs repeatedly during the years between the fire and the Anita Bryant protests. Paul went on to donate $1000 toward the documentary, *The Celluloid Closet*, as well as contribute toward the memorial UpStairs Lounge plaque in the sidewalk on Iberville. Robert believes the fire was much more of a catalyst than previously thought.

Like most UpStairs researchers, Robert found that the story has taken an emotional toll on him. He's had to set boundaries and often asks himself when it might be appropriate to step aside and hand the story over to someone else. He had to be pushed to take up the story to begin with, not feeling qualified to write about it. Often during those first years of research, he felt like he was "learning how to fly a spaceship while flying it for the first time." He encourages others to push past their self-doubt and whatever worries they have about what they might have of value to contribute. There's still more to be learned and told about the UpStairs in particular, and far more about LGBTQ history in general.

Robert L. Camina has produced two documentaries on LGBTQ history. The first, *Raid of the Rainbow Lounge*, detailed a brutal police raid on a Fort Worth gay bar in 2009 that happened on the 40th anniversary of the Stonewall riots. The 2012 film was narrated by Meredith Baxter and was screened in multiple film festivals across the United States, Canada, and Mexico.

Robert said that "In late 2012/early 2013, someone who had seen the film and admired our activism contacted me out of the blue. He thought we told the story of the Rainbow Lounge raid in a balanced, respectful manner. He went on to ask if I knew about the Up Stairs Lounge arson, and I didn't! I was stunned. I thought I knew my Gay History. Given the success of *Raid of the Rainbow Lounge*, he thought we should be the ones to share this vital story with the world."

Camina's second documentary was *Upstairs Inferno*, narrated by Christopher Rice. It premiered in 2015 and won eighteen awards. Discussing his work, Robert has said that "When production began on *Upstairs Inferno*, nearly 40 years had passed since the fire. Many of the survivors had passed away. However, with the help of the Internet and Facebook, I was able to locate quite a few people who were survivors, friends/family members of the victims, or witnesses. From day one, it was my intent to honor the victims and survivors with this film.

"Once I located these people, I introduced myself and made sure they knew I wasn't looking to exploit them. I spent time building relationships and trust. Asking people to resurrect painful memories is a huge request and I had to respect their boundaries. With solid friendships in place, we were able to have conversations on camera, rather than interrogations. I think that comes across in the film and it makes their stories much more powerful.

"The research process had its own challenges because I researched this story from scratch. My technique is to start with original source documents. Documents, precious photographs, and contact information for victims' friends and families had been lost with the passage of time. Add in the devastation caused by Hurricane Katrina and even more pieces of the puzzle were lost or destroyed.

"While the Internet was very helpful in the research process, nothing replaces stepping into a library and flipping through newspapers, scrolling through microfilm, or thumbing through photographs. I made several trips to multiple libraries in New Orleans. I even traveled to the ONE National Gay and Lesbian Archives in Los Angeles and the New York Public Library to sift through their collection of documents about the Up Stairs Lounge fire. It was a treasure hunt at times, but "new" discoveries made it exciting.

"There was a time when I was sorting through files in New Orleans and came across a charred swatch of red-flocked wallpaper that was from the Up Stairs Lounge. That was a huge find! Another "new" discovery was the color news footage of the fire. I spent countless hours searching news broadcast archives, *hoping* to find some long-lost news coverage. I hit dead end after dead end. Then one day, while on a random news library aggregator website, I typed in a set of keywords into the search bar. The result was a description of a news clip that sounded a lot like the Up Stairs Lounge fire.

"The film had not been digitized yet, so I couldn't preview the footage to test my suspicion. I decided to take a gamble and spend hundreds of dollars to get a digitized version of the clip to review. The risk paid off. I had "discovered" color news footage of the Up Stairs Lounge fully ablaze, firefighters battling the massive flames, and first responders attending to the badly burned victims. This was footage that hadn't been seen in years!

"It's possible that the footage would have been properly identified at some point, but for the sake of preserving history, I am glad I was able to expedite the process. The footage is now accurately labeled in the news archives and has been licensed for use in countless other projects.

"While I experienced many additional challenges during production, including the horrific task of fundraising, one of the most challenging aspects of making *Upstairs Inferno* was accepting the realization I was not going to find some of the material or people I was looking for. When you start a project with a specific vision, and you exhaust every avenue to achieve it, it's a challenge to come to peace with the realization that you won't be able to fulfill your vision 100%.

"As a storyteller, I tried to remain objective and keep my emotions in check. However, I would be lying if I said there weren't times the sheer magnitude of the tragedy didn't get to me. One time in particular, a family member of one of the victims mailed me an original portrait of their loved one. As I held this 40+ year-old photo in my hands and looked into his eyes, I broke down in tears. Physically touching the heirloom made this story extremely personal.

"I've gotten to know the families of many of the victims and I now consider them part of my extended family. I've also grown very close to many of the survivors. The people I've met along this journey, especially the survivors, have touched my life immeasurably and I am honored to call them my friends. They have taught me about life, love, and forgiveness.

"I didn't want to create a stagnant documentary, with only an exposition of facts. I wanted to humanize the story and show the real impact the fire had on the victims' friends, families, and the LGBTQ movement. It's easy to trivialize a situation when you gloss over a headline in a newspaper (or a Facebook post). There is something about *seeing* and *hearing* the story from those who experienced an event that truly makes it "real." That's what possesses the potential to create change.

"*Upstairs Inferno* was not the first telling of this story and I knew it would not be the last. A single literary work or work of art can only go so deep into a subject. Historians will be uncovering stories and facts for years to come. My documentary had its World Premiere in New Orleans on June 24, 2015: the 42nd anniversary of the deadly arson. The audience was full of survivors, friends/family members of victims, and witnesses. Many traveled across the country to attend the screening.

"As the names and pictures of the victims appeared on the screen at the end of the film, audience members stood up in respect. That was followed by a standing ovation, tears, hugs, and "thank yous." I'm incredibly grateful for how much the New Orleans LGBTQ community embraced me and the film.

"Prior to the World Premiere, the Louisiana State Fire Marshal's office contacted me and we worked together to examine the case and evaluate options regarding the investigation. After an internal review, much deliberation and consultations with legal experts, they decided not to reopen the case. However, they took this evaluation very seriously. I was honored that Louisiana State Fire Marshal "Butch" Browning flew in from Baton Rouge to attend the World Premiere to personally talk to the audience about the recent re-examination of the case.

"I was completely shocked but extremely humbled when the Fire Marshal presented me with an honorary medallion called the "Champion Coin" for my work and dedication to the Up Stairs Lounge fire story. It's a moment I will always cherish, and the medallion is something I will always treasure. To this day, it's on display on a shelf above my desk."

For the past eight years since his documentary was released, Robert Camina has continued working with survivors and family members of those killed and was instrumental in learning the most likely identity of one of the "unidentified white males" buried alongside Ferris, Larry Frost. If the location of those burial plots can finally be discovered, DNA analysis may be able to provide closure for another family as well.

Hunter Burke earned a BFA in Performing Arts-Theater from the University of Louisiana and has appeared in the films *The Big Short* and *One Night in Miami*. He's also appeared in several TV series, including *Bosch*, *Claws*, and *Sweet Magnolias*. He co-wrote the screenplay for *Lost Bayou*, which won Best Narrative Feature at the Santa Fe International Film Festival. He's now written a full-length screenplay, *The Fire UpStairs*, which was a Quarterfinalist for the 2021 Academy Nicoll Fellowship (essentially the Oscars for unproduced scripts). Here is some of his connection to the story:

I first learned about the fire in the fall of 2010. I had just moved to New Orleans from Lafayette, where I was born and raised. I bring this up only because I had spent my entire life in Louisiana and never once heard about the fire. Within the first month of living in New Orleans, I picked up a local weekly lifestyle newspaper (I think it was *The Gambit*) and it was the front page story. I can't remember the thesis of the article, but it provided general information regarding the events, which in turn provided the urge to seek out more information, which inevitably led me to your book.

Of all the atrocities and heartache I could point to that occurred around the fire, the thing that impacted me the most was the enduring love and community that the UpStairs Lounge bar provided to its customers. It was the love within the chosen family that thrived in the midst of hate and chaos. It is the detail that keeps me coming back to this story.

The decision to write our screenplay was not something I immediately arrived at. At first, it was just a passive inkling that the story of the UpStairs Lounge arson would make for a great film, but I wasn't the one to write it. But as the years went by and I worked on other projects, I would come back to the story of the UpStairs in my leisure time to research more. The more that was revealed, the more I became taken by it.

Yet I was still waiting on someone else to write the script. It wasn't until a conversation with my brother from another mother, Robert Larriviere, in which he insisted I at least make an attempt. Robert and I share a Cajun culture and a specific thing that occurred in our people's history is that the Cajun language was almost erased due to Americanization after WW2, yet was thankfully saved by a few dedicated culture bearers. The point he made was that I was actively contributing to the possibility of this story disappearing, if I didn't at least try to do it. So at his insistence, I began to put some words on the page.

The focus of our screenplay revolves around Johnny Townsend's journey in writing what would become, to my knowledge, the first written account of the UpStairs Lounge arson, called *Let the Faggots Burn*. In our script, the story unfolds almost as a detective story would in that we learn about the characters and events of the fire in 1973 through Johnny's "investigation" in 1989/1990. In dramatizing Johnny's interviews with survivors and those adjacent to the fire, we jump back and forth between 1973 and 1989 to tell the story of not only the fire, but also those dedicated archivists who've kept this story alive and heard, including Johnny Townsend, Clayton Delery, Robert Camina, Robert Fieseler, Royd Anderson, and Sheri Wright.

In these early stages of producing our film, the significant obstacle has been appealing to and amassing a team of collaborators who both believe in the project and have the production clout to get the film financed and greenlit. The journey so far has been locating those filmmakers (actors, directors, producers, etc.) who see the power in this story enough to dedicate years of hard work to make the film a reality.

Joey Gray studied acting at David Mamet's Atlantic Theater Company. He's appeared in the film *Party Monster* and in several TV series, including *7th Heaven*, *Malcolm in the Middle*, *Weeds*, and *Desperate Housewives*. He's also earned a master's degree in Cultural Reporting and Criticism from New York University. He started a queer political zine called *HARDY*, named after his gay grandfather. He's working on a queer podcast called *"Dear Uncle Vito,"* with the first series dedicated to the UpStairs Lounge. And he's written a feature-length narrative screenplay about the fire.

Brad Dalton wrote a sixty-five minute theatrical reading for five actors to be accompanied by a jazz pianist, based on Robert Fieseler's book *Tinderbox*. The five actors represent fifteen characters: Buddy Rasmussen, Adam Fontenot, Bill Larson, Troy Perry, Stewart Butler, Dexter Brecht, Roger Nunez, Michael Scarborough, Steve Duplantis, Claudine Rigaud, Ricky Everett, Rusty Quinton, Henry Kubicki, Anita Bryant, and Jerry Falwell.

Brad describes the inspiration for the piece as almost a mystical experience: "Sitting around during the pandemic, I reread Robert's book and I suddenly saw the piece clearly before me in a flash. I saw five actors delivering the text, passing it around to tell the story with little to no actual staging. And I heard the sound of a live jazz pianist. I followed the call. I never questioned it for a moment.

Although I had never done an adaptation of a book into a dramatic format, I just knew it would work."

Since that time, Brad has created similar adaptations of other works of literature.

To whittle the huge story of the UpStairs Lounge down to a manageable size, Brad left out sections about the national gay scene and concentrated on New Orleans. As he tells it, "The structure is: Introduction to the camaraderie and community and fun at the Up Stairs Lounge before the fire, then exploring the anti-gay environment of the 70's, the FIRE as the center of the piece, the depressing aftermath followed by the rise of gay liberation and finally, the recognition of the victims with the memorial marker being placed on Iberville for all to see in 2003."

His website, *braddalton.com*, provides a portion of his impressive background:

Brad Dalton's original productions have been produced widely throughout the United States and abroad in opera houses such as Lyric Opera of Chicago, Los Angeles Opera, the Barbican in London (with the LSO), the State Opera of South Australia, Carnegie Hall, Washington National Opera, San Diego Opera, San Jose Opera, Opera Santa Barbara, New Orleans Opera, Hawaii Opera Theatre, Austin Lyric Opera and Opera Boston.

In 2003, Dalton was awarded the prestigious Helpmann Award for "Best Direction of an Opera in Australia" for his direction of the Australian premiere of *Dead Man Walking*.

Dalton has received critical acclaim for his "ravishingly theatrical" production of *A Streetcar Named Desire* starring Renee Fleming, which has been seen in London, New York, Los Angeles, and Chicago.

In 2017, Dalton directed the American premiere of Alma Deutscher's *Cinderella*, available on Sony DVD and Blu Ray. New opera productions include *Alceste, Don Giovanni, The Magic Flute, Cosi Fan Tutte, La Clemenza di Tito, Idomeneo, Rigoletto, Il Trovatore, Tosca, La Boheme, Madama Butterfly, Faust, Romeo and Juliet, Carmen, Cavalleria Rusticana, Pagliacci, Anna Karenina, Albert Herring, A Streetcar Named Desire, The Flying Dutchman, Romeo and Juliet and* Alma Deutscher's *Cinderella.*

Dalton is a graduate of Harvard University and the National Shakespeare Conservatory. He has directed numerous productions of theatre and musical theatre as well as opera.

Monica Ordoñez cofounded Mélange Dance Company in 2014 along with Alexa Erck Lambert. She then choreographed and conceptualized a twenty-minute dance performance based on the UpStairs Lounge fire, later expanding the multi-media production to an hour and twenty minutes.

The performance was nominated for the Big Easy Classical Arts Award for Outstanding Modern Dance Presentation and described as "a valuable and radical work" by *Nola Dance Reader.*

Monica studied ballet as a child and graduated from Tulane University with a double major in Dance and Paralegal Studies.

To select which characters to portray, Monica explained, "The stories I feature are ones with details that inspire an organic visualization bringing them to life through a combination of the right music, storytelling, and choreography. Having visual details helped pique my interest; like Buddy Rasmussen's infamous Halloween photo, and how he would playfully speak on his microphone announcing the names of patrons walking in and established this fun and comfortable safe haven for the gay community.

"Of course the story of Reggie and Regina's interracial and queer love and their incredibly haunting final moment had to be honored.

"I kept coming back to the story of John and Jane. There were so many unique details to their story that really stimulated my imagination—John's life as a vet and the life they built together, from their family, to the activities they did together, their sweet relationship despite John being gay, and the complexity of their dynamic of love—the drama and emotion of it really stirred my feelings to make it a compelling piece to create.

"The details of the final spaghetti that Jane made John really got me as I pictured that eerie scenario where Jane said her final goodbye. It was so heart wrenching to imagine, and any audience member could really connect with this as a human being. As a woman I deeply connect with Jane's story as I consider what it might have been like at that time when women couldn't even own a credit card in their name, let alone survive on their own without financial support from their husband. I think Jane stayed with John out of necessity, but mostly out of love. She was supportive and continued to be, even in the aftermath of John's death and the fire, and though she wasn't a patron of the lounge, she is still a strong witness and storyteller to the tragedy. In my latest rendition of UpStairs, Jane really fulfilled this full circle narrative."

Monica used a multi-media approach to enhance the story, working with filmmakers Royd Anderson, Sheri Wright, and Robert Camina to incorporate imagery of the lounge and faces and voices of the actual patrons. She edited a pre-show film incorporating footage of surviving patrons, families, and activists speaking along with photos of the patrons to give the audience some context to begin their journey.

"Once the dance starts," Monica explained, "the dancers tell the story through choreography, text, live narration, and singing. I chose to add projections of a simulated UpStairs Lounge scene with the flocked red wallpaper, beefcake posters, etc., as a backdrop to help illustrate the feeling of being in the lounge, along with set design, and incorporated actual footage of the fire/news clips during the fire scene. There is also a montage of the patrons who passed courtesy of Robert Camina to honor the patrons and allow the audience to see the faces of these real human beings and solidify the connection that the dancers established."

One of Monica's goals is to reach people who might not read a book or watch a documentary. She says, "I've heard a lot of feedback like 'I didn't know I liked dance!' I'm passionate about creating dance works that tell stories that can transcend boundaries and inspire audiences to feel and connect in our shared humanity; stories that move, entertain, educate, and inspire. People who know about the fire may be discouraged by the horrific tragedy to learn more, but through dance we encourage audiences to open themselves to the stories of the lounge and the patrons that gave it life, providing an uplift that one might not feel without dance.

"Someone may have read that the lounge put on theatrical performances, had tricycle races, and even prayed together, singing proudly, 'United We Stand', but to see it come to life through this magic of dance, music, and human connection on stage can make one feel it more deeply. Through dance we have allowed audiences to see the celebration, the humor, the depth, the love, and the hope that lives in the stories of the lounge."

***

My own UpStairs story has ebbed and flowed over the years. I evacuated for Hurricane Katrina with one suitcase and never saw my apartment again. Fortunately, my family was able to go into the building when it was reopened and send several items to my new place in Seattle. One of those items was a floppy disk with my original UpStairs manuscript.

I hadn't even thought about publishing for years, the last interaction I had with the story occurring back on the 25th anniversary of the fire, when I was part of a panel discussion at the New Orleans Mint, along with survivor Courtney Craighead, journalist Clancy DuBos, and Fire Chief William McCrossen.

With four degrees and a recent breakup behind me, I was under a great deal of stress at the time, dealing with my fourth med school rejection as well. Life takes a toll, and I gave up on the story, placing my unpublished manuscript in the Historic New Orleans Collection, hoping some other researcher would be able to use the material for their own work.

Then Royd Anderson contacted me for an interview, and I thought, "Why not pull out that floppy disk and see what I can do?"

But once I'd published my book, I sat back and let others take over.

I was excited when Clayton Delery, Robert Camina, and Bobby Fieseler contacted me about their projects, only too happy to pass the baton, a tremendous weight off my shoulders. I've shared photos and knowledge as best I could.

But as we approach the 50th anniversary, I decided it was time to update the manuscript. There were several glaring deficiencies in my first edition. Chapter titles too often didn't accurately convey the information in those chapters. "Black Momma, White Momma," for instance, covered the homophobic response of the city and investigators. "Bill Richardson" covered the memorial service. So I've come up with better titles for several chapters.

An even bigger problem was that nowhere in the entire book was there a list of those killed, a rather basic bit of information. And in that first edition, I wasn't able to include even a single photo of the many I'd gathered over the years.

I certainly am not up to researching the story from scratch, but I've at least tried to address the most pressing issues in that first edition, and I've been able to add new information about Ferris LeBlanc, Mitch Mitchell, and the McAnears.

I did most of my research on the fire pre-internet. My first option at the time was to talk to people and have them refer me to other people they knew, a rather hit-or-miss strategy. I also read microfiche at the public library near City Hall. From the newspaper articles, I learned the hometowns of several victims and then pulled out phone books for each of those towns. I mailed physical letters to everyone in those towns with the same last name.

This was back when long-distance phone calls cost more than local calls. For the local victims, I grabbed the New Orleans phone book and started dialing. I'd go down the list one by one making cold calls until I found a relative.

"Hi, my name is Johnny Townsend, and I'm looking for anyone who knew a John Golding who died in a fire in 1973."

"That would be my husband," one woman said.

Yikes! What should I say now?

I quickly learned to prepare for awkward conversations.

I headed back to the third floor of the main branch of the library—the Louisiana division—and asked to see the coroner's reports. The librarian brought them out but forbid me to take notes in ink to reduce the chance I'd damage the documents. Photocopies were a whopping twenty-five cents each, a significant sum when there were so many pages, even more of an issue when I tracked down the lengthy fire investigation in an office near Baton Rouge.

But even after finding the coroner's reports, my problems weren't solved. There was no cause of death for Rodger Nunez. Odd, since that seemed one of the main functions of such a report. "Excuse me," I said to the librarian, "is something missing? I heard Nunez committed suicide."

The librarian then went in back and brought out the page he'd been censoring.

The school librarian in Abbeville responded to my questions by sending a photo of Rodger Nunez while a school librarian in Dallas sent me two photographs of Reggie Adams. Many friends and relatives of the victims graciously shared their personal photos. I met with journalist Ronnie LeBouef and purchased rights to publish four of his photos for $100 each, an enormous sum for me, but I didn't even think to draw up a contract of any kind and was therefore unable to include them in my first edition.

When I met Gerry Arnold, another journalist with a treasure trove of photos, I asked to purchase publication rights to several of his as well, but he told me to wait until I had a book contract. That journalist has since died, and I have no idea if his photos survived either his death or Hurricane Katrina.

As the family historian, I once borrowed a couple of dozen old photographs in my grandmother's possession to make copies for everyone in the family. This was pre-digital age, when often one member of the family was privileged with owning the photos while no one else enjoyed access.

I found a photographer Uptown named Peggy Stewart who could copy old photos, so when Napoleon and Stanley loaned me several of their personal snapshots from the UpStairs Lounge, I brought those to Peggy as well. After I explained what they were, she gasped. "I knew Skip Getchell!" she said, running off to grab a photo she'd taken of him in her studio.

Peggy also invited me to a party of older lesbians and gay men, where I found several more people to interview. During the eighteen months in 1989 and 1990 when I conducted the bulk of my research, I was so focused I'm sure I frequently came across as stranger than usual.

"You doing okay tonight?" someone might ask me at a bar.

"I'm good. And you?"

The guy might shrug and then say something like, "It's nice enough here. But I think I'm going to head home. Want to come along?"

"Sure." We'd start heading for the exit, where I'd add casually, "By the way, did you know anyone who died at the UpStairs Lounge?"

Perhaps I wasn't quite that bad, but my behavior wasn't far off. I must have interviewed well over a hundred people during that year and a half. Even when I didn't get new information, I was often able to confirm details I'd already heard.

I deeply regret not keeping an official list of those interviews, the names, dates, and so forth, but here are the people I distinctly remember interviewing at the time:

Regina Adams

Gerry Arnold

Nick Banner

Wayne Barras

Marti Bates

Pat Burke

Stewart Butler

J.C. Carrier

Rose Clark

Courtney Craighead

David Crumley

Preston Davis

Richard Davis

Phil Esteve

Ricky Everett

Miss Fury

Frank Gaalema

Jane Golding

Bill Goodrum

Jason Guidry

Benjamin Hambrick

Suzanne Joslyn

Paul Killgore

Irby Landreneau

Denny LeBouef

Ronnie LeDouef

Mildred Leingang

Brobson Lutz

Kerry Lyn

Marcy Marcell

Adolph Medina

Stanley Plaisance

Buddy Rasmussen

Larry Raybourne

Rose Revaldo

Bill Richardson

Ronnie Rosenthal

Michael Scarborough

Jim Schexnayder

Charlene Schneider

David Schwartz

Charles Selber

Tom Solieri

Peggy Stewart

Terry Stone

Tom Struve

Rod Wagener

Richard West

Jimmy Willemet

George and Keith (I don't remember their last names)

That's forty-nine people, but I interviewed at least sixty others during that period, and in recent years, I've also interviewed a handful more, including:

Skip Bailey

Duane Mitchell Jr.

Paul Villien

When I spoke with Rod Wagener, Bud Matyi's partner, he quizzed me about the fire before he would tell me anything at all. When I answered all his questions adequately, he nodded. "Okay, you've done your homework. I'll talk to you."

I behaved insensitively when interviewing Rose Clark, Adam Fontenot's cousin. As we concluded a long, productive interview, she asked a last question, and I told her Buddy's account of looking up at the bar from the street and seeing Adam still on his barstool, waving his arms and screaming amidst the flames.

Rose visibly blanched, and I realized that although I'd lived with these details for quite some time, she hadn't, and this was her beloved cousin I was talking about, not some unknown stranger. I made a concerted effort to speak with more delicacy in my interviews thereafter.

But I still messed up. When interviewing Regina Adams and Marcy Marcell, I asked for Regina's birth name. She wouldn't give it. As an ignorant cis man, I thought it odd to pretend Regina's former life as a male didn't exist.

Since we'd belonged to the same Mormon congregation in Metairie, I simply asked other congregants her name. It was inappropriate of me, and I've eliminated the dead name from this edition.

In that interview with Regina, when asking about the Warrens, I said that some other UpStairs regulars suggested the two young men might have been hustlers. My tone must have sounded judgmental, as both Regina and Marcy shut the interview down immediately. Another faux pas on my part.

And speaking of inappropriate behavior...

Interviewing Courtney Craighead presented a unique challenge. While he was open about the details of his past, he'd only offer a few at a time. He never allowed me inside his home on Chartres near St. Roch, instead insisting he drive me around town as we chatted.

But he wanted the interview to serve two purposes. While he drove me about, he reached over to unzip me and give me a long, protracted hand job. And this wasn't just one interview. He'd drop me off and say, "Oh, I still have more to tell you," and we'd arrange another time to meet, where the same bizarre interview process took place again. I suppose I could have said no, but I didn't want to risk offending him and have him stop talking.

Whatever it takes to get the story, right?

Perhaps this is information I should have kept to myself, but when people read Courtney's chapter now, the account he tells of all the sex he had with straight men might ring a little truer. He could be rather persistent.

One other interview that left a profound impression was one I had with Troy Perry. Courtney had let me know he was coming to town, and I called to ask if we could meet to talk about the UpStairs. "I'll be at the MCC dinner this weekend," he told me. "Meet me there."

I went to the dinner and found a moment to approach Rev. Perry. "Oh, just buy my book," he said dismissively. He'd just published *Don't Be Afraid Anymore*, which contained a chapter on the fire. "Everything I know is in there." He waved me away, and that was the extent of the interview.

I bought the book and was thoroughly shocked by what I read. By this point, I'd done extensive research and felt I knew a great deal about the fire. But there were names I'd never heard. Who was Andre? And Luther Boggs was now a teacher who'd been fired after school officials learned he'd been injured in a gay bar. Another burn victim was shown joking with nurses, while Jim Hambrick's brother had been a firsthand witness in the hospital and given a very different account.

Completely by chance, I ran into Troy at the airport in Oakland, California over a decade later and asked him point blank about the details in that chapter of his book. "Oh, I made most of that up," he said. To be honest, I already suspected as much and was frankly a bit surprised to hear him state it so directly. It seems likely the details of his own participation in the memorial service were accurate and that he only created composite characters to offer a fictional representation of the kind of regulars who'd been at the bar to help readers relate. Fair enough, I suppose. But that wasn't my goal.

Whatever the case might be, I went home and edited out every detail I could from my manuscript that I'd "learned" from his book. Troy Perry has done an incredible amount of great work for the LGBTQ community, and I don't want to tarnish his reputation for this solitary issue. Explaining our encounters, though, felt unavoidable.

I'm a tertiary character in the story of the UpStairs Lounge, but it's had a profound impact on me for the past five decades. I was a month shy of my twelfth birthday when the fire occurred. I remember seeing the front page of the newspaper the following morning, Rusty Quinton's face turned upward, staring in absolute horror. I didn't need to see the horror myself. It was evident in his eyes.

I was too ignorant to understand that the UpStairs was a gay bar, only horrified to imagine anyone being trapped by flames. Ever since, I've taken a few moments whenever I step inside a building to locate two or three alternate exits. These days, I continue the practice, though I now also look for possible items to use as weapons, active shooters having taken over as the most likely cause of a mass casualty event.

Society evolves, I suppose, or devolves, as the case may be.

Of the many people I talked to who were part of the original UpStairs saga, I've only been able to develop a meaningful friendship with two. I spent many evenings at PFLAG meetings with Bill Richardson and his partner Alex Jacobs. We were close enough after our interviews that they invited me over one morning for "nude coffee."

I didn't turn them down because of their age or the fact they were a couple, not even because of the nudity. I simply don't like coffee. But I regret not joining them and simply asking for a glass of milk instead.

I feel deeper regret over the situation with Buddy Rasmussen. He was only ever kind and generous to me, but after the story exploded with so many books and films over the space of a few years, he was hounded by reporters. I never gave out his contact information, but he wasn't hard to track down, and people simply showed up at this door thrusting cameras and microphones in his face.

Pro-tip:

Sheesh, *Amateur*-tip: Don't be a jerk.

Buddy and Bill are still together fifty years after the fire. To me, that's the single most powerful illustration of what we all lost the night of June 24th. It's easy to dismiss the UpStairs as a sleazy French Quarter gay bar. But real people met there, full of human frailties and strengths, fully capable of love and commitment, which are not, after all, sex-linked traits.

Lives were lost that night, to be sure, but love was lost as well.

Tragedy by itself doesn't convey meaning. We must invest meaning into it. How we choose to do so both as individuals and as a community will reveal who we truly are.

All of us, unfortunately, are today witnessing another critical moment in LGBTQ history. Let's record what we witness, but more importantly, let's act to make sure our community survives the current attacks and that we leave the world a better place for all who follow.

Appendix: The Up Stairs Lounge Fire 50th Anniversary

In 2023, the LGBT+ Archives Project of Louisiana, in partnership with the Historic New Orleans Collection and St. Mark's Methodist, presented a three-day memorial for the Up Stairs Lounge fire victims, from June 23 to June 25. The events were held at the Marriott Hotel on Canal Street, directly across from the UpStairs Lounge, as well as at 410 Chartres, at 520 Royal Street, at St. Mark's on North Rampart, and in front of the former bar at 604 Iberville.

The Commemoration Planning Committee met frequently at The Faerie Playhouse, the home of Stewart Butler and Alfred Doolittle, to coordinate. That committee included Brett Buck, Rev. Lonnie Cheramie, Kathleen Conlon, Rev. Ed Cooper, Clayton Delery, Jimmy Gale, Jessie Hicks, Robert Fieseler, Guy LaMothe, Ryan Leitner, Jim Meadows, Frank Perez, Tim Reynolds, Courtney Sharp, Rev. Cory Sparks, Robert Ticknor, Amy Williams, and Gregor Young.

Sponsors for the three-day event included the LGBT+ Archives Project, The Historic New Orleans Collection, Crescent City Leathermen, The Big Easy Sisters of Perpetual Indulgence, St. Mark's Methodist Church, Louisiana Endowment for the Humanities, St. George's Episcopal Church, PFLAG New Orleans, Ambush Magazine, Metropolitan Community Church of New Orleans, Krewe of

Evexia, French Quarter Journal, The National WWII Museum, Crescent City Tour Booking Agency, NAMI New Orleans, Odyssey House Louisiana, Greater New Orleans Foundation, Chez Nous, Crossing, New Orleans Tourism and Cultural Fund, The Corner Pocket, New Orleans and Company, American Townhouse Restaurant, Dr. David Campbell, The Faerie Playhouse Family, Rev. Guy LaMothe, and Mr. Michael J. Dolan.

Not officially part of the program, Hunter Burke and fifteen other actors performed a reading of his screenplay, *The Fire Upstairs*, on Wednesday, June 21.

Throughout the events, members of the Krewe of Evexia were on hand to offer emotional support to attendees impacted by the trauma of reliving the tragedy.

The first event on Friday, June 23, 2023, was a panel discussion in the Williams Research Center at 410 Chartres featuring authors Johnny Townsend, Clayton Delery, and Robert Fieseler, followed by a reception at 520 Royal Street.

Multiple events were scheduled for June 24, the 50th anniversary itself. The first three were panel discussions held in Galleria 6 at the Marriott on Canal Street.

From 10:00 to 11:00, the first panel, "Commemorating the Up Stairs Lounge Throughout the Decades," featured historian Roberts Batson, Rev. Dexter Brecht, Tim Reynolds, Rev. Carole Cotton Winn, and Robert Linné. The session was moderated by Rev. Cory Sparks.

From 11:30 to 12:30, the second panel, "Artistic Interpretations of the Up Stairs Lounge," featured actor/screenwriter Hunter Burke, director/writer Brad Dalton, choreographer/dancer Monica Ordoñez, and playwright/lyricist Max Vernon. The session was moderated by Kathleen Conlon.

From 1:30 to 2:20, the third panel, "The Spiritual Legacy of the Up Stairs Lounge," featured Rev. Paul Breton, Rev. Ed Cooper, Rev. Lonnie Cheramie, and Rev. Cory Sparks. The session was moderated by Guy LaMothe.

At 3:30, a commemoration service was conducted at St. Mark's Methodist Church at 1130 North Rampart Street. Bishop Delores J. Williamston, Rev. Ed Cooper, and Rabbi Edward P. Cohn offered prayers. The New Orleans Gay Men's Chorus sang "Amazing Grace" and "United We Stand." Members of Crescent City Leathermen produced black banners with the names of the Up Stairs Lounge victims. A bell rang out after each name was read. Jimmy Gale organized the name bearers to get representation from different parts of the community. Members of the Crescent City Leathermen, the Big Easy Sisters of Perpetual Indulgence, and several other volunteers from the Southern Decadence Entourage gathered in front of the church, each holding a banner.

From there, the group conducted a jazz funeral and second line across the French Quarter to the site of the Up Stairs Lounge at 604 Iberville.

At 6:45, Robert L. Camina began his introductory remarks at the Williams Research Center at 410 Chartres before airing his 96-minute documentary *Upstairs Inferno*. A brief Q&A session followed.

Not officially part of the program but occurring simultaneously, the Mélange Dance Company performed *The UpStairs Lounge: United We Stand* under the direction of Monica Ordoñez in the Lapis Theater at the New Orleans Museum of Art.

On Sunday, June 25, 2023, five events were held in Galleria 6 at the Marriott.

From 10:00 to 11:00, the first panel, "Documenting the Up Stairs Lounge," featured Royd Anderson, Joey Gray, and Sheri Wright. The session was moderated by Mark Bologna.

From 11:30 to 12:30, the second panel, "Contemporary Recollections, Then & Now," featured Clancy DuBos and Dr. David Campbell. The session was moderated by Clayton Delery.

From 1:30 to 2:30, the third panel, "Archiving the Up Stairs Lounge and Queer History in General," featured Joshua Burford, Leon Miller, Wayne Phillips, and Maigen Sullivan. The session was moderated by Jim Meadows.

From 3:00 to 4:15, there was a screening of the short ABC documentary *Prejudice and Pride*, followed by Max Vernon singing a song from *The View UpStairs*, which was then followed by a screening of Royd Anderson's short documentary, *The Upstairs Fire*.

At 4:30, *Tinderbox*, a dramatic reading by Brad Dalton with musical accompaniment, concluded the official events for the 50th anniversary memorial of the Up Stairs Lounge fire.

Bibliography/Resources

"22 fire dead identified positively; 3 tentatively." *The Advocate.* Los Angeles: 18 July 1973:8.

"30th Bar Blaze Victim Dies, Eight Remain Unidentified." *The States-Item.* New Orleans: 29 June 1973:3.

"5 Sisters Asking $625,000 in Suit." *The Times-Picayune.* New Orleans: 24 June 1974.

"Aid asked for fire survivors." *The Advocate.* Los Angeles: 18 July 1973:9.

Anderson, Royd. *New Orleans Disasters: Firsthand Accounts of Crescent City Tragedy.* The History Press· Cheltenham, UK. Nov. 2021.

Anderson, Royd. *The Upstairs Lounge Fire.* Documentary short. Producer and director Royd Anderson. June 2013.

"Arson Suspected—Charred Rubble Sifted for Clues." *The States-Item.* New Orleans: 26 June 1973, sec. 1:1.

"Bar Suit Fire Is Charging 11." *The Times-Picayune.* New Orleans: 11 June 1974.

"Bar's funky decor, clutter created instant firestorm." *The Advocate.* Los Angeles: 1 August 1973:6.

"Benefits boost N.O. fund." *The Advocate.* Los Angeles: 24 October 1973.

Biedenharn, Isabella. "The View UpStairs: EW stage review." *Entertainment Weekly.* 2 March 2017.

"Blaze Victim No. 12 Positively Identified." *The States-Item.* New Orleans: 28 June 1973, sec. 1:1.

"Blaze Victim Seeks Damages." *The Times-Picayune.* New Orleans: 21 June 1974.

Boileau, Lue. "'United We Stand': 50 Years After the UpStairs Lounge Fire That Claimed 32 LGBTQ+ Lives." *Verite.* New Orleans: 24 June 2023.

Bologna, Mark. "Fire at the Up Stairs Lounge—Episode #66." Podcast featuring Clayton Delery and Robert Fieseler. *beyondbourbonst.com.* 20 June 2018.

Bouden, Barbara. "Fire Reveals Bias." Letter. *The Times-Picayune.* New Orleans: 29 June 1973.

Camina, Robert L. "Striking Back Over Allegations of Investigative Negligence." *Advocate.* 15 Sept 2019.

Camina, Robert L. "Unknown Victim of Deadly 1973 Arson in Gay Bar Finally Identified." *Advocate.* 15 Nov 2018.

Camina, Robert L. *Upstairs Inferno.* Documentary film. Producer and director Robert Camina. June 2015.

Caron, Christina. "Overlooked No More: Bill Larson, Who Became a Symbol of Gay Loss in New Orleans." *New York Times.* 26 June 2019.

Chavez, Roby. "A 'forgotten tragedy' at a New Orleans gay bar and a new effort to honor victims' remains." PBS News Hour. 18 Aug 2022.

"Chief Feels Fire Arson." *The Times-Picayune.* New Orleans: 16 July 1973, sec. 1:1.

"Closeted Gay Bishop Dies of AIDS." *The Voice of Integrity.* Spring 1991. Reprinted from *Texas Monthly* 1987. 8-10.

Cooper, Alex. "50 Years Ago, the Fire at the Up Stairs Lounge Gay Bar in New Orleans Killed 32." *The Advocate*. 24 June 2023.

Crew, Louie, editor. "Second Bill's Story." *A Book of Revelations.* Washington: Integrity, 1991. 189-90.

Delery, Clayton and Robert Fieseler. "It's Too Soon to Identify the UpStairs Lounge Fire's Unknown." *Advocate*. 15 Sept 2019.

Delery-Edwards, Clayton. *The Up Stairs Lounge Arson: Thirty-Two Deaths in a New Orleans Gay Bar, June 24, 1973.* McFarland: Jefferson, NC. June 2014. 216 pages.

Desombre, Auriane. "Interview: Max Vernon on Queer History, Activism, and 'The View UpStairs.'" *StageBuddy.com*. 27 February 2017.

Dias, Elizabeth and Jim Downs. "The Horror Upstairs." *Time*. 1 July 2013.

Downs, Jim. "Before Orlando, There Was New Orleans." *New York Times*. 13 June 2016.

Downs, Jim. "New Evidence Shows That During the 1973 UpStairs Lounge Arson, Gays Had to Take Rescue Efforts into Their Own Hands." *Slate*. 22 June 2018.

Downs, Jim. *Stand by Me: The Forgotten History of Gay Liberation*. New York: Basic Books. March 2016. 272 pages.

DuBos, Clancy. "29 Killed in Quarter Blaze—Blood, Moans: Charity Scene." *The Times-Picayune*. New Orleans: 25 June 1973, sec. 1:1.

Dufrene v. Guarino, 343 So. 2d 1097 (Louisiana Court of Appeals 4th Circuit 1977). *Id.* at 1101 (Morial, J., dissenting).

Epstein, Brian and Peter Madden, producers. *Prejudice and Pride: Fire at the Upstairs Lounge.* 2018. ABC documentary. 29 minutes.

"European Premiere of The View UpStairs to Open at Soho Theatre." *Theatre Weekly.* 5 February 2019.

"Fatal Fire Probe Continues." *The Times-Picayune.* New Orleans: 28 June 1973.

"Feeding On Hope in New Orleans—Yesterday's dreams, today's ghosts." *The Advocate.* Los Angeles: 13 February 1974: 12+.

Fieseler, Robert W. "32 People Died in the UpStairs Lounge Fire in 1973. Why Was it Forgotten?" Interview by Jeremy Hobson. WBUR radio. 6 May 2019.

Fieseler, Robert W. "A Deadly Fire, an Indifferent Cop, and an Escaped Arsonist." CrimeReads.com. February 11, 2019.

Fieseler, Robert W. "Soldier in a Tinderbox: Ferris LeBlanc, World War II, and the Up Stairs Lounge Fire." Nationlww2museum.org. 1 Oct 2020.

Fieseler, Robert W. "This Mass Murder of Gay People Sparked a Mass Movement 43 Years Before Pulse." BuzzFeedNews.com. 30 May 2018.

Fieseler, Robert W. *Tinderbox: The Untold Story of the Up Stairs Lounge Fire and the Rise of Gay Liberation.* Liveright: New York. June 2018. 384 pages.

Fieseler, Robert W. "The UpStairs Lounge Fire Killed 32 People. Its Legacy Still Haunts Black Gay New Orleans." *The Daily Beast*. 13 May 2019.

"Fifty Years Later, New Orleans Honors Those Lost in Upstairs Lounge Fire." *wwltv.com*. New Orleans: 24 June 2023.

Finch, Susan. "Suzanne J. Fosberg, artist, playwright." *The Times-Picayune*. New Orleans: 2 July 1998. B-4.

"Fire IV: The Slight Latin & Rumor Control." *Vieux Carré Courier*. 20-26 July 1973:3.

"Fire Inspectors Count up 594 Violations of Codes." *The Times-Picayune*. New Orleans: 17 July 1973.

"Fire fund gives \$13,800." *The Advocate*. Los Angeles: 3 July 1974.

Fire Prevention Division of the New Orleans Fire Department. "Investigation Report of Fire." (Fire Report) L. W. Bergeron. 6-24-73. 9 pages.

"Fire victims: more than just names." *The Advocate*. Los Angeles: 1 August 1973:17.

"First gay dollars reach New Orleans fire victims." *The Advocate*. Los Angeles: 13 February 1974:2+.

Fosberg, Suzanne Joslyn. "It's a Faggot Bar—Did I Tell You?" *Vieux Carré Courier*. New Orleans: 29 June-5 July 1973:7.

Frazer, Tom. "Sons of Fire Victim Sent Home—Unaware of Father's Death." *The States-Item*. New Orleans: 26 June 1973.

"Fund exceeds \$16,500." *The Advocate*. Los Angeles: 19 December 1973.

"Fund near $15,000." *The Advocate.* Los Angeles: 10 October 1973:6.

"Fund passes $15,500, slows." *The Advocate.* Los Angeles: 7 November 1973:4.

"Fund tops $1400 in 9 days." *The Advocate.* Los Angeles: 1 August 1973:2.

"Gays Begin Relief Funds for Upstairs Fire Victims." *The Daily Record.* New Orleans: 27 June 1973:1.

Glaviano, Ann. "The UpStairs Lounge & the Return of Narrative Dance." *Nola Dance Reader.* 7 April 2015.

Gray, Joey. *The Fire UpStairs, Chapter One: The Story.* Podcast. Spotify. 28 minutes. 21 June 2023.

Gray, Joey. *The Fire UpStairs, Chapter Two: The History.* Podcast. Spotify. 45 minutes. 28 June 2023.

Griffin, Gareth. "Flames of Hate: The Upstairs Lounge Fire, June 24, 1973." Master's Thesis. Louisiana University at Lafayette, 2008. 75 pages.

Guild Guide 1972, USA and International. Washington: Guild Press, 1971.

Handley, Rachel. "'They turned their backs on him': Woman Remembers Lover Lost in UpStairs Lounge Fire." *wwltv.com.* New Orleans: 24 June 2023.

Helton, Glenn. "Nine Fire Victims Positively Identified." *The Daily Record.* New Orleans: 27 June 1973:1.

Helton, Glenn. "Thirty-First Fire Victim Dies." *The Daily Record.* New Orleans: 12 July 1973.

Hoekstra, Dave. "A gay actor from Palatine died in the UpStairs Lounge." *Chicago Tribune.* 13 June 2022.

"How the Media Saw It." *Vieux Carré Courier*. New Orleans: 29 June-5 July 1973:5.

Hunter, John Francis. *The Gay Insiders*. Stonehill, New York, 1972. 364-74.

Hurst, David. "The View UpStairs—A New Musical." *New York Arts Review*. 28 February 2017.

Indest, Susan. "The UpStairs Lounge Fire." Music.

"Inquiries Continue for Quarter Fire." *The Daily Record*. New Orleans: 26 June 1973:1+.

Katz, Allan. "Labeling the Dead: An Impossible Job?" *The States-Item*. New Orleans: 25 June 1973, sec. 1:6.

Katz, Allan. "New Charity Burn Unit Aids Fire Victims." *The States-Item*. New Orleans: 27 June 1973.

Landstroem, Lina. "Queer History on Stage: A Review of The View UpStairs by Max Vernon." *PublicSeminar.org*, 1 March 2017.

Laplace, John and Ed Anderson. "Arson Possibility Is Raised." *The Times-Picayune*. New Orleans: 25 June 1973, sec. 1:1.

Laplace, John. "Scene of French Quarter Fire Is Called Dante's 'Inferno,' Hitler's Incinerator." *The Times-Picayune*. New Orleans: 25 June 1973, sec. 1:1.

Larty, Jamiles. "Forty five years ago, a fire in New Orleans gay bar took 32 lives—and was met with apathy." *The Guardian*. July 6, 2018.

Lee, Vincent. "Gay Leaders Plan Aid for Victims of Bar Fire." *The Times-Picayune*. New Orleans: 27 June 1973, sec. 1:14.

Lilly, Christiana. "City of New Orleans Officially Recognizes Men Killed in 1973 UpStairs Lounge Fire." *South Florida Gay News*. 29 June 2022.

Lind, Angus. "Fire Bares the Grisly Face of Death." *The States-Item*. New Orleans: 25 June 1973, sec. 1:6.

Lind, Angus, Lanny Thomas, and Walt Philbin. "29 Dead in Quarter Holocaust—Fire Victims Are Identified." *The States-Item*. New Orleans: 25 June 1973, sec. 1:1+.

MacCash, Doug. "Upstairs Lounge fire is remembered in a musical by composer Wayne Self." *Nola.com*. 31 May 2013.

Markus, Eric. "The Untold Story of the Up Stairs Lounge Fire—Episode 229." Podcast featuring Robert Fieseler. *nypl.org*. 2 September 2018.

McConnaughey, Janet. "New Orleans Searches for remains of 4 victims of 1973 gay bar fire that killed 31." CBSNews.com. 6 Aug 2022.

McDaniel, Mike. "Remembering the Upstairs Lounge Fire." WWLTV.com. 21 Nov 2022.

Meis, Vincent Traughber. *The Mayor of Oak Street*. NineStar Press: New Mexico. 2021. Fiction. 373 pages.

"Memorial fund coming to an end—'We'll Know Next Time.'" *The Advocate*. Los Angeles: 31 July 1974.

"Memorial fund passes $10,000." *The Advocate*. Los Angeles: 12 September 1973.

"Memorial fund tops $7200." *The Advocate*. Los Angeles: 30 August 1973.

Minsky, Dave. "Today Marks 47 Years Since Nearly 3 Dozen Were Killed in the UpStairs Lounge Fire." *The Quarter Rat.* 24 June 2020.

Moeed, Naveed. "Theatre Review: Queer Life Then and Now in 'The View UpStairs.'" *Chatham Life & Style.* 18 March 2023.

"National Outpouring—Aid mounts for New Orleans." *The Advocate.* Los Angeles: 15 August 1973:2+.

"New church building from ashes of tragedy." *The Advocate.* Los Angeles: 13 March 1974:10.

Newhouse, Eric. "32 Perished in Up Stairs Bar Fire Year Ago Today." *The Times-Picayune.* New Orleans: 24 June 1974.

New Orleans Department of Police. General Case Report. Fire Fatality. Item # F-21149-73. Det. Charles Schlosser. Det. Sam Gebbia, reporting officers; Lt. Edward O'Donnell. supervisor. Date of report 8-30-73. 64 pages

New Orleans Fire Department 1973 Annual Report. William J. McCrossen, Superintendent. Dept. of Fire. 317 Decatur Street, New Orleans.

"N.O. fund almost $16,000." *The Advocate.* Los Angeles: 5 December 1973:4.

Nolan, Bruce and Chris Segura. "Memorial for Fire Dead Has Forgiveness Theme." *The Times-Picayune.* New Orleans: 26 June 1973, sec. 1:3.

Nolan, Bruce. "Past Underlines *Tragedy* of French Quarter Fire." *The Times-Picayune.* New Orleans: 25 June 1973, sec. 1:2.

Nolan, Bruce. "Service remembers Upstairs fire victims." *The Times-Picayune.* New Orleans: 25 June 1998, sec. B:1,2.

"Official Does Not Suspect Arson in New Orleans Fire." *The New York Times.* 27 July 1973.

"One Still Hospitalized—Outlook brightens for fire victims." *The Advocate.* Los Angeles: 10 October 1973:6+.

"Orleans fire confessor 'didn't do it.'" *The Advocate.* Los Angeles: 5 December 1973:1.

Osenlund, R. Kurt. "*The View UpStairs*: Why the Diverse Queer Musical is Vital for Our Times." *Out Magazine.* 3 May 2017.

"Over 800 Fire Code Violations Reported." *The Times-Picayune.* New Orleans: 18 July 1973.

Parish of Orleans, the State of Louisiana. Criminal District Court for the Parish of Orleans. Conviction and Prosecution Records for Rodger Dale Nunez.

Parris, Pat. "Mom, we found him—and it's horrible." *kgun9.com.* 30 June 2023.

Perez, Frank. "After UpStairs Lounge fire, gay and straight New Orleans changed." Nola.com. June 22, 2013.

Perez, Frank. *Political Animal: The Life and Times of Stewart Butler.* University Press of MS. Sept 2022. 320 pages.

Perez, Frank. "Reggie, Regina, and the 50th Anniversary of the UpStairs Lounge Fire." *Ambush Magazine.* 8 May 2023.

Perez, Frank. "UpStairs Lounge Fire 50th Anniversary Commemoration Activities Announced." *Ambush Magazine.* 10 Feb 2023.

Perry, Reverend Troy D., with Thomas L. P. Swicegood. *Don't Be Afraid Anymore.* New York: St. Martin's Press, 1990.

Philbin, Walt. "First the Horror—Then the Leap." *The States-Item*. New Orleans: 25 June 1973, sec. 1:6.

Polk's New Orleans City Directory. Dallas: R.L. Polk & Co. Pub. 1967.

Polk's New Orleans City Directory. Dallas: R.L. Polk & Co. Pub. 1973.

Pope, John. "Arsonist never found in fire that killed 32." *The Times-Picayune*. New Orleans: 26 June 1988.

"'Pray for those who did this.'" *The Advocate*. Los Angeles: 18 July 1973:8.

Reed, Roy. "Arson Suspected in Deaths of 29 in New Orleans Bar." *The New York Times*. 26 June 1973.

Reed, Roy. "Flash Fire in New Orleans Kills at Least 32 in Bar." *The New York Times*. 25 June 1973, sec. 1:1.

Richardson, Rev. William P., Jr. "More On the Closeted Gay Bishop." *The Voice of Integrity*. Summer 1991:2.

Romero, Michaela. "City Council Considers Resolution Honoring LGBTQ Victims." WGNO.com. 21 June 2022.

Rübsam, Henning. "Impressions of 'The View UpStairs': A New Off-Broadway Musical by Max Vernon at Lynn Redgrave Theater at Culture Project." *The Dance Enthusiast*. 21 March 2017.

Rushton, Bill. "After the Fire Up Stairs..." *Vieux Carré Courier*. New Orleans: 29 June-5 July 1973:1+.

Rushton, Bill. "Fire Three: Who the Victims Were." *Vieux Carré Courier*. New Orleans: 13-19 July 1973:6-7.

Rushton, Bill. "Fire tragedy confuses both straights, Gays." *The Advocate*. Los Angeles: 18 July 1973:2+.

Rushton, Bill. "How quickly memories fade." *The Advocate.* Los Angeles: 31 July 1974:1.

Rushton, Bill. "Mystery Unravels in New Orleans Bar Fire." *The Advocate.* Los Angeles: 22 October 1975:16.

Rushton, Bill. "New Orleans fire probe stalled; agencies at odds." *The Advocate.* Los Angeles: 10 October 1973:6.

Rushton, Bill. "New Orleans officials still silent on fire." *The Advocate.* Los Angeles: 15 August 1973:2+.

Rushton, Bill. "New Orleans toll 32; arson evidence cited." *The Advocate.* Los Angeles: 1 August 1973:1+.

Rushton, Bill. "Society real culprit in New Orleans tragedy?" *The Advocate.* Los Angeles: 18 July 1973.

Samuels, Monroe and Frank Minyard. Coroner's reports. June, July 1973, November 1974.

Schwandt, George. "Holocaust in New Orleans." *The Advocate.* Los Angeles: 18 July 1973:2+.

Sciallo, Andrew. "50 Years Later, the UpStairs Lounge Fire Is More Important to Remember Than Ever." *The Nation.* New York: 22 June 2023.

Sears, James T. *Rebels, Rubyfruit, and Rhinestones: Queering Space in the Stonewall South.* New Brunswick, NJ: Rutgers University Press. July 2001. 420 pages.

Segarra, Edward. "Remembering the Upstairs Lounge Fire 47 Years Later." Watermarkonline.com. 24 June 2020.

Segura, Chris. "Black, Empty Windows Stare." *The Times-Picayune.* New Orleans: 26 June 1973, sec. 1:3.

Segura, Chris. "Cleric Says Oppression Problem for Homosexuals." *The Times-Picayune*. New Orleans: 2 July 1973, sec. 2:7.

Segura, Chris. "Devastating French Quarter Fire Probed By 3 Agencies." *The Times-Picayune*. New Orleans: 26 June 1973, sec. 1:1.

Segura, Chris. "'Positive Identifications' Made for 9 Fire Victims." *The Times-Picayune*. New Orleans: 27 June 1973.

Sehgul, Paul. "In 1973, an Arsonist Killed 32 People at a Gay Club. Why Has History Shrugged?" Book review of *Tinderbox* by Robert W. Fieseler. *New York Times*. 29 May 2018.

Self, Wayne. "Remembering the History of the UpStairs Lounge." *The Advocate*. 6 June 2017.

Self, Wayne. *Upstairs: A Musical Eulogy* Theatrical production.

"Set Orleans fire, man tells police." *The Advocate*. Los Angeles: 21 November 1973:1.

Shannon, Patrick, III. "Meditations By Charlene Schneider." *Ambush Magazine*. New Orleans: 3-16 August 1990:1+.

Shapiro, Dean M. "Deadly 1973 Arson at UpStairs Lounge Inspires Performance by Melange Dance Company." *Nola.com*. 20 June 2023.

Sims, Shannon. "A Fire Killed 32 at a New Orleans Gay Bar. This Artist Didn't Forget." Review of Skylar Fein art exhibit. *New York Times*. 9 July 2018.

"Six More Victims of Fire Identified, Coroner Says." *The Times-Picayune*. New Orleans: 29 June 1973.

"Six of 15 Injured in Serious Condition." *The States-Item.* New Orleans: 25 June 1973, sec. 1:6.

State Fire Marshall's report. Edward S. Hyde, William M. Roth, Jr., and John M. Fischer. File #464-73. Presented to DA 7-22-75. 429 pages (includes the 64 pages of the New Orleans Police Department investigation).

Stewart, Greg. "Review: The View UpStairs at Soho Theatre." *Theatre Weekly.* 25 July 2019.

St. John, Martin. "'A part of our souls was ignited...'" *The Advocate.* Los Angeles: 1 August 1973:1, 16-17.

"Suit Is Brought in Lounge Fire." *The Times-Picayune.* New Orleans: 18 June 1974.

"Supplemental Information—The Upstairs Lounge Fire, New Orleans, Louisiana, June 24, 1973." On file at Fire Department Headquarters, 317 Decatur St., New Orleans.

"Survivor discovers her true friends." *The Advocate.* Los Angeles: 3 July 1974.

"Suspect Is Cleared in New Orleans Fire." *The New York Times.* New York: 16 November 1973.

Swindall, Sharon. "Dead Man Was Pastor To Other Fire Victims." *The Daily Record.* New Orleans: 26 June 1973:1,8.

Swindall, Sharon. "Fire Victim Dies, Nine More Identified." *The Daily Record.* New Orleans: 29 June 1973:1.

Swindall, Sharon. "Fire Victim Identified." *The Daily Record.* New Orleans: 30 June-1 July 1973:1.

Swindall, Sharon. "One More Fire Victim Identified." *The Daily Record.* New Orleans: 11 July 1973:1.

Swindall, Sharon. "Rookie Fireman Describes Fire." *The Daily Record.* New Orleans: 28 June 1973:1.

Swindall, Sharon. "Tourist Recalls Nightmare." *The Daily Record.* New Orleans: 27 June 1973:7.

Tabone, Eleanor. "Tragic Upstairs Lounge Fire Being Remembered 50 Years Later." *wwltv.com.* New Orleans: 23 June 2023.

Tabone, Eleanor. "'We Found Him—It's Horrible': For 42 Years the Family of a WW2 Vet Didn't Know He Died in N.O." *wwltv.com.* New Orleans: 25 June 2023.

Thomas, Lanny. "Fun...Drink...Song...with Death at the Piano." *The States-Item.* New Orleans: 25 June 1973:6.

Thomas, Lanny. "Have Labels Overshadowed 29 Deaths?" *The States-Item.* New Orleans: 28 June 1973.

Thomas, Lanny. "No Arson Evidence, Police Say." *The States-Item.* New Orleans: 27 June 1973:1.

Townsend, Johnny. *Inferno in the French Quarter: The UpStairs Lounge Fire.* 2011, 2023.

Townsend, Johnny. "That's Mentir, Not Mentor." *Impact.*

Townsend, Johnny. "UpStairs Lounge fire." Presentation at the University of North Carolina—Wilmington, Oct 2012, as part of the Stonewall Lecture Series.

Townsend, Johnny. "Will We Learn from Orlando? We Didn't Learn from New Orleans," published in the 19 June 2016 issue (June 18 online) of the *Salt Lake Tribune.*

Uddin, Shahamat. "The UpStairs Lounge Fire in New Orleans Was a Deadly Attack on the Local LGBTQ+ Community." *Teen Vogue.* 27 June 2023.

"Upstairs fire ruling upheld in appeal." *The States-Item.* New Orleans: 13 January 1977.

"Upstairs Is Hit by Biggest Suit." *The Times-Picayune.* New Orleans: 20 June 1974.

"UpStairs Lounge Fire." Panel discussion on the 25th anniversary of the fire on 24 June 1998, at the U.S. Mint in New Orleans. Fire Chief William McCrossen, journalist Clancy DuBos, survivor Courtney Craighead, and historian Johnny Townsend.

Vernon, Max. *The View UpStairs.* Musical. 2017. 105 minutes.

"Victim's Address Corrected." *The States-Item.* New Orleans: 30 June 1973.

Vincentelli, Elisabeth. "Review: A Gay Nightclub Tragedy, Decades Before Orlando, in 'The View UpStairs.'" *The New York Times.* 7 March 2017.

Wallace, Wayne N.; National Archives and Records Administration, National Personnel Records Center, Military Personnel Records, 9700 Page Blvd., St., Louis, MO 63132.

Wang, Lucas. "Review: The View UpStairs at The Soho Theatre." *pocketsizetheatre.com.* 24 July 2019.

Weiss, Ken. "Blaze Victims' Names Sought." *The Times-Picayune.* New Orleans: 26 June 1973:3.

"'We Knew Them as People,' Pastor Tells Gay Mourners." *The States-Item.* New Orleans: 26 June 1973.

Wells, Carlie Kollath. "50 Years after deadly Up Stairs Lounge fire: New Orleans LGBTQ+ community still seeks answers." *Axios.* 23 June 2023.

Willey, A. Elwood. "The Upstairs Lounge Fire—New Orleans, Louisiana." *Fire Journal.* National Fire Protection Association. Quincy, MA: January 1974:16-20.

Woods, Byron. "A Surprisingly Upbeat Musical Commemorates the UpStairs Lounge Fire." *Indy Week.* 8 March 2023.

WVUE, T.V. news transcripts, New Orleans ABC affiliate. 24-25 June 1973.

Books by Johnny Townsend

Thanks for reading! If you enjoyed this book, could you please take a few minutes to write a review online? Reviews are helpful both to me as an author and to other readers, so we'd all sincerely appreciate your writing one! And if you did enjoy the book, here are some others I've written you might want to look up:

Mormon Underwear

A Gay Mormon Missionary in Pompeii

The Golem of Rabbi Loew

Sexual Solidarity

Gayrabian Nights

Invasion of the Spirit Snatchers

Sins of the Saints

Gay Gaslighting

Escape from Zion

A Mormon Motive for Murder

Mormon Misfits

Going-Out-of-Religion Sale

Breaking the Promise of the Promised Land

Out of the Missionary's Closet

The Mysterious Madness of Mormons

I Will, Through the Veil

Marginal Mormons

Am I My Planet's Keeper?

Have Your Cum and Eat It, Too

Strangers with Benefits

Constructing Equity

Wake Up and Smell the Missionaries

Racism by Proxy

Orgy at the STD Clinic

Please Evacuate

Recommended Daily Humanity

The Camper Killings

Inferno in the French Quarter: The UpStairs Lounge Fire

Kinky Quilts: Patchwork Designs for Gay Men

An Eternity of Mirrors: Best Short Stories of Johnny Townsend

Latter-Gay Saints: An Anthology of Gay Mormon Fiction (co-editor)

Available from your favorite online or neighborhood bookstore.

Wondering what some of those other books are about? Read on!

Invasion of the Spirit Snatchers

During the Apocalypse, a group of Mormon survivors in Hurricane, Utah gather in the home of the Relief Society president, telling stories to pass the time as they ration their food storage and await the Second Coming. But this is no ordinary group of Mormons—or perhaps it is. They are the faithful, feminist, gay, apostate, and repentant, all working together to help each other through the darkest days any of them have yet seen.

Gayrabian Nights

Gayrabian Nights is a twist on the well-known classic, *1001 Arabian Nights*, in which Scheherazade, under the threat of death if she ceases to captivate King Shahryar's attention, enchants him through a series of mysterious, adventurous, and romantic tales.

In this variation, a male escort, invited to the hotel room of a closeted, homophobic Mormon senator, learns that the man is poised to vote on a piece of anti-gay legislation the following morning. To prevent him from sleeping, so that the exhausted senator will miss casting his vote on the Senate floor, the escort entertains him with stories of homophobia, celibacy, mixed orientation marriages, reparative therapy, coming out, first love, gay marriage, and long-term successful gay relationships.

The escort crafts the stories to give the senator a crash course in gay culture and sensibilities, hoping to bring the man closer to accepting his own sexual orientation.

Inferno in the French Quarter: The UpStairs Lounge Fire

On Gay Pride Day in 1973, someone set the entrance to a French Quarter gay bar on fire. In the terrible inferno that followed, thirty-two people lost their lives, including a third of the local congregation of the Metropolitan Community Church, their pastor burning to death halfway out a second-story window as he tried to claw his way to freedom.

A mother who'd gone to the bar with her two gay sons died alongside them. A man who'd helped his friend escape first was found dead near the fire escape. Two children waited outside a movie theater across town for a father and "uncle" who would never pick them up. During this era of rampant homophobia, several families refused to claim the bodies, and many churches refused to bury the dead.

Author Johnny Townsend pored through old records and tracked down survivors of the fire as well as relatives and friends of those killed to compile this fascinating account of a forgotten moment in gay history.

This second edition on the 50th anniversary of the fire includes additional research and information not available previously.

A Gay Mormon Missionary in Pompeii

What is a gay Mormon missionary doing in Italy? He is trying to save his own soul as well as the souls of others. In these tales chronicling the two-year mission of Robert Anderson, we see a young man tormented by his inability to be the man the Church says he should be. In addition to his personal hell, Anderson faces a major earthquake, organized crime, a serious bus accident, and much more. He copes with horrendous mission leaders and his own suicidal tendencies. But one day, he meets another missionary who loves him, and his world changes forever.

The Golem of Rabbi Loew

Jacob and Esau Cohen are the closest of brothers. In fact, they're lovers. A doctor tries to combine canine genes with those of Jews, to improve their chances of surviving a hostile world. A Talmudic scholar dates an escort. A scientist tries to develop the "God spot" in the brains of his patients in order to create a messiah. The Golem of Prague is really Rabbi Loew's secret lover. While some of the Jews in Townsend's book are Orthodox, this collection of Jewish stories most certainly is not.

Am I My Planet's Keeper?

Global Warming. Climate Change. Climate Crisis. Climate Emergency. Whatever label we use, we are facing one of the greatest challenges to the survival of life as we know it.

But while addressing greenhouse gases is perhaps our most urgent need, it's not our only task. We must also address toxic waste, pollution, habitat destruction, and our other contributions to the world's sixth mass extinction event.

In order to do that, we must simultaneously address the unmet human needs that keep us distracted from deeper engagement in stabilizing our climate: moderating economic inequality, guaranteeing healthcare to all, and ensuring education for everyone.

And to accomplish *that*, we must unite to combat the monied forces that use fear, prejudice, and misinformation to manipulate us.

It's a daunting task. But success is our only option.

Orgy at the STD Clinic

Todd Tillotson is struggling to move on after his husband is killed in a hit and run attack a year earlier during a Black Lives Matter protest in Seattle.

In this novel set entirely on public transportation, we watch as Todd, isolated throughout the pandemic, battles desperation in his attempt to safely reconnect with the world.

Will he find love again, even casual friendship, or will he simply end up another crazy old man on the bus?

Things don't look good until a man whose face he can't even see sits down beside him despite the raging variants.

And asks him a question that will change his life.

Please Evacuate

A gay, partygoing New Yorker unconcerned about the future or the unsustainability of capitalism is hit by a truck and thrust into a straight man's body half a continent away. As Hunter tries to figure out what's happening, he's caught up in another disaster, a wildfire sweeping through a Colorado community, the flames overtaking him and several schoolchildren as they flee.

When he awakens, Hunter finds himself in the body of yet another man, this time in northern Italy, a former missionary about to marry a young Mormon woman. Still piecing together this new reality, and beginning to embrace his latest identity, Hunter fights for his life in a devastating flash flood along with his wife *and* his new husband.

He's an aging worker in drought-stricken Texas, a nurse at an assisted living facility in the direct path of a hurricane, an advocate for the unhoused during a freak Seattle blizzard.

We watch as Hunter is plunged into life after life, finally recognizing the futility of only looking out for #1 and understanding the part he must play in addressing the global climate crisis…if he ever gets another chance.

Recommended Daily Humanity

A checklist of human rights must include basic housing, universal healthcare, equitable funding for public schools, and tuition-free college and vocational training.

In addition to the basics, though, we need much more to fully thrive. Subsidized childcare, universal pre-K, a universal basic income, subsidized high-speed internet, net neutrality, fare-free public transit (plus *more* public transit), and medically assisted death for the terminally ill who want it.

None of this will matter, though, if we neglect to address the rapidly worsening climate crisis.

Sound expensive? It is.

But not as expensive as refusing to implement these changes. The cost of climate disasters each year has grown to staggering figures. And the cost of social and political upheaval from not meeting the needs of suffering workers, families, and individuals may surpass even that.

It's best we understand that the vast sums required to enact meaningful change are an investment which will pay off not only in some indeterminate future but in fact almost immediately. And without these adjustments to our lifestyles and values, there may very well not be a future capable of sustaining freedom and democracy…or even civilization itself.

The Camper Killings

When a homeless man is found murdered a few blocks from Morgan Beylerian's house in south Seattle, everyone seems to consider the body just so much additional trash to be cleared from the neighborhood. But Morgan liked the guy. They used to chat when Morgan brought Nick groceries once a week.

And the brutal way the man was killed reminds Morgan of their shared Mormon heritage, back when the faithful agreed to have their throats slit if they ever revealed temple secrets.

Did Nick's former wife take action when her ex-husband refused to grant a temple divorce? Did his murder have something to do with the public accusations that brought an end to his promising career?

Morgan does his best to investigate when no one else seems to care, but it isn't easy as a man living paycheck to paycheck himself, only able to pursue his investigation via public transit.

As he continues his search for the killer, Morgan's friends withdraw and his husband threatens to leave. When another homeless man is killed and Morgan is accused of the crime, things look even bleaker.

But his troubles aren't over yet.

Will Morgan find the killer before the killer finds him?

Racism by Proxy

Are you biased? Am I?

The short answer is yes. We all are.

Having bias isn't a choice. We can't avoid it. We prefer members of our religion, our country, our political party, and speakers of our native language. We're taught bias unintentionally by people who aren't conscious of their biases, and we in turn unintentionally pass them on to others.

So it's not a "sin" to be biased. It's inevitable.

What matters is not allowing our unchosen biases to exert absolute control over our decisions and behavior. To do that, however, we must recognize and accept them as real.

In *Racism by Proxy*, essayist Johnny Townsend pushes past shame, guilt, and other useless approaches to show how all of us, even white people of varying privilege, benefit from increasing equity and social justice throughout our communities.

What Readers Have Said

Townsend's stories are "a gay *Portnoy's Complaint* of Mormonism. Salacious, sweet, sad, insightful, insulting, religiously ethnic, quirky-faithful, and funny."

D. Michael Quinn, author of *The Mormon Hierarchy: Origins of Power*

"Told from a believably conversational first-person perspective, [*A Gay Mormon Missionary in Pompeii's*] novelistic focus on Anderson's journey to thoughtful self-acceptance allows for greater character development than often seen in short stories, which makes this well-paced work rich and satisfying, and one of Townsend's strongest. An extremely important contribution to the field of Mormon fiction." Named to Kirkus Reviews' Best of 2011.

Kirkus Reviews

"The thirteen stories in *Mormon Underwear* capture this struggle [between Mormonism and homosexuality] with humor, sadness, insight, and sometimes shocking details....*Mormon Underwear* provides compelling stories, literally from the inside-out."

Niki D'Andrea, *Phoenix New Times*

"Townsend's lively writing style and engaging characters [in *Zombies for Jesus*] make for stories which force us to wake up, smell the (prohibited) coffee, and review our attitudes with regard to reading dogma so doggedly. These are tales which revel in the individual tics and quirks which make us human, Mormon or not, gay or not…"

A.J. Kirby, *The Short Review*

"The Rift," from *A Gay Mormon Missionary in Pompeii*, is a "fascinating tale of an untenable situation…a *tour de force.*"

David Lenson, editor, *The Massachusetts Review*

"Pronouncing the Apostrophe," from *The Golem of Rabbi Loew*, is "quiet and revealing, an intriguing tale…"

Sima Rabinowitz, Literary Magazine Review, *NewPages.com*

The Circumcision of God is "a collection of short stories that consider the imperfect, silenced majority of Mormons, who may in fact be [the Church's] best hope….[The book leaves] readers regretting the church's willingness to marginalize those who best exemplify its ideals: those who love fiercely despite all obstacles, who brave challenges at great personal risk and who always choose the hard, higher road."

Kirkus Reviews

In *Mormon Fairy Tales*, Johnny Townsend displays "both a wicked sense of irony and a deep well of compassion."

Kel Munger, *Sacramento News and Review*

Zombies for Jesus is "eerie, erotic, and magical."

Publishers Weekly

"While [Townsend's] many touching vignettes draw deeply from Mormon mythology, history, spirituality and culture, [*Mormon Fairy Tales*] is neither a gaudy act of proselytism nor angry protest literature from an ex-believer. Like all good fiction, his stories are simply about the joys, the hopes and the sorrows of people."

Kirkus Reviews

In *Zombies for Jesus*, "Townsend isn't writing satire, but deeply emotional and revealing portraits of people who are, with a few exceptions, quite lovable."

Kel Munger, *Sacramento News and Review*

Selling the City of Enoch is "sharply intelligent...pleasingly complex...The stories are full of...doubters, but there's no vindictiveness in these pages; the characters continuously poke holes in Mormonism's more extravagant absurdities, but they take very little pleasure in doing so....Many of Townsend's stories...have a provocative edge to them, but this [book] displays a great deal of insight as well...a playful, biting and surprisingly warm collection."

Kirkus Reviews

In *Sex among the Saints,* "Townsend writes with a deadpan wit and a supple, realistic prose that's full of psychological empathy....he takes his protagonists' moral struggles seriously and invests them with real emotional resonance."

Kirkus Reviews

Marginal Mormons is "an irreverent, honest look at life outside the mainstream Mormon Church....Throughout his musings on sin and forgiveness, Townsend beautifully demonstrates his characters' internal, perhaps irreconcilable struggles....Rather than anger and disdain, he offers an honest portrayal of people searching for meaning and community in their lives, regardless of their life choices or secrets." Named to Kirkus Reviews' Best of 2012.

Kirkus Reviews

The stories in *The Mormon Victorian Society* "register the new openness and confidence of gay life in the age of same-sex marriage....What hasn't changed is Townsend's wry, conversational prose, his subtle evocations of character and social dynamics, and his deadpan humor. His warm empathy still glows in this intimate yet clear-eyed engagement with Mormon theology and folkways. Funny, shrewd and finely wrought dissections of the awkward contradictions—and surprising harmonies—between conscience and desire." Named to Kirkus Reviews' Best of 2013.

Kirkus Reviews

"This collection of short stories [*The Mormon Victorian Society*] featuring gay Mormon characters slammed [me] in the face from the first page, wrestled my heart and mind to the floor, and left me panting and wanting more by the end. Johnny Townsend has created so many memorable characters in such few pages. I went weeks thinking about this book. It truly touched me."

Tom Webb, *A Bear on Books*

Dragons of the Book of Mormon is an "entertaining collection....Townsend's prose is sharp, clear, and easy to read, and his characters are well rendered..."

Publishers Weekly

"The pre-eminent documenter of alternative Mormon lifestyles...Townsend has a deep understanding of his characters, and his limpid prose, dry humor and well-grounded (occasionally magical) realism make their spiritual conundrums both compelling and entertaining. [*Dragons of the Book of Mormon* is] [a]nother of Townsend's critical but affectionate and absorbing tours of Mormon discontent." Named to Kirkus Reviews' Best of 2014.

Kirkus Reviews

In *Gayrabian Nights*, "Townsend's prose is always limpid and evocative, and…he finds real drama and emotional depth in the most ordinary of lives."

Kirkus Reviews

Gayrabian Nights is a "complex revelation of how seriously soul damaging the denial of the true self can be."

Ryan Rhodes, author of *Free Electricity*

Gayrabian Nights "was easily the most original book I've read all year. Funny, touching, topical, and thoroughly enjoyable."

Rainbow Awards

The Washing of Brains has "A lovely writing style, and each story [is] full of unique, engaging characters….immensely entertaining."

Rainbow Awards

Lying for the Lord is "one of the most gripping books that I've picked up for quite a while. I love the author's writing style, alternately cynical, humorous, biting, scathing, poignant, and touching.... This is the third book of his that I've read, and all are equally engaging. These are stories that need to be told, and the author does it in just the right way."

Heidi Alsop, *Ex-Mormon Foundation Board Member*

In *Lying for the Lord*, Townsend "gets under the skin of his characters to reveal their complexity and conflicts....shrewd, evocative [and] wryly humorous."

Kirkus Reviews

In *Missionaries Make the Best Companions*, "the author treats the clash between religious dogma and liberal humanism with vivid realism, sly humor, and subtle feeling as his characters try to figure out their true missions in life. Another of Townsend's rich dissections of Mormon failures and uncertainties..." Named to Kirkus Reviews' Best of 2015.

Kirkus Reviews

In *Invasion of the Spirit Snatchers*, "Townsend, a confident and practiced storyteller, skewers the hypocrisies and eccentricities of his characters with precision and affection. The outlandish framing narrative is the most consistent source of shock and humor, but the stories do much to ground the reader in the world—or former world—of the characters....A funny, charming tale about a group of Mormons facing the end of the world."

Kirkus Reviews

"Townsend's collection [*The Washing of Brains*] once again displays his limpid, naturalistic prose, skillful narrative chops, and his subtle insights into psychology...Well-crafted dispatches on the clash between religion and self-fulfillment..."

Kirkus Reviews

"While the author is generally at his best when working as a satirist, there are some fine, understated touches in these tales [*The Last Days Linger*] that will likely affect readers in subtle ways....readers should come away impressed by the deep empathy he shows for all his characters—even the homophobic ones."

Kirkus Reviews

"Written in a conversational style that often uses stories and personal anecdotes to reveal larger truths, this immensely approachable book [*Racism by Proxy*] skillfully serves its intended audience of White readers grappling with complex questions regarding race, history, and identity. The author's frequent references to the Church of Jesus Christ of Latter-day Saints may be too niche for readers unfamiliar with its idiosyncrasies, but Townsend generally strikes a perfect balance of humor, introspection, and reasoned arguments that will engage even skeptical readers."

Kirkus Reviews

Orgy at the STD Clinic portrays "an all-too real scenario that Townsend skewers to wincingly accurate proportions…[with] instant classic moments courtesy of his punchy, sassy, sexy lead character…"

Jim Piechota, *Bay Area Reporter*

Orgy at the STD Clinic is "…a triumph of humane sensibility. A richly textured saga that brilliantly captures the fraying social fabric of contemporary life." Named to Kirkus Reviews' Best Indie Books of 2022.

Kirkus Reviews

"Johnny Townsend's 'Partying with St. Roch' [in the anthology *Latter-Gay Saints*] tells a beautiful, haunting tale."

Kent Brintnall, Out in Print: Queer Book Reviews

Gayrabian Nights is "an allegorical tour de force…a hard-core emotional punch."

Gay. Guy. Reading and Friends

In *Dead Mankind Walking*, "Townsend writes in an energetic prose that balances crankiness and humor....A rambunctious volume of short, well-crafted essays..."

Kirkus Reviews